D1365685

THE
FIRST WORLD WAR

IN ASSOCIATION WITH
IMPERIAL WAR MUSEUMS

GARY SHEFFIELD

ANDRE
DEUTSCH

MAP KEY

Common symbols used on maps in this book:

NATIONAL COLOURS

- British, Dominion & Empire
- French
- German
- Belgian
- American

SIZE OF MILITARY UNITS

- XXXX Army
- XXX Corps
- XX Division
- X Brigade
- III Regiment
- II Battalion

MILITARY TYPES

- Infantry
- Tanks
- Cavalry

MILITARY SYMBOLS

- XXXXX   Army group boundary line
- XXXX   Army boundary line
- XXX   Corps boundary line
- XX   Division boundary line
- →   Troops attacking
- ↪   Unsuccessful attack
- ←   Planned withdrawal

To my nephew, Dominic

THIS IS AN ANDRE DEUTSCH BOOK

Text copyright © Gary Sheffield 2008, 2014, 2017
Design & map copyright © André Deutsch Limited 2008, 2014, 2017

Imperial War Museum photographs and memorabilia
© Imperial War Museum

This edition published in 2018
First published as *The First World War Remembered* in 2014
by André Deutsch Limited,
a division of the Carlton Publishing Group,
20 Mortimer Street, London W1T 3JW

Material from this book was originally published in
The Western Front Experience by Gary Sheffield in 2008

Printed in Dubai

A CIP catalogue for this book is available from the British Library

ISBN: 978 0 233 00532 4

CONTENTS

INTRODUCTION

THE CENTENARY OF THE FIRST WORLD WAR HAS REMINDED US THAT IT WAS THE SINGLE EVENT THAT MORE THAN ANY OTHER CAN BE SAID TO HAVE SHAPED THE WORLD IN WHICH WE LIVE. THE SECOND WORLD WAR GREW OUT OF THE FIRST. IT WAS NOT A "GIVEN" THAT A SECOND GREAT WAR WOULD OCCUR, BUT THERE WAS SUFFICIENT UNFINISHED BUSINESS FROM 1914–18 TO MAKE IT LIKELY.

The global spread of the First World War was such that almost no part was left untouched, either directly or indirectly. The resources of great empires were mobilized to fight a total war. Soldiers came from tropical North Queensland and West Africa to fight for Britain and France against Germany in Belgium. Labourers from South Africa, China and Vietnam were sent to work on the Western Front. Men from the far reaches of the Russian and Austro-Hungarian Empires battled each other in the Carpathians.

As the public and media interest over the centenary years shows, unlike most historical events, the First World War continues to excite passions among non-experts. The war continues to affect us all. In Britain, opinion is sharply polarized between those who see the war as a monstrous tragedy which should never have happened, and those who agree it was a tragedy but say that it was not of Britain's making and Britain had no choice but to get involved. From a French or German perspective it can be seen

as the second round in a Franco-German war that began in 1870 and only ended in 1945. An American might view it as the moment when the USA finally stepped onto the world stage; an Australian, New Zealander or Canadian as the time when their nations began to emerge from under the protective wing of the mother country. Citizens of states such as Poland, the Czech Republic and Latvia can look back to 1914–18 as the beginning of, in some cases an extremely prolonged, process of achieving national self determination. The powder keg that is the modern Middle East has its origins in British and French meddling in the ruins of the Ottoman Empire. German Nazism, Italian Fascism, Soviet Communism and the Cold War were all by-products of the First World War.

The generals of the war still excite passionate debates, with individuals lined up for and against. Haig and Pétain remain controversial figures, although for very different reasons; and historians still debate the merits of Conrad, Foch, French, Pershing, Brusilov, Kemel,

Joffre, Currie and Monash as commanders. But increasingly the ordinary soldier has taken centre stage. And we should not forget the civilians – women, older men, and children – whose support for the war was critical. As historians are increasingly realizing, home front and battle front were closely intertwined.

This book enables us explore the First World War through text, pictures and memorabilia. I hope that it gives readers some idea of the issues at stake, the strategies, tactics and battles, and the lives of the people who were there.

GARY SHEFFIELD, University of Birmingham, 2017

OPPOSITE: Canadian troops guard German prisoners as they use a stretcher and a light railway truck to transport wounded soldiers to get medical attention, Vimy Ridge, April 1917.

ABOVE: Soldiers from 2nd Special Regiment at the Guet Post in the frontline trenches in front of La Pompelle in 1916.

SLIDE TOWARDS CONFLICT

THE ORIGINS OF THE WAR

THE EVENTS THAT PLUNGED EUROPE INTO WAR IN 1914 MOVED
WITH DIZZYING SPEED. ON 28 JUNE, ARCHDUKE FRANZ FERDINAND OF
AUSTRIA-HUNGARY WAS ASSASSINATED BY A YOUNG SERB, GAVRILO
PRINCIP. A MONTH LATER, AUSTRIA DECLARED WAR ON SERBIA,
WHICH VIENNA BLAMED FOR THE MURDER, AND BY 5 AUGUST
THE MAJOR STATES OF EUROPE WERE AT WAR.

1914

OTTO VON BISMARCK
(1815–98)

Bismarck was instrumental in uniting the disparate German states into an empire under the leadership of Prussia. He used a series of wars against Denmark (1864), Austria (1866) and France (1870–71) to establish the new state, with the King of Prussia being proclaimed as Kaiser (Emperor) Wilhelm I in the Hall of Mirrors at Versailles in 1871. Bismarck's subtle diplomatic skills, which played a large part in keeping Europe at peace in the last quarter of the nineteenth century, were sorely missed after his dismissal by Wilhelm II in 1890.

The immediate trigger for the First World War was thus rivalry between states in the Balkans. Russia backed Serbia, the latter state posing as the protector of the Serbs in the polyglot Habsburg Empire. Austria risked war with Russia to preserve its influence in the Balkans, having received on 5 July a firm promise of support from its ally Germany. Russia, alarmed by the threat to its security and prestige, mobilized its forces, followed by Germany and then France, Russia's ally since 1892. The German attack on Belgium on 4 August then brought Britain into the war. In retrospect, the war seemed to many to be almost accidental, with states slipping into an unwanted conflict.

However, there were wider issues at play. The German defeat of Napoleon III's France in 1870–71 had destroyed the existing international balance of power. But Germany, despite its ever increasing economic power, chose, under the leadership of the "Iron Chancellor", Otto von Bismarck, to live within the new situation it had created, and to avoid threatening its neighbours, while keeping France isolated. All this changed when the young and mentally unbalanced Kaiser Wilhelm II came to the throne in 1888. In 1890 Wilhelm dismissed

Bismarck, and the system of treaties that the Chancellor had carefully constructed to protect Germany began to unravel. Wilhelm's bellicose *Weltpolitik* (world policy) led to diplomatic encirclement, having thoroughly frightened Britain, France and Russia. The British government abandoned its policy of non-alignment and established an Entente – although not a formal alliance – with France and Russia in 1904.

By 1914, Germany had backed itself into a corner. Many historians agree that Germany took advantage of the situation in the Balkans to attempt to break up the Entente, even at the risk of a major war. Others argue that Germany actually desired and planned for war. Russia, defeated by the Japanese in 1904–05, was rapidly rebuilding its military strength, and some of the German élite favoured a war to prevent it from re-emerging as a rival. At the very least, the ambitious programme of annexations and the creation of de facto economic colonies across Europe that was drawn up by Germany shortly after the Russo-Japanese War began indicates that it was willing to take advantage of the opportunity to undertake aggressive expansionism. Likewise, there was nothing accidental about Austria-Hungary's decision

OPPOSITE: Franz Ferdinand and his wife Sophie are photographed getting into a car just minutes before their murder by Gavrilo Princip (inset left).

ABOVE TOP: Napoleon III led France to a humiliating defeat by Germany in 1870–71. Desire for revenge was a factor in 1914.

ABOVE: Admiral von Tirpitz masterminded the creation of the fleet that turned Germany into a great naval power but alarmed the British.

to crush Serbia, regardless of the risks of wider war. The Austrians, excluded over the previous century from spheres of influence in Germany and Italy, believed that they could not afford to be marginalized in the Balkans. Striking a blow against nationalism, a force that threatened to rot the multi-national Habsburg Empire from within, was also highly attractive.

There, were of course, other factors in the outbreak of the First World, War. Although arms races do not in themselves cause wars, military competition before 1914 added to the sense of impending crisis. The Anglo-German naval rivalry was particularly dangerous. Britain's primary defence force was the Royal Navy, and the German fleet-building programme initiated under Admiral Tirpitz posed a direct threat to the security of the British homeland and the British

Empire. In response, the British drew closer to France and Russia and, in 1906 launched HMS *Dreadnought*. This revolutionary new battleship, the brainchild of Admiral Sir John "Jacky" Fisher, was superior to anything else afloat. It forced the Germans to respond, ratcheting the naval race to a more dangerous level.

Domestic politics were also significant. Sir Edward Grey, British Foreign Secretary, has been accused of failing to deter Germany by not sending strong enough signals concerning British intentions; yet his hand was weakened by the unwillingness of many of his Liberal colleagues in the Cabinet to contemplate war. In France, Germany's decision to seize the province of Alsace and Lorraine in 1871 caused lasting resentment. In Germany, the rise of the Social Democrats alarmed the Imperial government and may have contributed to a desire for a popular

TSAR NICHOLAS II
(1868–1918)

Russia played a key role in the outbreak of the war. Humiliated at their impotence during the crisis engendered by the Austrian annexation of Bosnia in 1908, in 1914 the Russian leaders were determined to stand firm in the Balkans. In part this was linked to domestic factors. Under Tsar Nicholas II, who ruled from 1894–1917, Russia became politically unstable, with an abortive revolution breaking out in 1905. In the July 1914 crisis, the Russian government was keen to demonstrate to domestic critics as well as foreign enemies that it was capable of strong action.

war. Above all, a pan-European current of militarism, and a general belief in Social Darwinism – the idea that the survival of the fittest applied to nations and peoples – led to a febrile atmosphere in which resorting to war to settle disputes came to be seen as natural and acceptable. For all that, when article 231 of the 1919 Treaty of Versailles (that ended the war in the West) blamed Germany and its allies for the outbreak of the war, it encapsulated an essential truth.

OPPOSITE ABOVE: HMS *Dreadnought* was the first of the "all big gun" battleships, brought into service by Fisher.

OPPOSITE BELOW: A pickelhaube (spiked bonnet) belonging to a German officer of Infantry Regiment No. 8.

RIGHT: A German military handbook: *The Good Comrade* by Major von Klass. This nineteenth edition was published in 1914.

MOBILIZATION

THE OUTBREAK OF WAR

FOR YEARS BEFORE 1914, GENERAL STAFFS IN EUROPE HAD PREPARED ELABORATE PLANS FOR MOBILIZATION IN THE EVENT OF WAR. DURING THE NINETEENTH CENTURY, MOST STATES HAD ADOPTED A SYSTEM OF CONSCRIPTING MEN INTO THE ARMY FOR A SET, OFTEN FAIRLY SHORT, PERIOD OF TIME, THEN SENDING THEM BACK TO CIVILIAN LIFE.

1914

These reservists were then recalled to the colours in time of emergency. This arrangement allowed armies to put vast numbers of men into the field. Germany's field army of 82 infantry divisions included 31 reserve formations; the French had 73 divisions, 25 of which were composed of reservists. The major exception was Britain, which relied on a long-service regular army backed up by a volunteer part-time Territorial Force, rather than on conscription. Shortly after the war began, the new Secretary of State for War, Field Marshal Lord Kitchener called for volunteers for a new, mass army. This ensured that by 1916 Britain had an army comparable in size to its allies and enemies. But in August 1914, Britain could only put a mere six infantry divisions in the field – in addition, of course, to the might of the Royal Navy.

The war plans of the Great Powers dictated that no time could be wasted between mobilizing and fighting. The German pre-war plan, developed under General Alfred von Schlieffen, was designed to compensate for the fact that Germany would face a war on two fronts. Hurling the bulk of its forces westwards, and invading neutral Belgium to outflank the French frontier defences, Germany would defeat France in a matter of weeks. Its forces would then redeploy via the strategic railway system to face the Russian Army, which the Germans calculated

ABOVE: British recruitment poster. All feature Field Marshal Earl Kitchener of Khartoum, Secretary of State for War and a British national icon.

would be slow to move. That infringement of Belgian territory was likely to bring the British into the war was discounted. The operational concept was based on the idea of encirclement, a favourite German military gambit that served them well in the Franco-Prussian War of 1870–71 (and was to be repeated on numerous occasions in the

ENTENTE CORDIALE

In 1898, the Fashoda Incident, a confrontation between British and French troops in southern Sudan, brought the two countries close to war. A desire to settle colonial disputes and increasing fear of Germany brought the British and French together. An agreement (the "Entente Cordiale") was signed in 1904, and by 1914 their military plans were being co-ordinated. The French navy deployed in the Mediterranean, leaving the Royal Navy to protect the Channel coast. The arrival in August 1914 of the BEF to fight alongside the French Army was the logical outcome of this rapprochement.

Second World War). If the French advanced into Lorraine, so much the better; the German trap would close behind them. The Schlieffen Plan, hotly debated by historians in recent years, stands as an example of a gamble of breathtaking proportions. If it failed, Germany would be in deep trouble.

The French army pinned its hopes on Plan XVII, a strategy developed by the French general staff under the leadership of General Joseph Joffre. Plan XVII was founded on the concept of the all-out offensive, an aggressive

ABOVE: A large proportion of the British battalions that went to war in 1914 were composed of reservists, like these men.

ABOVE: German troops on a pre-war training exercise. They are wearing the spiked helmet replaced during the war by the "coal-scuttle".

THE FRENCH ARMY IN 1914

French soldiers went to war in 1914 wearing antiquated uniforms of blue coats, and bright red trousers that symbolized the élan of the army. By contrast, the Germans had dull, grey uniforms that made their soldiers less conspicuous. The British took this trend the furthest, wearing practical khaki ("dust-coloured") clothing. During the course of the war, the French switched to a more sensible "horizon blue" uniform, and the Germans similarly modified their dress, swapping the spiked pickelhaube for the "coal scuttle" steel helmet.

ABOVE TOP RIGHT: Among this crowd in Munich in August 1914 was the young Adolf Hitler, captured, by a remarkable coincidence, in this photograph.

ABOVE: Alfred von Schlieffen died before he saw the disaster that his plan inflicted upon his country and Europe.

RIGHT: This French poster of 1914 announces general mobilization, which includes requisitioning of animals and vehicles for service with the military.

military doctrine associated with Lieutenant General (later Marshal) Ferdinand Foch. Both Joffre and Foch were to go on to play extremely prominent roles during the First World War. On the outbreak of war, major French forces would surge into Lorraine to recapture the provinces lost to Germany after the Franco-Prussian War, while others would advance farther to the north. Everywhere, the French would carry the war to the enemy. As the consequence of secret talks between the British and French staffs, it was decided that the British Expeditionary Force (BEF), too small to carry out an independent strategy, would take its place on the left of the French Army, a decision reluctantly confirmed by an ad hoc war council of politicians and generals convened on the outbreak of war. The Belgian Army, less than 120,000 strong in 1914, could do little but resist the Germans as best they could until joined by Franco-British forces.

The French, British and German armies were armed with broadly similar weapons – bolt-action, magazine rifles capable of rapid fire; modern, quick-firing artillery; and a limited number of machine guns. All retained considerable numbers of cavalry, armed with both firearms and swords, for reconnaissance and the charge. Every army also had a small number of primitive airplanes. General staffs had studied the most recent military campaigns, in South Africa (1899–1902) and Manchuria (1904–05), and had incorporated the perceived lessons into their thinking. None were unaware of the devastating power of modern weapons, or the difficulty in

overcoming fixed fortifications. To strike first and win quickly, before the front could congeal into trench warfare, seemed a logical extrapolation from recent wars; and the Russo-Japanese War apparently demonstrated that determined troops with high morale could overcome entrenched defenders, albeit at a heavy cost in casualties. The French were the most extreme exponents of the cult of the offensive and the "moral battlefield", in which heavy emphasis was placed on morale (the words being used interchangeably at this time), but these concepts also influenced the British and Germans. These pre-war doctrines were not entirely wrong, but undoubtedly contributed to the huge "butcher's bill" in the early months of the war.

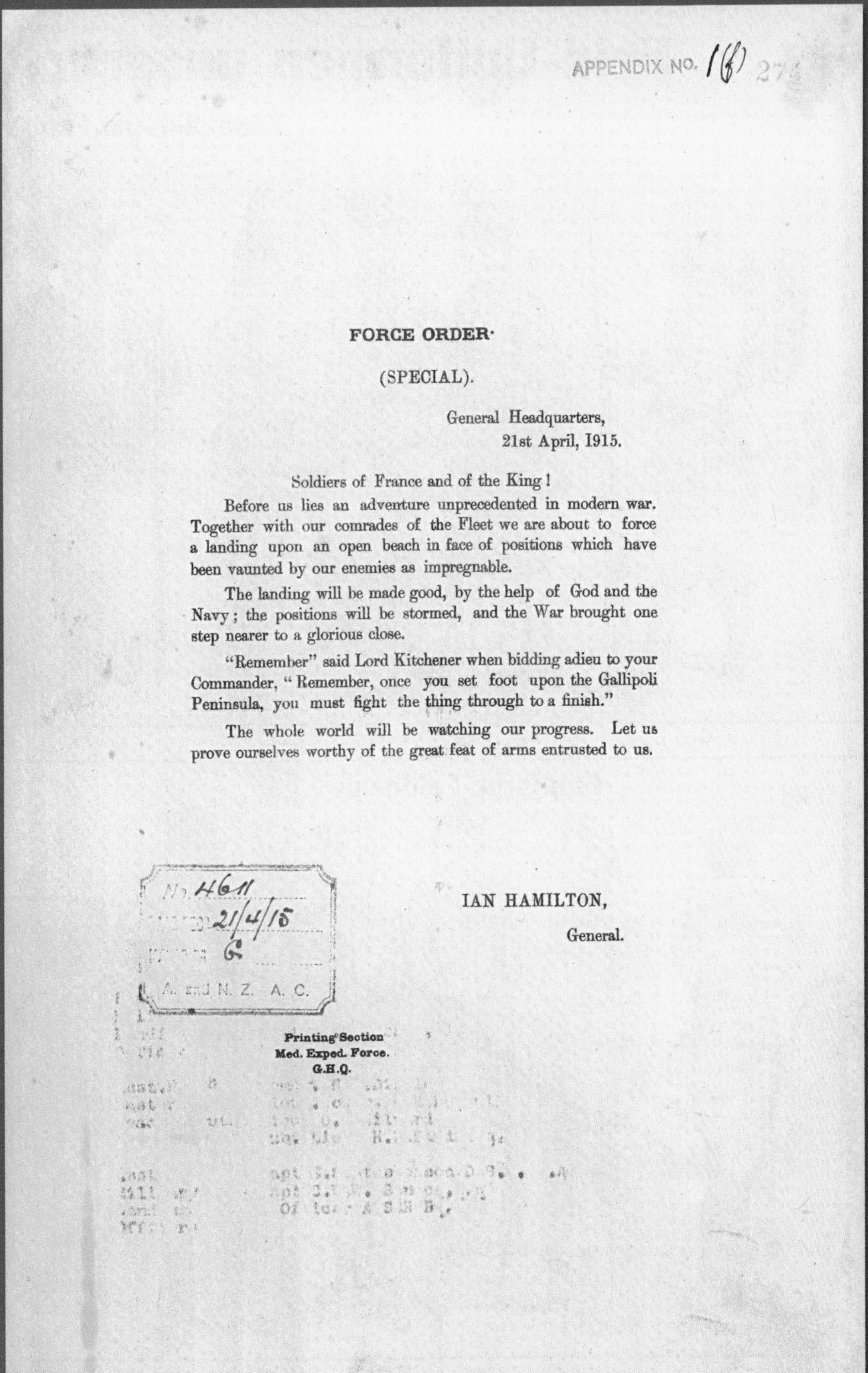

FORCE ORDER.

(SPECIAL).

General Headquarters,
21st April, 1915.

Soldiers of France and of the King!

Before us lies an adventure unprecedented in modern war. Together with our comrades of the Fleet we are about to force a landing upon an open beach in face of positions which have been vaunted by our enemies as impregnable.

The landing will be made good, by the help of God and the Navy; the positions will be stormed, and the War brought one step nearer to a glorious close.

"Remember" said Lord Kitchener when bidding adieu to your Commander, "Remember, once you set foot upon the Gallipoli Peninsula, you must fight the thing through to a finish."

The whole world will be watching our progress. Let us prove ourselves worthy of the great feat of arms entrusted to us.

IAN HAMILTON,

General.

No. 4611
21/4/15
G
A. & N. Z. A. C.

Printing Section
Med. Exped. Force.
G.H.Q.

General Sir Ian Hamilton's Force Order

General Sir Ian Hamilton wanted this order to be read to all troops before the Gallipoli Landing to inspire them.

Feld-Uniformen unserer Fein

Kriegsbilderbogen Nr. 4.

Französische Feldarmee.

Dragoner.   Infanterist.   Jäger zu Pferd.   Artillerist.   Kürassier.   Alpenjäger.   Kavallerie-Offi

Englische Feldarmee.

Fußtruppe.   Infanterie-Offizier.   Offizier,   Soldat,   Kavallerist.   Stabsoffizier i. Mantel.   Indische Hilfstruppe.
Schottische Hochländer-Truppe.

im Westen.

...er der Fußtruppe.   Zuave.   Turko.

Belgische Feldarmee.

...artillerist.   Jäger zu Fuß,   Jäger zu Pferd,   Infanterist.
             Offizier.   Unteroffizier.

Allied uniform recognition poster

A German poster of Allied uniforms from 1914. The drab khaki clothing of the British, the product of experience in colonial warfare, contrasts with the colourful French and Belgian uniforms.

The Active-Service French Book for Soldiers & Sailors

An English–French phrase book used by soldiers of the British Expeditionary Force fighting in France.

1914

THE
ACTIVE-SERVICE
FRENCH BOOK
FOR
SOLDIERS & SAILORS.

CONTAINING

The SOLDIERS' LANGUAGE MANUAL. By AJAX.

FRENCH FOR THE FRONT. By E. F. HARRIS.

PRICE SEVENPENCE NET.

London:
E. MARLBOROUGH & Co., 51, Old Bailey, E.C.
[All rights reserved.]

NOTE.

A soldier fighting in a foreign land has to meet a real and constant difficulty when unable to converse with the inhabitants. The drift of war carries him from where his own tongue is understood and he is brought into touch with many people who know nothing of English. The acquaintance of even a few of the most ordinary words and phrases of every-day life, and especially of every-day military life, will not only be an immense help but will render him a far more efficient soldier. Indeed, if by duty or misfortune he gets isolated from his comrades, it may go far to enable him to bring his business through with success, or to secure him succour and relief.

With this in view, The Soldiers' Language Manual has been prepared; much thought and care have been exercised in compiling the Vocabularies and Phrases; and just enough notes on the grammar have been given to help in the formation of simple sentences for ordinary requirements.

For the Phonetic Pronunciation Marlborough's "Self-Taught" System has been used. It is simple and with practice will speedily remove any diffidence in making first attempts to speak French, while, with a little attention, the sounds of the same language spoken by others will soon be understood. The system is more fully explained in "French Self-Taught," as mentioned in footnote on page 2.

L'ORAISON DOMINICALE.
The Lord's Prayer.

Notre Père, qui (vous) êtes aux cieux :
Our Father, who (you) are in the heavens

Que votre nom soit sanctifié :
That Your Name be hallowed :

Que votre règne arrive : Que votre
That Your Kingdom come : That Your

volonté soit faite sur la terre comme
will be done on the earth as

au ciel : Donnez-nous aujourd'hui
in the heaven : Give us to-day

notre pain quotidien : Et
our bread of every day (daily): And

pardonnez-nous nos offenses, comme
forgive us our trespasses, as

nous pardonnons à ceux qui nous ont
we forgive them who us have

offensés : Et ne nous laissez pas succom-
offended : And us leave not to give way

ber à la tentation ; mais délivrez-nous
to the temptation ; but deliver us

de mal. Amen.
from evil. Amen.

PRECAUTIONS *continued.*

77. SHARPSHOOTERS (*Tirailleurs*).

FRENCH.	HOW TO SAY IT.	ENGLISH.
Il y a des tirailleurs dans le jardin,	eel-yah dai tee-rah-yerr dahn ler zhar-dahn	There are sharp-shooters in the garden,
Derrière les haies ;	derryair lai hai ;	Behind the hedges ;
Ils sont là, depuis ce matin ;	eel son lah, derpeuce ser mat-an ;	They have been there all the morning !
Tirez, ou prenez-les!	teereh, oo prer-neh lai !	Fire, or take them !

SCOUTS AND SPIES. (*Manual,* 12-15.)

78. SPY ? (*Espion*).

FRENCH.	HOW TO SAY IT.	ENGLISH.
Espion ? Moi ?	esp'yon ? mwah ?	A spy ? I ?
Je ne le suis pas !	zher ner ler seuee pah !	I'm not !
Je suis anglais,	zher seuee-zahn-glai,	I am English,
Simple soldat.	sahnpl' sol-dah.	A private (soldier.)

79. PRISONER ? (*Prisonnier ?*)

FRENCH.	HOW TO SAY IT.	ENGLISH.
Prisonnier ? Moi ?	pree-zonn-yeh ? mwah ?	Prisoner ? I ?
Et pourquoi ?	eh poor-kwah ?	And why ?
Je suis ami,	zher seuee-zam-ee,	I am a friend,
Anglais ! Soldat !	ahnglai ! sol-dah !	Englishman ! Soldier !

80. HUNS ARE THERE, THE (*Les Boches sont là*).

FRENCH.	HOW TO SAY IT.	ENGLISH.
Venez avec moi	verneh-zav-ek mwah	Come with me,
Et ne parlez pas !	eh ner parr-leh pah !	And don't speak !
Marchez à quatre pattes,	marr-sheh-zah katr' pat	Go on all fours,
Les boches sont là.	lai bosh son lah.	The Germans (brutes) are there.

81. COVER, SEEK (*Cherchez un abri*).

FRENCH.	HOW TO SAY IT.	ENGLISH.
Traversez par ici	travairseh par eesee	Cross this way
Et cherchez un abri,	eh shairsheh-zern abree	And seek cover (a shelter),
Les Allemands nous volent !	lai-zalmahn noo vwah !	The Germans see us !
Silence aussi !	see-lahnss oh-see !	Silence, too !

(24)

WAR CRIES.

82. VICTORY, TO ! (*A la victoire!*).

FRENCH.	HOW TO SAY IT.	ENGLISH.
A la victoire !	ah lah vik-twahr !	To victory !
Vive le drapeau !	veev ler drap-oh !	Success to our flag !
Combattons bien	con-batton b'yan	Let us fight well
Pour le drapeau.	poor ler drap-oh.	For our flag.

83. KING, LAW AND LIBERTY (*Le Roi, la Loi, la Liberté*).

FRENCH.	HOW TO SAY IT.	ENGLISH.
Le Roi, la Loi,	ler rwah, lah lwah,	King, Law,
La Liberté !	lah libairteh !	Liberty !
Nous nous battons pour les trois,	noo noo batton poor lai trwah,	We fight for the three,
Nous tous Alliés !	noo too-zal-yeh !	All we Allies !

84. LONG LIVE FRANCE, &c., (*Vive la France, &c.*)

FRENCH.	HOW TO SAY IT.	ENGLISH.
Vive la France, la Belgique,	veev lah frahns, lah Belzheek	Long live France, Belgium,
Et la Russie !	eh lah Reussee!	And Russia !
Vive l'Angleterre	veev lahn-gler-tair	Long live England
Et l'Italie !	eh leetahlee !	And Italy !

WATER, SUPPLY OF.

85. WATER, PURE (*De l'eau, pure*).

FRENCH.	HOW TO SAY IT.	ENGLISH.
Etes-vous bien sûr Que cette eau soit pure ?	ait-voo b'yan seur ker set oh swah peur ?	Are you quite sure That this water is pure ?
Est-elle empoison-née ?	ait-el ahm-pwah-zonneh ?	Is it poisoned ?
Pouvons-nous l'employer pour le thé ?	poovon noo lahn-ployeh poor ler teh ?	Can we use it for the tea ?

86. WATER-BOTTLE FILLED (*Bidon rempli*).

FRENCH.	HOW TO SAY IT.	ENGLISH.
Je veux remplir	zher ver rahnpleer	I wish to fill
Ma gourde d'eau ;	mah goord doh ;	My water-bottle ;
Donnez-moi de l'eau	donneh mwah der loh	Give me some water
Dans un seau.	dahn-zun so.	In a pail.

WOUNDED (RED CROSS). (*Manual,* pp. 10, 11.)

87. HAND BROKEN (*La main cassée*).

FRENCH.	HOW TO SAY IT.	ENGLISH.
Main	mahn	Hand
Cassée !	kasseh !	Broken !
Écharpe,	eh-sharrp.	Sling,
S'il vous plaît !	seel voo plai !	Please !

(25)

WOUNDED (RED CROSS) *continued.*

101. DOCTOR, FETCH THE (*Allez chercher le médecin*).

FRENCH.	HOW TO SAY IT.	ENGLISH.
Mon camarade est blessé,	mon kamarahd eh blesseh,	My comrade is wounded,
Touché au bras ;	toosheh oh brah ;	Hit in the arm ;
Allez chercher le médecin,	alleh shair-sheh ler maidsan,	Fetch the doctor,
Et venez avec moi.	eh verneh-zavek mwah.	And come with me.

102. BULLET WOUND (*Touché par un balle*).

FRENCH.	HOW TO SAY IT.	ENGLISH.
Etes-vous touché par une balle ?	ait voo too-sheh pahr eun bal ?	Were you hit by a bullet ?
Où avez-vous mal ?	oo avveh voo mal ?	Where have you pain ?
Il vous faut aller	eel voo foh-talleh	You must go
Bien vite à l'hôpital.	b'yah veet ah lo-pee-tahl.	Quickly to the hospital.

103. WOUND, DRESS THE (*Pansez la plaie*).

FRENCH.	HOW TO SAY IT.	ENGLISH.
Blessé	blesseh	Wounded
Au pied ;	oh pee-ai ;	In the foot ;
Pansez	pahnseh	Dress
La plaie.	lah plai.	The wound (sore).

104. FOOT, WOUNDED IN (*Blessé au pied*).

FRENCH.	HOW TO SAY IT.	ENGLISH.
Blessé ?	blesseh ?	Wounded ?
Oui !	oo-ee !	Yes !
Où ?	oo ?	Where ?
Au pied.	oh pee-ai.	In (at) the foot.

105. ARM, WOUNDED IN (*Blessé au bras*).

FRENCH.	HOW TO SAY IT.	ENGLISH.
Blessé au bras ?	blesseh oh brah ?	Wounded in the arm ?
Pas grave, je crois !	pah grahv, zher krwah !	Not serious, I think !
Je vais le bander	zher vai ler bahndeh	I am going to bandage it
Et guérir le bras.	eh gaireer ler brah.	And heal the arm.

106. SHRAPNEL WOUND (*Blessé par un obus*).

FRENCH.	HOW TO SAY IT.	ENGLISH.
J'ai été blessé	zhai ehteh blesseh	I was wounded
Par un obus	pahr ern obbeu	By a shell
A la jambe	ah lah zhanb	In the leg
Et au pied, Monsieur !	eh oh pee-ai mers'-yer !	And in the foot, Sir !

(28)

RHYMES FOR ACTIVE SERVICE.

The references are to *The Soldiers' Language Manual, English-French.*

ALLIES. (*Manual,* pp. 3, 7, 8.)

40. ALLIES (*Alliés*).

FRENCH.	HOW TO SAY IT.	ENGLISH.
Vous êtes français,	voo-zait frahn-sai	You are French,
Je suis anglais.	zher seuee-zahnglai.	I am English.
Nous sommes amis,	noo som-zam-ee,	We are friends,
Nous sommes alliés.	noo som-zal-yeh.	We are Allies.

41. ENGLISH, DO YOU SPEAK ? (*Parlez-vous anglais ?*).

FRENCH.	HOW TO SAY IT.	ENGLISH.
Je suis soldat anglais,	zher seuee sol-dah-tahnglai	I am an English soldier
Parlant peu français.	par-lahn per frahnsai.	Speaking little French.
Parlez-vous anglais ?	par-leh voo-zahnglai ?	Do you speak English ?
Oui ? C'est parfait !	oo-ee ? sai par-fai !	Yes ? That's perfect.

ASSISTANCE. (*Manual,* pp. 3, 4, 7.)

42. TRENCH, TO DIG A (*Creuser une tranchée*).

FRENCH.	HOW TO SAY IT.	ENGLISH.
Aidez-moi,	aideh-mwah,	Help me,
Je vais	zher vai	I am going
Creuser	crerzeh	To dig
Une tranchée.	eun trahnsheh.	A trench.

43. TOBACCO, PLEASE (*Tabac, s'il vous plaît*).

FRENCH.	HOW TO SAY IT.	ENGLISH.
Donnez-moi,	donneh-mwah,	Give me
S'il vous plaît,	seel voo plai	If you please
Du tabac	deu tabah	Some tobacco
A fumer.	ah feumeh.	To smoke.

44. TIRED (*Fatigué.*)

FRENCH.	HOW TO SAY IT.	ENGLISH.
Monsieur, je suis fatigué.	mers'yer, zher seuee fateegeh,	Sir, I am tired,
Je ne puis plus marcher,	zher ner peuce pleu marsheh,	I can no longer walk,
J'ai les pieds bien mouillés ;	zhai lai pee-ai b'yan mooyeh	I have very wet feet ;
Peut-être pourriez vous m'aider ?	per-taitr' poorri-ch-voo maideh ?	Perhaps you can help me ?

(17)

17

BATTLE OF THE FRONTIERS

LORRAINE AND THE SCHLIEFFEN PLAN

THE FIRST SHOTS OF THE WAR WERE FIRED BY THE AUSTRIANS AGAINST
THE SERBS ON 29 JULY, BUT THE OUTBREAK OF FIGHTING IN WESTERN
EUROPE WAS NOT LONG DELAYED. THE FIRST MAJOR CLASH CAME ON
5 AUGUST WITH THE GERMAN ATTACK ON THE BELGIAN FORTRESS OF
LIÈGE, WHICH HELD OUT UNTIL 13 AUGUST.

1914

Original-Aufnahme vom Kriegsschauplatz.
Die durch ein einziges 42 cm Geschoss zerstörten Betondecken
eines Panzerturmes des Forts Louch.

Kr. 86.

VERLAG VON
GUSTAV LIERSCH & C?
BERLIN, S.W.

ABOVE: The concrete roof of a gun emplacement on
one of the Liège fortresses, destroyed by a German
420mm shell.

OPPOSITE ABOVE: Belgian carabineers retreating to
Antwerp on 20 August 1914. Note the antiquated
uniforms and machine guns drawn by dogs.

This was highly significant, because the longer the Belgians could impede the German advance, the further behind schedule the Schlieffen Plan would fall. The Belgian Army held the line of the River Gette before retreating into the fortress of Antwerp on 20 August, and the Belgian capital, Brussels, was lost the same day. The Germans continued to advance, capturing the fortress of Huy (on the River Meuse) and beginning a short siege of Namur, which fell on 23 August.

Moltke, who had succeeded Schlieffen as Chief of the Great General Staff in 1906, was forced to deploy a sizeable force to mask Antwerp, and to protect the flank of the main German advance from a Belgian sortie. On 5 October, the port was reinforced by a British force, in a demonstration of British sea power. This further weakened and slowed the German main effort. Partly out of frustration, partly to discourage guerrilla activity, the Germans carried out *Schrecklichkeit*, a policy of terror that included sacking the medieval city of Louvain and killing civilians. The oft-mocked Allied propaganda about German atrocities, although frequently exaggerated, did have foundations in truth.

Plan XVII was initiated on 6 August with

the movement of a French corps into Alsace, only for it to be repulsed by the defenders. A follow-up attack under General Paul Pau resulted in the capture of Mulhouse on 8 August. The French troops were greeted by cheering crowds, glad to welcome their liberators. However, shortly afterwards the victorious French were ordered to abandon their gains so that troops could be switched to meet the growing crisis to the north. The major French offensive into Lorraine commenced on 14 August with two Armies (First and Second). This was a complex undertaking, as the further the French advanced, the wider their frontage of attack became. In spite of the fact that, according to the Schlieffen Plan, the German forces should have kept to the defensive, they went onto the attack and on 20 August defeated the French in the twin battles of Morhange and Sarrebourg, and then pushed on to the French frontier. Some French formations fought well. General Foch's XX ("Iron") Corps held its ground stubbornly at Morhange, and was preparing to counter-attack, when to Foch's astonishment it received orders to pull back. "You don't know what is happening to the neighbouring corps", his Chief of Staff, General Denis Duchêne, sourly commented. XX Corps,

JOSEPH JACQUES CÉSAIRE JOFFRE (1851–1931)

Joffre, Chief of the French General Staff 1911–14 and Commander-in-Chief 1914–16, oversaw the development and implementation of Plan XVII, but then was able to rescue the French army from the consequences of that plan. His legendary calmness reflected ability of a very high order to cope with the shocks of war. Joffre, the ruthless sacker of subordinates, was himself removed from command at the end of 1916, having failed to break the deadlocked Western Front over the previous two years.

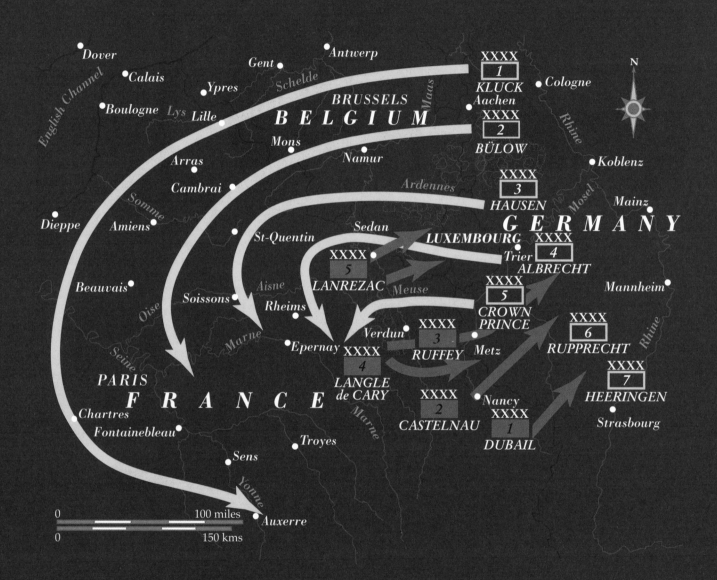

Dover
Calais
Ypres
Boulogne
Lille
Arras
Cambrai
Dieppe
Amiens
Beauvais
Soissons
PARIS
Chartres
Fontainebleau
Sens
Auxerre

Antwerp
Gent
Schelde
BRUSSELS
BELGIUM
Mons
Namur
St-Quentin
Sedan
Rheims
Epernay
Troyes

English Channel
Lys
Somme
Oise
Aisne
Seine
Marne
Yonne
Marne

Maas
Ardennes
LUXEMBOURG
XXXX 5
LANREZAC
Verdun
XXXX 4
LANGLE de CARY
XXXX 3
RUFFEY
Meuse
Metz
XXXX 2
CASTELNAU
Nancy
XXXX 1
DUBAIL

XXXX 1
KLUCK
Aachen
XXXX 2
BÜLOW
XXXX 3
HAUSEN
XXXX 4
ALBRECHT
Trier
XXXX 5
CROWN PRINCE
XXXX 6
RUPPRECHT
XXXX 7
HEERINGEN

GERMANY
Cologne
Koblenz
Mainz
Mosel
Mannheim
Rhine
Strasbourg

N

0   100 miles
0   150 kms

FRANCE

GERMAN & FRENCH WAR PLANS: 1914

→ Schlieffen Plan   → French plan XVII

weary but in good order covered the retreat of Second Army. A few days later, Foch's son, a junior officer with 131st Infantry Regiment, was killed in battle just a short distance away.

The French stabilized the situation, just as a new German offensive was getting underway. Joffre, the Commander-in-Chief (C-in-C) had ordered two armies to attack into the hilly, wooded terrain of the Ardennes in the belief that the German forces in this sector were weak. This misapprehension was based on an intelligence failure: the French had not realized the extent to which the Germans would use reserve troops to create new divisions. In encounter battles (unplanned meeting engagements) at Neufchâteau and Virton on 21–22 August, the attackers suffered further heavy losses and were pulled back behind the River Meuse.

Plan XVII was proving a bloody failure. Around 300,000 French soldiers became casualties in the Battle of the Frontiers. A report from Second Army in Lorraine stated: "The troops, infantry and artillery have been sorely tested. Our artillery is held at a distance by the long-range artillery of our enemy; it cannot get close enough for counterbattery fire. Our infantry has attacked with élan, but have been halted primarily by enemy artillery fire and by unseen enemy infantry hidden in trenches." In spite of the setbacks, "Papa" Joffre remained imperturbably calm, although he energetically sacked incompetent, or perhaps merely unlucky, commanders. In little more than a month, he removed 50 generals, including no less than 38 divisional commanders, and promoted talented, and by now battle-hardened leaders from further down the military hierarchy. One such officer was Ferdinand Foch, promoted to command Ninth Army.

By mid-August, both Joffre and Moltke were less focused on Alsace-Lorraine. Now they looked towards Belgium. For it was there, as the Germans advanced, that a major crisis was brewing.

ABOVE TOP RIGHT: Ruins of the Hotel de Ville in Louvain, September 1914. The German sack of the Belgian city caused international outrage.

ABOVE RIGHT: Soldiers of German 47th Infantry Regiment (10th Division), August 1914. Infantry losses were heavy in the opening months of the war.

HELMUTH VON MOLTKE "THE YOUNGER"
(1848–1916)

Von Moltke was the nephew of Helmut von Moltke "the elder", the German victor of the 1870–71 Franco-Prussian War. Although a belligerent advocate of war in the summer of 1914, he lacked his uncle's qualities of self-belief and ruthlessness. On campaign, finding it increasingly difficult to control the vast German armies, he collapsed with a nervous breakdown after the Battle of the Marne. He was blamed by contemporaries and some historians for meddling with Schlieffen's original plan. This is unfair as the plan was likely to fail on logistic grounds alone.

Lord Kitchener's BEF
orders to Sir John French

Instructions sent by Lord
Kitchener, British Secretary
of State for War, to Field
Marshal Sir John French,
Commander-in-Chief of the
British Expeditionary Force,
19 August 1914.

1914

Instructions for the General Officer Commanding the Expeditionary Force proceeding to France.

Owing to the infringement of the neutrality of Belgium by Germany, and in furtherance of the Entente which exists between this country and France, His Majesty's Government has decided, at the request of the French Government, to send an Expeditionary Force to France and to entrust the command of the troops to yourself.

The special motive of the Force under your command is to support, and co-operate with, the French Army against our common enemies. The peculiar task laid upon you is to assist the French Government in preventing, or repelling, the invasion by Germany of French and Belgian territory, and eventually to restore the neutrality of Belgium, on behalf of which, as guaranteed by Treaty, Belgium has appealed to the French and to ourselves.

These are the reasons which have induced His Majesty's Government to declare war, and these reasons constitute the primary objective you have before you.

The place of your assembly, according to present arrangements, is Amiens, and during the assembly of your troops you will have every opportunity for discussing with the Commander-in-Chief of the French Army the military position in general and the special part which your Force is able, and adapted, to play. It must be recognised from the outset that the numerical strength of the British Force – and its contingent reinforcements – is strictly limited, and with this consideration kept steadily in view it will be obvious that the greatest care must be exercised towards a minimum of losses and wastage.

Therefore, while every effort must be made to coincide most sympathetically with the plans and wishes of our Ally, the gravest consideration will devolve upon you as to participation in forward

movements

movements where large bodies of French troops are not engaged and where your Force may be unduly exposed to attack. Should a contingency of this sort be contemplated, I look to you to inform me fully and give me time to communicate to you any decision to which His Majesty's Government may come in the matter. In this connection I wish you distinctly to understand that your command is an entirely independent one, and that you will in no case come in any sense under the orders of any allied General.

In minor operations you should be careful that your subordinates understand that risk of serious losses should only be taken where such risk is authoritatively considered to be commensurate with the object in view.

The high courage and discipline of your troops should, and certainly will, have fair and full opportunity of display during the campaign, but officers may well be reminded that in this - their first-experience of European warfare a greater measure of caution must be employed than under former conditions of hostilities against an untrained adversary.

You will kindly keep up constant communication with the War Office, and you will be good enough to inform me as to all movements of the enemy reported to you as well as to those of the French Army.

I am sure you fully realise that you can rely with the utmost confidence on the whole-hearted and unswerving support of the Government, of myself, and of your compatriots, in carrying out the high duty which The King has entrusted to you and in maintaining the great traditions of His Majesty's Army.

Kitchener

19th August, 1914.

MONS AND LE CATEAU

FIRST ACTIONS OF THE BEF

THE KAISER, IN AN ORDER OF 19 AUGUST, REFERRED TO "GENERAL
FRENCH'S INSIGNIFICANT LITTLE ARMY". THE WORD "INSIGNIFICANT"
WAS TRANSLATED INTO ENGLISH AS "CONTEMPTIBLE". REVELLING
IN THE INSULT, THE BEF OF 1914 ACQUIRED ITS NICKNAME:
THE "OLD CONTEMPTIBLES".

1914

Wilhelm II's order illustrated how casually the German High Command regarded the British Army's presence on the Continent. In fact, Moltke welcomed the opportunity to defeat the BEF as well as the French Army. Given the disarray of the Allies, it seemed that this was a distinct possibility. Lanrezac's French Fifth Army pushed into Belgium with Sir John French's BEF on its left. But as French Third and Fourth Armies fell back, the flank of Lanrezac's Fifth Army was uncovered, and it found itself threatened by three German armies: from the east by Third Army (von Hausen); to the front by von Bülow's Second Army; and von Kluck's First Army to the west. In the Battle of the Sambre (21–23 August), the French met defeat. However, the manoeuvres of the three German armies were poorly synchronized and they were unable to profit fully from their successes.

OPPOSITE: British soldiers and French cavalrymen fraternize outside a café, 1914. The Mons campaign of August strained inter-Allied relations.

ABOVE: The 4th Royal Fusiliers resting in Mons, Saturday 22 August, 1914. On the next day the battalion saw heavy fighting.

SIR JOHN DENTON PINKSTONE FRENCH
(1852–1925)

Field Marshal French took the BEF to France in 1914 as its Commander-in-Chief. An Irish cavalryman, he established his reputation as an able commander of mounted troops during the South African (or Second Boer) War (1899–1902), when he forged an effective partnership with his chief of staff, Douglas Haig. He did not cope well with the demands of commanding the BEF and was replaced in December 1915 by Haig after the failure of the battle of Loos. French never forgave his former protégé.

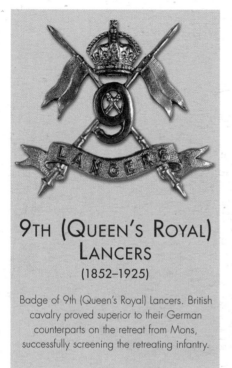

9TH (QUEEN'S ROYAL) LANCERS
(1852–1925)

Badge of 9th (Queen's Royal) Lancers. British cavalry proved superior to their German counterparts on the retreat from Mons, successfully screening the retreating infantry.

On Lanrezac's left, on 23 August the British fought their first battle in Western Europe since Waterloo, 99 years before. The problems encountered by Sir John French and Lanrezac – neither of whom was fluent in the other's language – in attempting to co-ordinate their operations reveals much about the challenges posed by fighting alongside allies, and the British and French in effect fought two separate but adjacent battles. Mons was

a classic encounter battle. Led by the 9th Lancers, the British II Corps under General Sir Horace Smith-Dorrien reached Mons on 21–22 August. Mons was a mining area of slag heaps and chimneys – not an ideal place to fight a battle. By the following day, 3rd and 5th Divisions had taken up positions along the banks of the Mons-Condé canal, in Mons itself and in outlying villages. The Cavalry Division was held in reserve. When German First Army appeared on the scene, they were taken by surprise, as Kluck believed the BEF was at Tournai. Mounting clumsy frontal assaults, the attackers were bloodily repulsed in most places. The sheer pressure of German forces and heavy artillery fire meant that the outnumbered BEF could not hold on indefinitely. Mons was not an affair in which generals calmly manoeuvred troops as if on a giant chessboard. Rather, individual units and sub-units fought a series of almost private battles. The machine gun section of the 4th Royal Fusiliers conducted a rearguard action at a bridge that resulted in the award of two Victoria Crosses, one posthumous.

Late on 23 August, II Corps began to fall back a new position. Lanrezac's Fifth Army was in full retreat. When French discovered this, the BEF too disengaged and slipped away from the Mons battlefield. Mons was a tactical victory for the British at the cost of 1,600 casualties (which was very light by later standards), but strategically the Germans had the upper hand and continued to drive

forward. Command and control was fragile. British I Corps, under General Sir Douglas Haig, remained in touch with Lanrezac's French Fifth Army, but Haig lost contact with Smith-Dorrien; and Sir John French at General Headquaters (GHQ) was able to exercise little control over the BEF's two corps. On 26 August, a German advance briefly threatened I Corps headquarters at Landrecies, causing some short-lived panic.

For the BEF, the retreat from Mons was a gruelling experience. Apart from the hard march under a hot sun, retreating from an enemy they believed they had defeated was demoralizing for many British soldiers. Spirits rose when, on 26 August, the order was given to halt and deploy for battle. With the Germans in pursuit, Smith-Dorrien was forced to turn and fight at Le Cateau, 50km (30 miles) south of Mons. Once again, II Corps inflicted a sharp tactical defeat on the Germans, who were as tired as the British. But this time British losses were much heavier – some 7,800. 1st Gordon Highlanders were accidentally left behind when the rest of the Corps retreated and were forced to surrender. The Germans, too, suffered badly and Smith-Dorrien was able to resume the retreat. The BEF was battered but intact and had fulfilled a vital role on the flank of French Fifth Army. French, however, temporarily lost his nerve and wanted to pull out of the line to refit. Kitchener had to cross over from England to forbid it. The end of August neared with the campaign still in the balance.

MAURICE JAMES DEASE VC

Lieutenant Dease, 4th Royal Fusiliers, was posthumously awarded the first Victoria Cross (VC) of the war for his actions at Mons.

SIDNEY FRANK GODLEY VC

After Dease was wounded, Private Godley took over a machine gun and held off the Germans. Awarded the VC, he lived until 1957.

Sir Horace Lockwood Smith-Dorrien
(1858–1930)

General Smith-Dorrien first saw action during the Zulu War of 1879, where he escaped from the Battle of Isandhlwana. His brilliant handling of II Corps in August 1914 played a major role in ensuring the survival of the BEF, but he was unfairly sacked by Sir John French during the Second Battle of Ypres that began on 22 April 1915. The two had fallen out before the war, and French was a vindictive man. Smith-Dorrien's reputation has endured rather better than French's.

ABOVE: Men of British 5th Cavalry Brigade on the retreat from Mons. British cavalry alternated between walking and riding to spare their horses.

THE MARNE AND THE AISNE

PUSHING BACK THE GERMAN OFFENSIVE

BY THE END OF AUGUST, JOFFRE HAD DECIDED HIS FORCE SHOULD GO
ONTO THE DEFENSIVE, AND FORMED A NEW ARMY (THE SIXTH, UNDER
GENERAL MAUNOURY) TO PLUG THE GAP ON THE LEFT OF THE BEF.
HOWEVER, LOCAL OFFENSIVES CONTINUED. AT GUISE ON 29 AUGUST,
FRENCH FIFTH ARMY MAULED THE FLANK OF GERMAN SECOND ARMY,
WHICH CAUSED BÜLOW TO HALT HIS ADVANCE FOR TWO DAYS.

1914

Lanrezac, shortly to be replaced by Franchet d'Esperey, had pulled back after the battle. Kluck, believing that Fifth Army was vulnerable and that the BEF no longer posed a threat, decide to wheel his army in front of Paris, rather than adhering to the letter of the Schlieffen Plan and encircling the French capital. On 3 September, Allied aircraft spotted that the direction of Kluck's advance had changed.

The French now had a golden opportunity to seize the strategic initiative by striking the German flank.

In Lorraine, too, the French were on the defensive. Crown Prince Rupprecht's forces advanced towards the 65-km (40-mile) gap between the fortresses of Épinal and Toul. Hampered by a stream of contradictory orders from Moltke's headquarters,

Rupprecht's advance was slowed by a tough fight near Nancy. In late August, at Verdun, the German Crown Prince, Friedrich Wilhelm's Fifth Army forces were battered by the French Third Army under General Sarrail. On 9 September, the Germans gave

ABOVE: A long column of German troops on the march, passing ambulances (note the red crosses on the flags) moving to the rear.

ABOVE: Erich von Falkenhayn (on the left) succeeded Moltke the Younger after the failure of the Schlieffen Plan.

ALEXANDER VON KLUCK
(1846–1934)

The 68-year-old General von Kluck commanded German First Army in 1914. He first saw service in the 1866 Austro-Prussian War (also known as the Seven Weeks War) and was noted as a particularly aggressive, even rash commander, who was prepared to take risks to get results. His relations with the cautious Karl von Bülow, commander of Second Army – and for a time Kluck's nominal superior – were often tense. His decision to alter the course of his army precipitated the first battle of the Marne. He was wounded in 1915.

ABOVE: French soldiers went to war in 1914 wearing the characteristic soft "kepi" as headgear. This example belonged to a sergeant of 132 Infantry Regiment.

RIGHT: The "taxis of the Marne", used to transport troops during the fighting, have become an enduring symbol of the battle.

up and fell back to their starting positions of 17 August.

In the northern sector, it did not prove easy to reverse the Allied retreat. Some troops, including the BEF, continued southwards after the order to turn around had been issued. Fortunately, the military governor of Paris, General Gallieni, moved up Sixth Army on 4 September, two days ahead of Joffre's order for a general offensive. The Germans were poorly placed to respond to the Allied attack. Kluck, after prodding from Moltke, was slowly deploying to protect the flanks of Second and Third Armies when advanced elements of Maunoury's forces attacked on 5 September. The rest of Sixth Army, plus Fifth Army and the BEF joined the battle on the following day. What became known as the First Battle of the Marne was a hard struggle. At one stage the French were reinforced by "the taxis of the Marne", which ferried a brigade of troops from Paris. The battle was ultimately decided not on the

Dover

English Channel

Calais

Boulogne

Ypres

front line stretches
to sea as sides
attempt to out-
flank each other

Lille

Arras

Cambrai

Dieppe

Amiens

Somme

Beauvais

FRANCE

Soissons

Rheims

Aisne

XXXX
1

XXXX
6

MAUNOURY

Oise

Seine

PARIS

Chartres

XXXX
BEF

FRENCH

Marne

Epernay

XXXX
5

LANREZAC/
FRANCHET d'ESPEREY

Gent

Antwerp

Schelde

BRUSSELS

BELGIUM

Mons

Namur

Le Cateau

St-Quentin

XXXX
2

Langres

XXXX
BEL

ALBERT

Maas

Liège

Ardennes

Sedan

LUXEMBOURG

Meuse

Trier

Verdun

XXXX
4

LANGLE
de CARY

XXXX
3

SARRAIL

XXXX
2

CASTELNAU

Metz

XXXX
1

DUBAIL

XXXX
1

KLUCK

Cologne

XXXX
2

BÜLOW

Koblenz

Rhine

XXXX
3

HAUSEN

GERMANY

Mainz

XXXX
4

WURTTEMBERG

Mosel

XXXX
5

CROWN
PRINCE

Mannheim

XXXX
6

RUPPRECHT

Nancy

Rhine

Strasbourg

XXXX
7

HEERINGEN

Freiburg

Mulhouse

0   60 miles

0   100 kms

N

WESTERN FRONT: 1914–15

| German positions | — | 29 August 1914 | Allied positions | — | 1 September 1914 |
| | --- | 1 September 1914 | Front line | — | January–December 1915 |

Had they been unable to hold the line there, they would have retreated some 65 km (40 miles). As a by-product of the Aisne, trench warfare was begun – it was to endure for another four years.

Moltke was sacked on 14 September, and his successor, Erich von Falkenhayn, went on to the offensive by attempting to outflank the Allied left. Joffre replied in kind, and there followed a series of attempts to turn the enemy's flank as the centre of the struggle moved steadily to the north. This is erroneously known as the "Race to the Sea"; the generals were not seeking to reach the coast, but to get round their opponent's flank. One such action took place at Dixmude in Belgium in mid October. Here, the defenders included French marines and Tirailleurs Sénégalais (Senegalese light infantry). Between 2 and 15 October, the BEF was transferred to Flanders, and from 10 October onwards its corps came into battle in places whose names were to become dreadfully familiar over the next four years – La Bassée, Messines, Armentières. The fall of Antwerp on 10 October released German troops for use in Flanders. These, together with some newly raised divisions, allowed the Germans to make one last attempt to smash through the congealing trench lines.

ABOVE: Scottish troops (1st Cameronians, 19 Brigade) are passed by French cavalry during the so-called race to the sea, October 1914.

JOSEPH SIMON GALLIENI
(1849–1916)

General Gallieni built his reputation as a commander in colonial conflicts in Africa, Madagascar and Indochina. Appointed military governor of Paris in August 1914, when he became aware that Kluck's army was exposing its flank he immediately grasped the possibilities, and his foresight and energy deserve a share of the credit for the success in the battle of the Marne. Gallieni became Minister of War in October 1915, but was shut out of high-level decision making by his rival Joffre. He resigned in March 1916.

ground, but in the minds of the German High Command. Moltke was startled by the reappearance of the BEF, which he had thought destroyed, advancing alongside French Fifth Army into the lightly defended gap between Bülow's and Kluck's forces. As the result of the visit of one of Moltke's staff officers, Colonel Hentsch, it was decided that German Second Army would retreat if the Allies crossed the Marne. On 9 September, the BEF did just that. Bülow fell back, with Kluck conforming to the retreat. The Germans had been stopped at the Marne. It was a great strategic victory. Some called it a miracle.

The Allies followed the retreating Germans and briefly victory seemed in sight. On reaching the heights above the River Aisne on 12–13 September, however, the Germans were discovered to be occupying primitive trenches. Joffre on 15 September realized that it was "no longer a question of pursuit, but of methodical attack". The Aisne was another strategic victory, this time for the Germans.

RIGHT: A German gravemarker. This identified the resting place of Peter Kollwitz (207th Reserve Infantry Regiment) killed on 23 October 1914 at Dixmude. His artist mother, Kathe, created the famous Mourning Parents sculpture.

BELOW: A French 75mm gun in action, October 1914. This photograph shows the moment of firing – the barrel is at full recoil.

THE BATTLE OF TANNENBERG

RUSSIANS GO ON THE OFFENSIVE

IN AUGUST 1914, GERMANY FACED THE NIGHTMARE OF FIGHTING ON
TWO WIDELY-SEPARATED FRONTS. THE SCHLIEFFEN PLAN GAMBLED THAT
FRANCE COULD BE DEFEATED IN THE WEST BEFORE RUSSIAN FORCES
ATTACKED GERMANY IN STRENGTH IN THE EAST.

1914

THE NAME OF THE BATTLE

The name "Tannenberg" refers to a wooded
hill. It was the site of a battle fought in
1410 between the Teutonic Knights and a
Polish-Lithuanian force. The Knights were
defeated, and although the 1914 battle
was fought some miles away, it was given
the name "Tannenberg" as a belated form
of symbolic revenge for the earlier defeat.

The assumption was that the "Russian steamroller" would be slow to mobilize, and massive forces could be rushed from France by rail. But the Russian mobilization proved to be surprisingly swift, and in mid-August two armies struck against East Prussia. The German plan was unravelling.

The commander of German Eighth Army, Maximilian von Prittwitz, had been planning to retreat before the Russian advance into East Prussia but an aggressive corps commander, Hermann von François, attacked Paul von Rennenkampf's Russian First Army at Gumbinnen (20 August 1914). After initial success, the Germans were forced back, and Prittwitz lost his nerve. Fearing that he was about to be encircled by Alexander Samsonov's Russian Second Army, he ordered a retreat that would have meant abandoning large tracts of East Prussia. He

ABOVE LEFT: Russian troops fording a stream, August 1914.

ABOVE: General Paul von Hindenburg (middle), Colonel Max Hoffmann and Major-General Erich Ludendorff (right) at "command post Tannenberg", 24 August 1914.

OPPOSITE ABOVE: Infantry on the march, August 1914.

OPPOSITE BELOW: German soldiers in position in a house, August 1914.

was promptly sacked by Moltke, and a retired general, Paul von Hindenburg, was sent to replace him, with Erich Ludendorff, who had recently come to prominence at the siege of Liège, as his chief-of-staff.

In spite of their success, the Russians were facing severe problems. The strategic challenges of coordinating enormous armies across multiple fronts across hundreds of miles would have taxed the most efficient general staff in the world, and the Russian army's was far from that. The infrastructure of the Russian empire was poorly developed, which presented serious logistical problems. One of the attractions of invading East Prussia was that it was rich territory, but the presence of the Augustów Forest and the Masurian

Lakes forced the Russians to split their forces to move either side of these two awkward obstacles in the border area, as a result of which they could not offer mutual support.

Two factors exacerbated this problem. First, Russian communications were primitive even by the standards of 1914. This meant that, by default, much responsibility was devolved to formation commanders; the commander-in-chief, Grand Duke Nicholas, could do little to influence the East Prussian campaign once it had begun. Moreover, the highest echelons of the Russian officer corps was riven with factionalism. Unfortunately, Samsonov and Rennenkampf were bitter rivals, and there was no effective overall commander to keep them in check.

OPPOSITE ABOVE: Soldiers of the Russian Second Army in Austria, following their defeat and capture by the Germans at the Battle of Tannenberg, 30 August 1914.

OPPOSITE BELOW: Russian General Paul von Rennenkampf, pictured in 1905.

ABOVE: The ruins of a destroyed town in the battle area.

Alerted that Rennenkampf had failed to capitalize on his success, the new German command team – and Colonel Max Hoffman of Eighth Army - saw the opportunity to win an offensive battle of manoeuvre by attacking Samsonov, who was pushing forward, oblivious to any possible German threat. On 27 August, the Germans struck.

The Germans outflanked Samsonov's army, cutting the roads. François's I Corps was moved by rail around the Russian left. XX Corps fixed Samsonov to the front, and XVII Corps marched around the Russian right flank. It was a classic example of the favourite German operational gambit of encircling the enemy. The Germans knew, because the Russians sent radio messages

without being encoded, that Rennenkampf would not be able to support his rival; he was marching away from Samsonov. The German assault achieved surprise, and on 28 August Samsonov tried to retreat. But the Russians found themselves facing enemy forces on three sides. Many of the soldiers were demoralized and the army began to disintegrate. Faced with catastrophe, Samsonov committed suicide.

Tannenberg was a great German victory. For fewer than 20,000 losses, the Germans inflicted losses of 130,000, including 100,000 prisoners. Despite the failure of the Schlieffen Plan, the Russian threat to East Prussia was halted, and the Germans had gained the initiative in the East. And in Hindenburg, Germany had a new hero.

THE FIRST BATTLE OF YPRES

BLOODY STALEMATE

THE GERMAN ATTACK OF 20 OCTOBER 1914 INITIATED A SERIES OF ENGAGEMENTS THAT HAVE BECOME KNOWN TO HISTORY AS THE FIRST BATTLE OF YPRES. IT WAS AN OFFENSIVE ON A LARGE SCALE, FROM THE BÉTHUNE AREA TO THE COAST. RUPPRECHT'S SIXTH ARMY, RECENTLY TRANSFERRED FROM LORRAINE, ATTACKED TOWARDS THE NORTHEAST FROM THE DIRECTION OF LILLE.

1914

ABOVE: French soldiers in Ypres, October 1914. First Ypres was a genuinely
Allied battle, involving the French, British and Belgian armies.

The newly created Fourth Army moved west on a front between Ypres and Nieuport. In an extremely fortuitous piece of timing, Haig's I Corps arrived at Ypres from the Aisne on 20 October and helped stabilize the situation there. In the La Bassée-Messines sector, II and III Corps also repulsed German attacks. The heavy losses among young and inexperienced German volunteers caused the fighting to be dubbed the *Kindermord* ("massacre of the innocents"). The attackers had far more success against the Belgians on the River Yser: Nieuport and Dixmude were held (the former by French 42nd Division, the latter by the French marines); but elsewhere the Belgians were forced back to hold the line of the Dixmude-Nieuport railway. This terrain is extremely low-lying, and in desperation, in late October, the sea defences were deliberately breached and the sea allowed to flood the land. This created a highly effective barrier to a further German advance; so much so, that for the rest of the war this was a relatively quiet sector of the Western Front.

On 31 October, the Germans tried again. This time they concentrated on Ypres, using seven divisions commanded by General von Fabeck to assault the front between Messines and Gheluvelt. Under the cover of a heavy bombardment, the Germans made good progress. Haig's I Corps and Allenby's cavalry were in the path of the attack and, exhausted, began to give way. The Germans seized and held Messines Ridge, a battle in which the London Scottish became the first battalion of the Territorial Force, a reserve army of part-time soldiers originally raised for home defence, to go into battle. Further north, a chance shell fatally wounded the commander of British 1st Division and stunned his 2nd Division counterpart. Haig, receiving information that his line had been broken, mounted his horse and rode forward to the front. Briefly, Ypres was within the reach of the Germans, but they failed to grasp the opportunity.

ABOVE RIGHT: Civilian buses, complete with incongruous advertisements for soap and whisky, pressed into service to transport troops on the Western Front.

SIR DOUGLAS HAIG
(1861–1928)

General (later Field Marshal) Haig made his name as a corps commander at First Ypres. He became Commander-in-Chief of the BEF in late 1915. The most controversial general in British history, Haig has been condemned for the attritional battles of Passchendaele and the Somme, but rarely given the credit for the victory in 1918. He claimed that without the wearing down of the German army in 1916–17, the final victory would have been impossible, an argument that has never been satisfactorily refuted by historians.

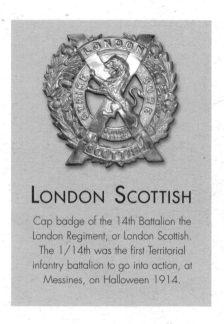

LONDON SCOTTISH

Cap badge of the 14th Battalion the London Regiment, or London Scottish. The 1/14th was the first Territorial infantry battalion to go into action, at Messines, on Halloween 1914.

Delays in bringing forward troops and the general chaos of battle allowed the 2nd Worcesters to counter-attack at Gheluvelt and restore the situation. Foch, appointed by Joffre as commander of the French left wing, fed in reserves, including French XVI and IX Corps, and put General D'Urbal in command of all French troops in the Ypres sector. The Allies had survived the crisis – for the moment.

While the fighting did not die away entirely, both sides spent the next few days regrouping, a breathing space for which the Allies were profoundly grateful. On 1 November, the new commander of 1st Division reported to Haig that his men could not resist an "organized attack". Over the next few days, more Allied troops reached Ypres, but the Germans, too, brought up another corps,

which attacked on 11 November. South of the Menin Road, the British fought off the attacks, but north of it a fresh crisis developed. Once again, Haig's I Corps was brought to the point of defeat as the Prussian Guards smashed through the weakened defenders. In the process, the attackers were themselves weakened and the impetus of the assault diminished. The artillery of 2nd Division, its covering screen of infantry having vanished, continued to pound away at the attackers. A force of batmen, cooks, headquarters staff and other "odds and ends" mounted a desperate counter-attack that did just enough, just in time, and then the 2nd Oxfordshire and Buckinghamshire Light Infantry made a decisive intervention. The battle dragged on until 22 November, but the Allied line had been stabilized and Ypres, one of the few Belgian cities still in Allied

hands, had been held. The French and British held an awkward salient around the city, surrounded on three sides by the Germans.

The campaigns in the West since August 1914 had been shockingly costly: perhaps 300,000 Frenchmen had been killed; the BEF had lost 86,000 men killed, wounded and missing; the Germans lost at least 134,000 (19,600 of them dead) at First Ypres alone. The attempt to win a rapid war of movement had ended in trench deadlock. A French offensive that began on 14 December (the First Battle of Artois) did nothing to break it. But there was a common belief that this was only a temporary phase. As British, French and German soldiers held their trenches, their generals planned for a resumption of mobile warfare in the New Year.

OPPOSITE: Belgian civilians flee their homes during the fighting at Messines, October 1914. Many eventually went to France or Britain.

ABOVE LEFT: An officer of the 2nd Argyll and Sutherland Highlanders, Captain Moorhouse, firing his Short Magazine Lee-Enfield rifle, Bois Grenier sector, near Ypres, November 1914.

ABOVE RIGHT: A Highland "Balmoral", named after the Royal residence in Scotland, the bonnet of the Black Watch (The Royal Highlanders).

The Christmas Truce

Over Christmas 1914, a number of British and German – and to a lesser extent, French – units observed strictly unofficial truces. The Christmas Truce has been much mythologized. It was by no means universal; 2nd Grenadier Guards were involved in some tough fighting on Christmas Day. But it is clear that in some places fighting ceased, soldiers fraternized in No Man's Land, and, according to a persistent story, German and British soldiers played football. Although a truce on such a scale never reoccurred, low-level fraternization took place throughout the war.

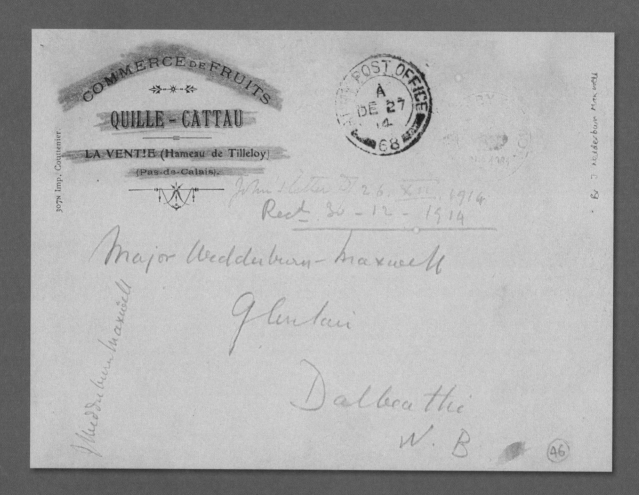

2nd Lieutenant Maxwell's 1914 Christmas letter

A letter from 2nd Lieutenant John Wedderburn-Maxwell,
5th Battery, XLV Brigade, Royal Field Artillery, describing
the 1914 Christmas Truce.

26 XII '14   5th battery 45" "B" R.F.A.

Sending home King Xmas Card and Lady Revolution to be kept

Rec. 30. XII. 14   VIII Divn B.E.F.

My dear Father

Very many thanks for your last and to all for their Xmas presents. Very little time to write but must tell you the most wonderful thing of the war I should say. On Xmas eve the Germans lined their trenches with lights & had several Xmas trees all lit up. Of course we stopped firing & both sides sang Carols. Early Xmas morning one of the RIR Tommies shouted out 'take a tip & chuck it' to which they replied:-

come over. An RIR sergeant went across to their lines & they gave him a box of cigars & sent him back after arranging not to fire till midnight. Then parties of both sides came out & met in the middle, exchanging cigarettes, buttons, what not! They wanted to have a football match yesterday afternoon but couldn't get a ball. Noon told me all this last night when the battery all 5 officers had dinner together - I came up last night at 10 pm for my turn at the Observation station, & walked down beside our trenches & saw Germans & English still up above ground, tho the 'Soldiers Truce' was over at midnight, when one of our officers fired a

very Pistol as signal that this was up, and a volley over their heads - However both sides are still quite friendly. They said - so a captain in a London Territorial regiment told me - the French are no good, they give in; the Russians are no good. They think they have an enormous victory in Poland & that the war will be over in 3 weeks. They say we are very good fighters & our artillery gives them no rest. They were quite cheerful and well fed, & their trenches were rather less muddy than ours, wider & shallower. I think it's the most extraordinary show I've ever heard of & refused to believe it for a long while. Micky O'Sullivan, the

vet, was up here yesterday afternoon and now says the Germans held a bottle up on their lines, upon which Micky was off out of our trenches like a scalded cat, only to find the bottle empty! One was a waiter at the Ritz and wants to go home to London. They say we are their friends & wont shoot till we do.' If we don't take care there will be a german-cut peace without Generals or COs having any say in the matter. Some were very young, 16 or 17. I only hope I get a chance of talking to one but they kept by their own trenches this morning not in the middle and now - 12.30 - on the 3rd our battery are shooting. Off to lunch with RIR so very best love to all & a prosperous & happy N Year

THE WAR AGAINST TURKEY

FIGHTING IN THE CAUCASUS AND EGYPT

THE ENTRY OF THE OTTOMAN EMPIRE (TURKEY) IN NOVEMBER 1914
OPENED UP GLITTERING PROSPECTS FOR THE ALLIES. TURKEY HAD LONG
BEEN REGARDED AS THE "SICK MAN OF EUROPE", ITS TERRITORIES
RIPE FOR DISMEMBERMENT. RUSSIA HAD AMBITIONS TO TAKE OVER
CONSTANTINOPLE: THE SEIZURE OF THE OTTOMAN CAPITAL WOULD
ALLOW ITS SHIPS TO PASS UNHINDERED FROM THE BLACK SEA TO THE
MEDITERRANEAN. BRITAIN AND FRANCE WANTED TO ENLARGE THEIR
RESPECTIVE MIDDLE EASTERN EMPIRES AT TURKISH EXPENSE.

1914
1916

The Turks had mostly performed poorly in the recent Balkan Wars (1912–13), and their vast empire suffered from inadequate railways and roads. However, the Ottomans were to prove a tougher enemy than expected. Supported by German officers, some Turkish commanders were to prove highly competent, and their soldiers tough and resourceful.

On 21 December 1914 the Turks launched a major offensive against the Russians in the Caucasus. The Ottoman Third Army, comprised of three weak corps (about 66,000 fighting men), had to struggle against the harsh environment, mountainous terrain and appalling weather, as well as the enemy. Ottoman logistics were poor in the extreme, and their soldiers often lacked

ABOVE: The Kurdish cavalry of the Turkish army, stationed in the Caucasus and the Eastern Taurus in 1916.

OPPOSITE ABOVE: Turkish prisoners taken by the Russians in 1914.

OPPOSITE CENTRE: The fort of Erzurum in eastern Turkey, having been captured by the Russians in the Caucasus Campaign.

OPPOSITE BELOW: British mounted troops in the desert with camel-borne troops in the background.

THE BATTLE OF ROMANI

In August 1916, an Ottoman force, which included some German and Austro-Hungarian elements, all under the overall command of German General Kress von Kressenstein, made a determined advance towards the Suez Canal. It was opposed by the British 52nd (Lowland) Division and the Anzac Mounted Division. The Ottoman plan was to secure Romani, close to the coast. Capturing it would bring the Canal within artillery range. However, in heavy fighting on 4 August, the British Empire troops first halted the Turkish advance and then drove the enemy back. The Turks never again posed a serious threat to the Canal.

ABOVE: The German general, Friedrich Freiherr Kress von Kressenstein.

basic necessities such as warm clothing to protect against the snow. The Russians, with about 77,000 effectives, were initially under pressure – an appeal on 2 January 1915 from Russian high command to the British and French was one of the factors that led to the Gallipoli campaign – but they were able to contain the Turkish assaults. Then, in late December, the Russians struck back. Two out of three Turkish corps were severely

damaged, and subsequently the Russians pushed further forward, to Lake Van. Another major offensive began in the Caucasus in January 1916, when Russian forces commanded by General Nikolai Yudenich drove on to Ottoman soil and captured the cities of Erzurum (in February), Trebizond (April) and Erzingham (July). These were spectacular advances over territories that had been disputed between

the Russians and the Turks for two centuries. Having suffered calamitous losses, the Ottomans rushed reinforcements to the Caucasus, and in August-September the front became stalemated, as the Russians were at the end of a long and tenuous supply chain and were unable to extend their advance. At another extremity of their Empire, in February 1915 the Turks tried to take the Suez Canal. Egypt was critical to the security

ABOVE: *The Battle of Chunuk Bair, 8 August 1915* (Ion Brown), vividly depicts the Wellington Battalion's desperate fight on the crest. Not since 25 April had any Anzacs – and there were only a handful even then – laid eyes on the Narrows, which can be seen in the background.

of the British Empire, as possession of the Canal meant that ships sailing for Britain's southern hemisphere possessions could avoid a long detour around the southern tip of Africa. Thus, when the Turks moved along the central route across the Sinai desert, it was a potentially serious development, especially as a British defeat might have triggered an uprising in Egypt by Arab dissidents. In the event, the attack on the

Canal was easily defeated. Subsequently, it made strategic sense for the British to carry out forward defence, and a fresh Ottoman advance was smashed 32 kilometres (20 miles) from the Canal at the Battle of Romani (August 1916). The scene was set for the British advance westwards across the Sinai into Palestine.

WAR IN AFRICA

THE CLASH OF IMPERIAL AMBITIONS

BY 1914, THE "SCRAMBLE FOR AFRICA" WAS LONG PAST AND ALMOST THE ENTIRE CONTINENT WAS CONTROLLED BY THE EUROPEAN IMPERIAL POWERS. RIVALRIES WERE FIERCE. A CLASH OF AMBITIONS IN AFRICA HAD ALMOST CAUSED WAR BETWEEN FRANCE AND BRITAIN IN 1898, WHILE GERMANY HAD STOOD BY WITH ILL-CONCEALED SATISFACTION WHEN BRITAIN SUFFERED A SERIES OF EMBARRASSING DEFEATS AT THE HANDS OF THE WHITE BOER REPUBLICS IN THE SOUTH AFRICAN WAR (1899–1902).

1914
1916

Given the competing imperial ambitions, it was no surprise that Africa became a battlefield during the 1914–18 war. Apart from immediate objectives – such as securing wireless (radio) stations – the British and French sought to expand their empires at German expense, partly to achieve security for existing territories, but also from force of habit.

Germany was at a major disadvantage in the war for Africa. Allied – principally British – sea-power cut Germany's colonies off from the Fatherland, making it almost impossible

to reinforce them. It seemed that they could be captured at the Allies' leisure. As early as 6–7 August 1914, German Togoland was invaded by British and French-officered African troops from neighbouring colonies, with the campaign being over 20 days later. Modern Namibia (German South-West Africa) was attacked in September 1914 by forces from the Union of South Africa. The

ABOVE: A Boer detachment from Transvaal bear arms following the outbreak of the First World War in late 1914.

RIGHT: General Louis Botha, the first Prime Minister of South Africa from 1910 to 1919.

invasion was compromised by a rebellion in South Africa of 12,000 Boer "bitter enders", who had never been reconciled to the 1902 peace settlement with the British. Thirty thousand Union troops were deployed before the uprising was crushed at the end of January 1915. Led by the South African Prime Minister, General Louis Botha, the Union forces resumed the offensive in South-West Africa and by mid-July 1915 had conquered the territory.

It took from late August 1914 to February 1916, nearly 18 months of hard campaigning by British, French and Belgian troops – again mostly Africans officered by Europeans – before the German West African colony of the Cameroons was subdued. As in all the campaigns in Africa, in addition to the fighting troops the armies employed many African "porters" to carry supplies – perhaps 40,000 in this case. The harsh climate and disease were more formidable enemies than the Germans, with the porters suffering very badly, but despite these obstacles, in the end resistance was extinguished.

Things were very different in German East Africa. Here, in Tanganyika, African troops

(Askaris) under the command of Lieutenant-Colonel Paul von Lettow-Vorbeck waged a brilliant guerrilla campaign against the invading forces of the British Empire. He maximized the advantages which the difficult terrain bestowed on the defender and skilfully manoeuvred his lightly-equipped Askaris, consistently wrong-footing his British pursuers, who suffered badly from diseases such as malaria. The campaign was marked by poor British generalship, including the humiliating failure to capture the port of Tanga from 3 to 5 November 1914. Thereafter, Imperial forces increased steadily in size but could not inflict a decisive defeat on Lettow-Vorbeck. The campaign only ended when he voluntarily surrendered after he heard about the Armistice – two weeks after the end of the war in Europe. The German African empire had proved to be a far tougher nut than originally anticipated by the Allies.

ABOVE TOP LEFT: A fez headdress associated with African troops serving in the German Schutztruppe.

ABOVE LEFT: The tunic of a first lieutenant in the German colonial forces.

ABOVE: An artist's impression of an Askari band which was one of a series of images made for cigarette cards.

BELOW: Indian troops held as prisoners of war following the Battle of Tanga, in November 1914.

THE WAR AT SEA

THE NORTH SEA, ADRIATIC AND MEDITERRANEAN

IN 1914, BRITAIN'S ROYAL NAVY (RN) HAD DOMINATED THE OCEANS FOR MORE THAN A CENTURY. AT THE BEGINNING OF THE WAR, THE NAVY'S TRADITIONAL STRATEGY HAD SWUNG INTO PLACE. GERMANY WAS BLOCKADED TO PREVENT GOODS GETTING IN OR OUT OF ENEMY TERRITORY. SHIPS HEADING FOR ENEMY OR NEUTRAL PORTS WERE BOARDED AND CONTRABAND – ANYTHING FROM MUNITIONS TO FOOD – WAS SEIZED.

1914
1915

In November 1914, the British formally classified the North Sea as a war zone, giving notice that action might be taken against ships that entered the area. The French navy mounted a similar blockade of Austro-Hungarian ports in the Adriatic.

Although the blockade began to bite, and ultimately proved a critical factor in winning the war for the Allies, the British did not have it all their own way in the war at sea. In August 1914, two German cruisers, *Goeben* and *Breslau*, eluded the Royal Navy in the Mediterranean and escaped to Constantinople, where they played a role in bringing the Ottoman Empire into the war. On 28 August, three German light cruisers were sunk off the German island of

OPPOSITE: The battle cruisers *Aboukir*, *Hogue* and *Cressy* sinking in the North Sea after being torpedoed.

ABOVE LEFT: Rear Admiral "Jacky" Fisher.

ABOVE RIGHT: The Indefatigable Class battlecruiser HMAS *Australia*, flagship of the Royal Australian Navy.

1915

Heligoland, but among the embarrassing British naval losses were the antiquated cruisers *Aboukir*, *Hogue* and *Cressy*, torpedoed off the coast of the Netherlands on 22 September. Partly as a result of these setbacks, but also because of an outcry against his German background, Admiral Prince Louis of Battenberg was forced out of his position as head of the Royal Navy and replaced by the veteran Admiral "Jacky" Fisher. But more embarrassment was to follow: on 16 December, three towns on the east coast of England were shelled by German battlecruisers.

Across the globe the Royal Navy, supported by the Royal Australian Navy and the navy of Britain's ally Japan, mopped up German merchant and naval vessels, cut off from home with no hope of penetrating the British blockade. One such force was

Admiral von Spee's Pacific Squadron, which preyed on Allied shipping with some success: off Coronel (Chile) on 1 November, Spee destroyed an inferior British force. Vengeance was swift. At the Battle of the Falkland Islands (8 December 1914) Admiral Sturdee, reinforced with two state-of-the-art battlecruisers, destroyed all but one of von Spee's ships. The single escapee, the cruiser *Dresden*, was tracked down and sunk in March 1915.

The main focus of the war at sea in 1915 was the submarine war and the struggle at the Dardanelles (see separate sections), but there was one major clash between surface fleets. On 24 January, Admiral von Igenohl sent four armoured cruisers, supported by two flotillas of torpedo boats out on a raid into the North Sea. The ever-aggressive Admiral Sir David Beatty attacked the German force

off Dogger Bank with his battlecruisers and sunk an armoured cruiser, Blücher. Igenohl was replaced as commander of the High Seas Fleet by a more cautious admiral, von Pohl. For over a year, the two battle-fleets eyed each other warily, until in May 1916 the long awaited major battle took place, off Jutland.

ABOVE: SMS *Nurnberg* at Valparaiso, Chile, after the Battle of Coronel.

OPPOSITE ABOVE: The ruins of a house in Scarborough, destroyed during the 500 shell bombardment on 16 December, 1914.

OPPOSITE BELOW: Vice Admiral Sir Doveton Sturdee, on the quarterdeck of HMS *Hercules*.

THE NAVAL BOMBARDMENT OF BRITISH TOWNS

The German High Seas Fleet posed a threat not only to its Royal Naval counterpart but also to British civilians. On 3 November Great Yarmouth and Lowestoft were shelled from the sea, with little effect, but on 16 December it was the turn of Whitby, Scarborough, and the Hartlepool area. One hundred and twenty-seven people were killed, the victims' ages ranging from six months to 86 years. British propagandists made much of German barbarity, which helped to deflect criticism of the Royal Navy's failure to catch the raiders. Raids continued intermittently, with Lowestoft and Great Yarmouth again shelled in April 1916. Forty houses were destroyed and four people killed.

1915 SPRING OFFENSIVES

ARTOIS AND CHAMPAGNE

THE END OF MOBILE WARFARE IN 1914 LEFT THE GERMANS IN
CONTROL OF MOST OF BELGIUM AND OF SOME OF THE MOST
IMPORTANT INDUSTRIAL AREAS OF FRANCE. THE OPPOSING LINES
STRETCHED FROM THE CHANNEL COAST NEAR NIEUPORT ALL THE
WAY TO THE SWISS FRONTIER.

1914
1915

ABOVE: No Man's Land, Bois Grenier sector, June 1915.
British positions are marked with an "O" and German
lines with an "X".

At the beginning of 1915, the trench system was still fairly rudimentary – sometimes little more than holes in the ground hastily joined together. In some places the terrain was unsuitable for the digging of trenches. In the Vosges mountains they sometimes had to be cut into rock with explosives. At this stage the French provided by far the largest Allied army, although the BEF grew as new formations arrived.

French offensives continued over the winter. Joffre's strategy was one of constant offensives, "nibbling" (as he called it) the enemy. He aimed to pinch out the great bulge in the German line – the Noyon Salient – by attacking in Artois and Champagne. But the First Battle of Artois (27 September–10 October 1914), an ambitious attempt to capture key objectives, including the dominating heights of Vimy Ridge that overlooked the German-held Douai plain, made little headway and was ended in early January. Another offensive was begun in Champagne on 20 December 1914, which continued in stages until the end of March. Again, despite fierce fighting, the French had little to show for this effort except 240,000 casualties. The Germans captured the high ground of the Chemin des Dames ("Ladies's Road", named after Louis XV's daughters) running east and west in the département of the Aisne in November 1914, and in January

1915 a German attack seized the last French position on the plateau, Creute farm (later known as the Dragon's Cave). In the Vosges, a bitter struggle for the Hartmannsweilerkopf peak resulted in 20,000 French losses over four months before they secured the heights in April.

The early fighting in 1915 demonstrated how important heavy and accurate artillery fire was to battlefield success, particularly now the armies were faced with siege warfare. The

ABOVE: The Liverpool Scottish attack Bellewaerde on 16 June 1915.

RIGHT: A binocular periscope. Since it could be lethal to look over the parapet, trench periscopes were very common. Many of the early ones were improvised from whatever materials were available.

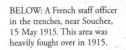

BELOW: A French staff officer in the trenches, near Souchez, 15 May 1915. This area was heavily fought over in 1915.

THE BATTLE OF NEUVE CHAPELLE
10 MARCH 1915

The Battle of Neuve Chapelle was the first major British offensive of 1915. Before the action, the Royal Flying Corps carried out photo-reconnaissance missions over the German trenches to produce maps that improved the accuracy of the British bombardment. The principles of traffic control, a mundane but essential facet of modern warfare, began to emerge as a result of the battle. The attack was carried out by IV Corps and Indian Corps, the latter consisting of Indian, British and Gurkha troops under Lieutenant-General Sir James Willcocks.

British offensive at Neuve Chapelle on 10 March gave further evidence confirming this reality. The battle was well planned by Haig's First Army staff: the initial bombardment, which was heavy by contemporary standards and lasted only 35 minutes, mostly overwhelmed the German infantry and allowed the British to take the front-line trenches. But resistance on the flanks, the difficulty of following up the initial success and the arrival of German reserves meant the

battle soon bogged down. A mere 1,100 m (1,200 yds) was gained for 13,000 British and 12,000 German casualties.

With the exception of the the German attack at Ypres in April (see pages 56–59), it was the Allies who remained on the offensive in Spring 1915. French First and Third Armies fought a bloody and unsuccessful battle to reduce the St-Mihiel salient (5–18 April), and Joffre launched another hammer blow in Artois in May. Bad news from the

Eastern Front – the Central Powers inflicted a major defeat on the Russians at Gorlice-Tarnów in early May – lent particular urgency to this offensive. It also offered an opportunity to strike in the West while the Germans were heavily committed in the East. Joffre ordered D'Urbal's Tenth Army to smash through the German defences in Artois and re-open mobile warfare. On 9 May, Tenth Army, with 1,075 guns (including 293 heavies), attacked Vimy Ridge

and positions flanking it. The main attack in the centre was assigned to Philippe Pétain's XXXIII Corps. The defenders wilted under the weight of the bombardment, and within 90 minutes, the 77th and Moroccan Divisions had pressed forward onto the crest of Vimy Ridge. Then, the problems of trench warfare reasserted themselves. Lacking modern radio communictions, reserves could not be summoned forward to exploit the gains. When they did arrive, it was too late as German reserves first shored up the front and then drove the attackers back.

On 9 May the BEF again attacked over the Neuve Chapelle battlefield after another brief bombardment. In a day's fighting Haig's First Army achieved nothing apart from casualties of 11,000 in what became known as the battle of Aubers Ridge. Sir John French was pressed by the French to continue offensive operations, and, after reverting to a bombardment that lasted four days, on 15–16 May, First Army attacked at Festubert with the aim of inflicting heavy casualties on the Germans and pinning their forces to this front. This brought some modest gains, but again at the price of heavy losses. Festubert was the first time the British fought a deliberately attritional battle, and the limited success helped to create the idea that "artillery conquers, infantry occupies" that was to have terrible repercussions in July 1916.

ABOVE: Two typical fantassins – French infantrymen – loaded with kit. Such men were the backbone of the French army in the war.

"Je les grignote" ("I keep nibbling them") JOFFRE

BELOW: German trench artillery, 1915: the Granatenwerfer (grenade thrower) and its Wurfgranaten missile, which weighed 1.8 kg (4 lb).

THE SECOND BATTLE OF YPRES

THE FIRST USE OF POISON GAS

IN THEIR SEARCH FOR A WAY TO BREAK THE DEADLOCK ON THE WESTERN FRONT, THE BELLIGERENTS MADE AMPLE USE OF NEW TECHNOLOGIES. GAS HAD FIRST BEEN TRIED ON THE EASTERN FRONT AT BOLIMOV IN JANUARY 1915 AND GAS CANISTERS HAD BEEN USED IN SHRAPNEL AT NEUVE CHAPELLE. THE FRENCH HAD ALSO PREVIOUSLY USED TEAR GAS CANISTERS BUT AT THE SECOND BATTLE OF YPRES THIS SEARCH SAW THE FIRST USE OF POISON GAS ON A LARGE SCALE.

1915

ABOVE: A cloud of gas moves across the battlefield during the Second Battle of Ypres, 1915.

ABOVE: A posed photograph of French troops during the Second Battle of Ypres. They are wearing a primitive form of gas mask.

POISON GAS

Following the first major use of gas at Second Ypres, both sides used chemical weapons freely. The original clumsy use of wind-borne agents was superseded later in the war by projectiles such as those fired by the British Livens Projector. Chlorine gas was superseded by phosgene, and later by mustard gas. Gas never became a decisive weapon, in part because anti-gas protection steadily improved. The soldiers of early 1915 had crude mouth and nose pads; by the end of the war soldiers were issued with more sophisticated respirators.

The fighting of October–November 1914 had left the Allies holding a vulnerable salient jutting out 8 km (6 miles) into German-held territory. Falkenhayn ordered a limited offensive at Ypres in April 1915 that would test a recently developed weapon, chlorine gas, and – it was hoped – would divert attention from the Eastern Front, where the main German effort was taking place. Fourth Army had 11 divisions in the area, but as this was not intended as a major attack, no further reserves were provided. The attackers faced two French, four British and the 1st Canadian Division, the latter having arrived on the Western Front in February 1915.

The German attack achieved almost complete surprise, no less than 5,830 metal cylinders containing the gas having been installed on the front lines without attracting attention. This represented a substantial intelligence failure on the part of the Allies. A German deserter had warned the French several weeks earlier of a plan to use gas, and similar reports arrived from other sources. Suspecting a deception operation, and rather naïvely

ABOVE: German troops discharging poison gas from canisters.

RIGHT: Later in the war, the German army was much better prepared for chemical warfare. Here, driver and horses are wearing respirators.

LOGISTICS

Logistics – the art and science of moving and supplying troops – is an unglamorous but vital facet of warfare. During the First World War, armies used a combination of horse-drawn and motor transport, backed up by light- and standard-gauge railways. Vast quantities of materiel had to be moved; before the French Sixth Army's attack on the Somme in July 1916, ammunition for 552 heavy guns had to be stockpiled. In the autumn of 1918, a robust and flexible logistic system would give the BEF an important advantage over the Germans.

of the French, Canadians and British helped hold the Allied position together. French reinforcements arrived, but nonetheless the situation was growing serious as the salient became steadily compressed. On 27 April, Smith-Dorrien, the local army commander, sensibly told Sir John French that he wanted to fall back to a more defensible position 4 km (2.5 miles) in the rear. French, who hated Smith-Dorrien, used this as an excuse to remove him from his command. Smith-Dorrien's replacement, V Corps commander Sir Herbert Plumer, recommended the same course of action, although more tactfully, and this time the French agreed to a retirement. Plumer, described by one historian as "almost an ideal general for siege warfare", was to command in the Ypres Salient for most of the next three years.

Although any chance of the Germans achieving a clean breakthrough had vanished, the Second Battle of Ypres had not yet finished. A French attack on 30 April gained about 180 m (200 yds), while on 8 May the Germans mounted a major assault on Frenzenberg Ridge. British 27th and 28th Divisions took the main force of the attack, and had to be reinforced by dismounted cavalry. In a week of intense fighting, the defenders were gradually forced back about 1,100 m (1,200 yds). One last spasm of fighting erupted around Bellewaarde on 24–25 May, and then the battle burned out. The Germans had forced the Allies back towards Ypres, but had failed to capitalize on the surprise gained by the initial gas attack. It was a great opportunity missed.

believing that the Germans would abide by the international law that forbade the use of such weapons, the French High Command ignored the warnings. The Germans relied on the wind blowing in the right direction for the gas to be effective, and in the late afternoon the atmospheric conditions were judged to be right. At 17:00 the defenders came under intense artillery fire, and the 45th (Algerian) and French 87th Divisions – the latter consisting of overage territorials – holding the northern part of the Ypres salient saw mist – described by some as bluish-white, by others as yellow-green – drift over from the German trenches. Utterly unprepared for a chemical attack, the French troops gave way and fled in rout. Faced with a 3.25-km (2-mile) gap in their line, the Allies seemed on the verge of a major defeat.

However, the Germans followed up their success with some hesitation, cautiously

advancing about 3.25 km (2 miles) and then, on reaching the gas cloud, digging in. This uncharacteristic lack of drive was probably related to the rudimentary anti-gas protection with which the German troops were provided. This German failure to exploit the Allied crisis bought valuable time for British and French reinforcements to reach the battlefield. The inexperienced Canadians, suddenly finding that their flank was open, were particularly vulnerable to a renewed German advance. Improvising gas masks out of cloth soaked in water or urine, ten British and Canadian battalions plugged the gap. On 23 April, the French and Canadians were able to link hands across the salient. The following day saw the Canadians again engulfed by a gas cloud, but they held their ground, their staunch behaviour proving that any fears that British regulars might have had about the reliability of this largely citizen force were groundless. The defensive actions

ABOVE: British soldiers of King's Liverpool Regiment in shallow "scrapes" during the Second Battle of Ypres.

OPPOSITE ABOVE: French victims of German gas at Second Ypres: the bodies of Zouaves, 22 April 1915.

OPPOSITE BELOW: No.8 Casualty Clearing Station, Bailleul, 1 May 1915. British victims of a gas attack at Hill 60, near Ypres.

MGP

ORIGINAL.

Copy sent to Dgams & Secy

POST OFFICE TELEGRAPHS.

Government Despatch No. 140   23 April 19

SB Priority 115 *

Given in at 6 57

at 8.48

Received in   9.10 at 6/18

Sent out for delivery at

This message has passed through the hands of

Telegraphist
Writer.

TO { Troopers War Office P.

Oai 948 23rd April Germans used powerful
asphyxiating gases very extensively in attack
on French yesterday with serious effect
aaa Apparently these gases are either
chlorine or bromine aaa will send
further details later but meanwhile strongly
urge that immediate steps be taken
to supply similar means of most
effective kind for use by our
troops aaa Also essential that our

Gas attack telegrams

The German gas attack at Ypres in April 1915 took the Allies by surprise. In this telegram Sir John French asks the War Office to provide anti-gas equipment for British troops.

1915

POST OFFICE TELEGRAPHS.

Government Despatch No. 140   Ap 23   19

Given in at ....

at ....

Received in 640 at ....

Sent out for delivery at ....

This message has passed through the hands of

Telegraphist

Writer.

TO {   Troopers P2

Troops should be immediately provided with means of counteracting effects of enemy gases which should be suitable for use when on the move aaa As a temporary measure am arranging for troops in trenches to be supplied with solution of bicarbonate of soda in which to soak handkerchiefs aaa

Chief S.H.S 5.50 pm

EASTERN FRONT BATTLES
EXPULSION OF THE RUSSIAN FORCES

THE EASTERN FRONT BATTLES OF 1915 WERE ON A HUGE SCALE AND
ENORMOUSLY BLOODY, BUT THEY ARE LITTLE KNOWN IN THE WEST.
IN OCTOBER–DECEMBER 1914, A SERIES OF CLASHES IN POLAND
ENDED WITH THE TSAR'S ARMIES IN THE ASCENDANT, THE AUSTRO-
HUNGARIAN ARMIES HAVING SUFFERED PARTICULARLY BADLY.

1915

However, at the end of the year the German army in the east was reinforced, and in February 1915 an offensive finally cleared the Russians out of East Prussia, although an attempt to encircle and destroy the retreating Russians only partly succeeded – there was to be no second Tannenberg.

Further south, on 23 January, the Austrians, supported by German forces, began an ambitious attempt to expel Russian forces from the Carpathian mountains. The Russian advance in 1914 had captured much Austrian territory. But Fortress Przemysl held out behind Russian lines, and the offensive aimed to relieve the 120,000-strong garrison. Mountain warfare is always testing; but fighting in mid-January, troops had to contend with dreadful weather while wearing wholly inadequate uniforms and lacking even basic equipment. The logistical problems of fighting in the mountains were a quartermaster's nightmare. The decision by Conrad, the Austrian de facto Commander-in-Chief, to launch and then continue this battle rates as one of the worse strategic decisions of the war.

Worse was to come. On 22 March 1915 Przemysl finally surrendered, releasing three Russian corps for a counter-offensive in the Carpathians. The ground captured at such

great cost by the Habsburg troops was lost. The Russian advance in turn was halted in mid-April as supply lines lengthened and German troops arrived. Austrian losses amounted to 800,000, including many irreplaceable experienced soldiers. Although there was some suspicion of the loyalty of non-ethnic German soldiers in Austrian forces, for the most part the army proved remarkably cohesive, enduring until the very end of the war.

The Germans were deeply worried about the poor performance of their ally. A process of colonization of the Austrian army began, with German soldiers taking key positions from high command downwards. General

Falkenhayn, the German Commander-in-Chief, decided to send troops east to make a major push to take the pressure off their allies. Von Mackensen's Eleventh Army was the spearhead formation, with the Austrian Fourth Army on the flank. Although lip-service was paid to Austrian sensitivities, the Germans were firmly in control. The Gorlice-Tarnów campaign began with a crushing artillery bombardment on 2 May 1915. Russian Third Army rapidly crumbled under the assault, as Mackensen's forces surged forward to the River San. By 10 May, 140,000 Russians were prisoners. The arrival of Russian reinforcements and inevitable logistic problems slowed the German-Austrian advance, but Russian counter-attacks were ultimately fruitless, in spite of good progress made by Ninth Army. Przemsyl was recaptured (this time, for good) on 4 June and two weeks later the Russians abandoned Galicia, with Central Powers troops capturing Lvov on 22 June. It was a stunning victory that stood in sharp contrast to the deadlock in the West.

OPPOSITE: A cossack patrol occupying a town in Poland shortly after it was evacuated by the Germans.

ABOVE TOP LEFT: An Austrian Skoda 305mm howitzer and crew in action in the Carpathian mountains in 1914.

ABOVE TOP RIGHT: Fortress Przemysl, the scene of fierce Austrian resistance and Russian attacks.

LEFT: Austrian Field Marshal Franz Conrad von Hoetzendorf, Chief of the Austrian General Staff.

ABOVE RIGHT: General von Falkenhayn (left), photographed after the war while commanding the Ninth Army on the Romanian Front.

INTERRELATION OF EAST AND WEST

Although separated by hundreds of miles, events on the Eastern and Western Fronts were closely interrelated. Russian pressure on the Austro-Hungarians helped buy time for the volunteer British armies to be raised and trained. Conversely, Falkenhayn, a "Westerner", authorized the May 1915 Gorlice-Tarnów offensive in the correct belief that the German positions on the Western Front could withstand an Anglo-French attack – although this did mean that few operational reserves were available to take advantage of the initial success of the gas attack at the Second Battle of Ypres in April 1915.

TOTAL WAR

THE HOME FRONTS

CIVILIANS, NOT JUST SOLDIERS, SAILORS AND AIRMEN, WERE CRITICAL TO THE WAGING OF THE FIRST WORLD WAR. THE WAR WAS A "TOTAL" CONFLICT THAT REQUIRED STATES TO MOBILIZE THEIR ECONOMIES AND POPULATIONS AS WELL AS THEIR ARMED FORCES. INDUSTRIAL PRODUCTION WAS VITAL, AND FACTORIES PRODUCING WAR MATERIALS SPRANG UP ACROSS THE BELLIGERENT COUNTRIES.

1914
1918

ABOVE: Workers surrounded by shells in a Nottinghamshire munitions factory, July 1917.

THE TREND TO TOTAL WAR

Total war involves mass mobilization and ruthlessness in the conduct of war. The French Revolutionary and Napoleonic Wars (1792–1815) showed signs of totality, as did the American Civil War (1861– 65), but 1914–18 was the first war in which modern industrialized states engaged in all-out conflict. Yet the Second World War was even more a total conflict in this regard. Many leaders in that war, including Winston Churchill, drew upon their experiences in 1914–18. Unlike in the First World War, the Second ended with the unconditional surrender of the beaten powers, Germany and Japan.

In particular, France, which lost most of its industrialized areas in the initial German advance, performed wonders in manufacturing munitions. Many women entered the workforce to replace men who were sent off to fight. Maintaining Home Front morale was all important, and all these factors led to the industrial working classes flexing their muscles and in some cases – notably in Britain – achieving significant social advances.

The popular image of Europeans celebrating the outbreak of war in August 1914 and rushing lemming-like to destruction is a caricature. While there was some enthusiasm, for the most part war was greeted warily. However, those actively opposed to the war

made little headway – socialist hopes of a Europe-wide general strike by workers were quickly dashed. Instead, competing groups within states made a show of unity, agreeing not to engage in active opposition to their governments' war policy. In France this was known as the "Sacred Union"; while Germany had the "Fortress Truce". Although industrial peace and an end to class conflict came under great strain in the years to come, one of the striking things about all the Home Fronts, with the exception of Russia, was how stable they were. Even the multi-national Austro-Hungarian Empire, which contained many minority groups who longed to be independent, held together until the end of the war.

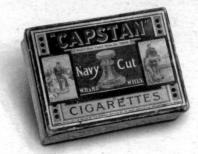

ABOVE LEFT: Firemen deal with the aftermath of a Gotha air raid on London in July 1917.

ABOVE TOP RIGHT: A German Gotha G IV. These heavy bombers were integral to the Gotha raids on London.

ABOVE: A tin of tobacco given to POW R. Holborrow by a German prison guard in 1918.

Civilians in all the European belligerent states had one thing in common: shortages of goods which had been easily available before the war. Rationing was commonplace, but Germany was particularly badly affected by the British naval blockade and many civilians went hungry. Ersatz (substitute) food, such as coffee made from acorns, became common, and 1916–17 was remembered as the "Turnip" winter. Failure of the German government to ensure the supply of basic foodstuffs to cities (increasingly farmers held on to the food they produced) was a significant factor in the decline of support for the Kaiser's regime.

The logical extension of the mobilization of civilians for the war effort was that they became targets. That was the rationale behind the British hunger blockade of German food supply lines, and also the bombing of enemy cities. The German Zeppelin raids against British cities that began in 1915 were succeeded by use of Gotha aircraft in 1917–18. The British Independent Air Force dropped 540 tons of bombs on Germany in 1918. The casualties that were caused were small in comparison to those of the Second World War, but they were seen at the time as shocking.

In 1917–18 the peoples of Europe were

war-weary. In Germany, the overambitious Hindenburg Programme of economic mobilization made thing worse, alienating many. By contrast the new, charismatic leaders in France and Britain, Clemenceau and Lloyd George, led a successful "re-mobilization" of their people. The War was won and lost on the Home Front as well as on the battlefront.

ABOVE: The leaders of Italy, Britain, France and the USA at the Paris Peace Conference in May 1919.

BELOW LEFT: RAF officers with the largest bomb dropped by the Air Force (1,650 lb) during the First World War.

BELOW RIGHT: Lloyd George, British Prime Minister during the second half of the First World War.

Fleury-Douaumont map

The 17 May Operations map used by General
Costantini at the HQ of the Fleury-Douaumont sector
on the right bank at Verdun.

AUTUMN 1915 BATTLES

ARTOIS, CHAMPAGNE AND LOOS

ALTHOUGH THE SUMMER OF 1915 WAS RELATIVELY QUIET ON THE WESTERN FRONT, THERE WAS STILL PLENTY OF FIGHTING IN "MINOR OPERATIONS". IN THE ARGONNE IN LATE JUNE, A GERMAN OFFENSIVE PENETRATED 225 M (250 YDS) INTO THE LINES OF XXXII FRENCH CORPS AND TOOK FONTAINE-AUX-CHARMES. FRENCH COUNTER-ATTACKS PREVENTED ANY FURTHER MAJOR ADVANCE, BUT BY MID-JULY THEY HAD SUFFERED 32,000 CASUALTIES. NEAR YPRES, THE GERMANS USED FLAMETHROWERS ON 30 JULY TO CAPTURE HOOGE FROM THE BRITISH. ACTIONS SUCH AS THESE WERE IN ADDITION TO THE EVERYDAY GRIND OF TRENCH WARFARE.

1915

Joffre's strategy for the autumn offensive aimed not so much at a clean breakthrough, but at pushing the enemy out of key positions and thus disrupting the continuity of his defences, compelling the Germans into a major retreat. In its final form, Joffre's strategy sought to pinch off the great German salient that had Noyon at its head by attacking from Artois, to the north – Vimy Ridge being a key tactical objective – and from Champagne, to the south. After heated debate, the BEF was committed to a simultaneous supporting attack at Loos, near Lens, despite the opposition of both French and Haig. This was coal-mining country, and the terrain of slag heaps and pit villages would be difficult ground for the British infantry to traverse. Nonetheless, Lord Kitchener, who was still the chief at the War Office, was persuaded that the problems being experienced by the Russians, and the threat of the current French government falling and being replaced by a ministry that would seek peace with Germany, meant that Loos had to go ahead. Haig, whose First Army would carry out the attack, warmed to the concept as he came to believe that the use of poison gas made a victory possible by

ABOVE: Fatigues and work parties were a never ending part of life on the Western Front. Here French troops fill sandbags behind the lines in Champagne.

THOMPSON ("TOMMY") CAPPER
(1863–1915)

General Capper, commander of British 7th Division, died of wounds sustained at the Battle of Loos in September 1915. He joined in the front line fighting on the second day of the battle and was hit by a bullet while organizing an attack, dying at a casualty clearing station on 27 September. Contrary to the myth that generals invariably kept out of harm's way in comfortable chateaux miles behind the lines, Capper was one of eight British generals killed, wounded or taken prisoner during the Loos offensive.

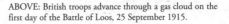

ABOVE TOP: The grim price of war: French dead after an attack in the Champagne sector.

ABOVE: British troops advance through a gas cloud on the first day of the Battle of Loos, 25 September 1915.

compensating for lack of artillery. On the other side of No Man's Land, the Germans built additional defences, and waited.

Expectations were high on the day of the great offensive, 25 September 1915. The Allies had a numerical advantage, but the battle demonstrated the extent to which the odds were stacked in the favour of the defender. On some sectors in Champagne the French infantry made some substantial gains. XIV Corps of Pétain's Second Army,

attacking across a narrow strip of No Man's Land, punched through the first belt of German defences to a depth of 4 km (2.5 miles). II Colonial Corps in Second Army gained about 3 km (2 miles). At the end of the first day, there was good reason for optimism in the French High Command. On the second day, some more gains were made, although not of the order of those gained on 25 September, and at the inevitable cost in heavy casualties. Thereafter, the battle reverted to attritional slogging.

In Artois, too, there was disappointment for the French. D'Urbal's Tenth Army attacked in bad weather, and took some positions on their left, around Arras. But the German positions were very strong, and on the right, south of Arras, the French infantry sustained heavy losses for paltry gains. On 26 September, D'Urbal decided to reinforce success rather than attempt to rescue failure, and attacked on his left. Souchez fell, and on 28 September French troops fought their way on to the crest of Vimy Ridge but were driven

THE FRENCH AT VIMY RIDGE
1914–1915

Vimy Ridge is about 8 km (5 miles) from Arras. Some 7 km (11 miles) long, it rises to a height of 145 m (475 ft) and dominates the surrounding countryside. The Ridge was fiercely contested between French and German troops in 1915, the near success of Pétain's XXXIII Corps in May helping to consolidate this commander's growing reputation. This whole area was the scene of heavy fighting in 1915. Nearby is the French National Memorial and cemetery at Notre-Dame de Lorette, vital high ground which was captured in stages during 1915.

1915

ABOVE TOP: An excellent shot of French soldiers in a trench, circa 1915. Note the variety of winter clothing.

ABOVE: The attack of 46th (North Midland) Division on Hohenzollern Redoubt, 13 October 1915. Note smoke and gas in the centre and left.

OPPOSITE: Scots Guardsmen in Big Willie Trench, Loos, October 1915. Three are preparing Mills Bombs (grenades) while others look at the camera.

back. Fighting continued into October, but the French made no further important gains.

For the BEF's attack at Loos, much depended on the wind's blowing in the right direction to carry chlorine gas over the German trenches. In the early morning of 25 September, Haig had to decide whether or not to order the gas to be released from the 5,000 cylinders that had been installed, and, despite worries about the wind, at 05:15 he gave the order. At 06:30, six British divisions attacked the enemy positions, only for the advancing infantry to find that, on the left and centre, the gas cloud had not delivered the anticipated benefits – indeed, in some places, such as the extreme left, it drifted back on to the attacking troops. For all that, Haig's troops did well. The 9th (Scottish) Division, part of Kitchener's New Army which was raised from volunteers in 1914, seized the powerful Hohenzollern Redoubt, while another captured the village of Loos. The German defences were in disarray, and the timely arrival of British reserves could have been devastatingly effective. But the reserves did not reach the battlefield until the following day, when they were decisively repulsed. Loos, like the offensive in Artois and Champagne, ended in disappointment. The outnumbered Germans held off the Allies with relative ease.

RIGHT: A disc grenade, produced to meet the demands of trench warfare. This one contained 65 grams (2.3 oz) of explosive.

"Votre élan sera irrésistible"
("Your élan will be irresistible")
JOFFRE TO HIS ARMY
SEPTEMBER 1915

BRITISH COMMAND

DOUGLAS HAIG TAKES OVER

SIR JOHN FRENCH'S REPUTATION HAD BEEN IN DECLINE THROUGH 1915, AND THE FAILURE AT LOOS WAS THE FINAL BLOW. THE LAST STAGE, THE ATTACK OF 13 OCTOBER, HAD PRODUCED, IN THE WORDS OF THE OFFICIAL HISTORIAN "NOTHING BUT THE USELESS SLAUGHTER OF INFANTRY".

1915

ABOVE: Early volunteers for Kitchener's Army, 1914, still in civilian clothes. This unit was the Grimsby Chums (10th Lincolns).

OPPOSITE: Lord Kitchener, 2 June 1916. Three days later he was killed on board HMS *Hampshire* when it hit a mine and sank.

French's misuse of the reserves – two New Army Divisions –which were held back well behind the lines on 25 September under his personal control, was seen as a major mistake. French publicly blamed Haig, a charge that Haig indignantly rebutted. In truth, Haig aimed for a decisive breakthrough while French anticipated a more methodical battle, in which there would be plenty of time to deploy the reserves when needed. The tension between these two concepts was never resolved.

French's clumsy attempt to pass the buck was followed by his replacement by Haig, who became Commander-in-Chief of the BEF on 19 December 1915. A few days later General Sir William Robertson became the Chief of the Imperial General Staff (CIGS), the professional head of the British Army. He was elevated as a means of marginalizing Kitchener's influence as Secretary of State for War, and in tough negotiations Robertson insisted on receiving enhanced powers before he would take the job. Both "Wully"

Robertson and Haig were "Westerners" – men who believed in the primacy of the Western Front. They formed a powerful team that in 1916 came into conflict with David Lloyd George, the Liberal politician who succeeded to the War Office after the death of Lord Kitchener in June 1916.

This clash grew more serious when Lloyd George succeeded Asquith as Prime Minister in December 1916. Lloyd George, although a proponent of total war, shrank from Haig's insistence on fighting attritional battles in the West, and at various times tried to clip Haig's wings by attempting to transfer the main effort away from the Western Front; placing him under a French general; and withholding troops from the BEF. Haig and Robertson

became more distant in the course of 1917. Robertson had wider strategic vision than Haig, and his job required him to oversee the global British war effort, not just the Western Front. Haig unfairly blamed the CIGS for dispersing troops away from the West, and refused to stand by him when Lloyd George sacked Robertson early in 1918. The Prime Minister's relations with Robertson's replacement, Sir Henry Wilson, deteriorated over time as they too clashed over civil-military issues.

Lloyd George would have liked to sack Haig, but the latter enjoyed support from the Press and the Conservative members of the Coalition government. After the disappointment of the battle of Cambrai in

late 1917 (see pages 192–195), and the near disaster of the German Spring Offensive of 1918 (see pages 196–203), Haig lost support and his position became weaker. Curiously, Lloyd George still refused to move against him. In the 1930s, after Haig was dead, Lloyd George in his War Memoirs inflicted lasting damage on the Commander-in-Chief's reputation.

Today, there is a popular perception that First World War generals presided over a series of failed battles in which the same outdated tactics were tried over and again. In reality, soldiers at all levels of the British, French and German Armies responded to the unexpected stalemate by experimentation and innovation, whether it was methods of

74

improvising hand grenades from jam tins, developing techniques of trench raiding or ordering, deploying and working out the tactics for sophisticated new weapons. Haig is often accused of being a military Luddite. Nothing could be further from the truth. He was very keen on technology, being an enthusiastic supporter of tanks and the Royal Flying Corps. If anything, the problem was that Haig expected too much of primitive technology; witness his belief that poison gas could help overcome the major disadvantages faced by the BEF at Loos.

Underpinning the narrative of the battles on the Western Front was a struggle by the armies to out-think the enemy by using new technology and tactics. In the process, the warfare of 1914 – which essentially looked back to Napoleonic warfare – was transformed into something recognizably modern. The BEF was some way down this track by the time Haig took over.

The great battles of 1916 and 1917 were to result, by 1918, in an all-arms team that included tanks, infantry, artillery, airpower, machine guns and chemical weapons, bound together by modern – if primitive – wireless communications and supported by effective logistics. By then, the Allies had moved decisively ahead of the Germans in the sophistication of their fighting. An updated version of this form of warfare remains in use to the present day.

OPPOSITE: General (later Field Marshal) Sir Douglas Haig, with a Guard of Honour for an Allied general, St Omer, March 1916.

BELOW LEFT: In becoming Prime Minister of a coalition government Lloyd George fatally split the Liberal Party. He fell from office in 1922.

HERBERT HENRY ASQUITH
(1852–1928)

Asquith was the Prime Minister who took Britain to war in August 1914. Formidably intelligent, he presided over a very talented Liberal government that included David Lloyd George and Winston Churchill, but was forced to form a coalition with the Conservatives in May 1915. In December 1916, Lloyd George replaced him as Prime Minister in an internal coup. Asquith's style of leadership was unfairly criticized by contemporaries and subsequent historians as being insufficiently vigorous, but in reality he deserves much credit for his war leadership.

THE SALONIKA CAMPAIGN
THE ALLIED OFFENSIVE

A COMPLEX MIX OF DIPLOMACY, POLITICS AND STRATEGY LED TO WHAT WAS PERHAPS THE MOST BIZARRE CAMPAIGN OF THE WAR. THE GENESIS OF THE "SALONIKA" CAMPAIGN WAS THE DEFEAT OF THE INVADING AUSTRIAN FORCES BY THE SERBS IN 1914. IN THE FOLLOWING YEAR, THE GERMANS SENT SUBSTANTIAL FORCES TO SUPPORT THE AUSTRIANS AND BULGARIANS IN CRUSHING SERBIA.

1915
1918

In response, in October 1915 the British and French sent an initial two divisions, which were quickly reinforced, to the Aegean port of Salonika (or Thessaloniki), in neutral Greek Macedonia, with the intention of advancing to the aid of the Serbs. It was too little, too late. The Serbian army was defeated, the king and government forced into exile, and the Allied force retired to Salonika.

Although the Greek government that had invited in the Anglo-French forces had fallen, and its successor was less friendly, the Allied commander, the French general Maurice Sarrail, built trenches around the port. Salonika remained an Allied enclave for the rest of the war, outside the control of the Greek authorities (indeed, providing a base for anti-government dissidents). Much to the disgust of some British commanders, the numbers of Allied troops in Salonika grew to some 160,000 by early 1916, and reached a huge 600,000 a year later. Sarrail's force included a British corps under General George Milne. Sarrail was an influential general and the politics of the French army demanded that he had an army-sized command away from the Western Front.

During 1916 and 1917 the "gardeners of Salonika" saw only limited action. A Bulgarian incursion at Florina in August 1916 disrupted Sarrail's plan for a major

attack, but in November the Serbian town of Monastir was taken by the Allies. A further push in April 1917, in the Monastir sector, was intended to support Nivelle's imminent offensive on the Western Front. It was a failure, not least because of the problems of co-ordinating a multi-national force which by this stage included Serbian, Russian and renegade Greek formations, as well as British and French. The German and Bulgarian defenders held on and by May the offensive had ground to a halt, with Russian and French forces affected by mutiny.

STANLEY SPENCER
(1891–1959)

Salonika was known as the Germans' biggest prison camp because of the large number of Allied troops tied up there, apparently to no good purpose. A humble member of these forces was Stanley Spencer (1891–1959), an artist in civilian life who served in the ranks of the Royal Army Medical Corps. One of his finest achievements is the Sandham Memorial Chapel in Berkshire. Built to commemorate Harry Sandham, a Salonika veteran, the chapel houses Spencer's extraordinary wall paintings of scenes from Salonika. These paintings are among the most important cultural artefacts to result from the British campaigns of the war.

OPPOSITE: Bulgarian infantry advancing under cover of an artillery barrage during the Salonika campaign, 1916.

ABOVE LEFT: General Sarrail, Commander-in-Chief of the large contingent of Allied forces at Salonika.

ABOVE RIGHT: *Travoys Arriving with Wounded at a Dressing-Station at Smol, Macedonia, September 1916.* An oil painting by Stanley Spencer.

RIGHT: Digging a drainage channel to counter the danger posed by malaria-carrying mosquitoes.

In June 1918 the Frenchman Franchet
d'Esperey, took command. Supported by a
strong Greek contingent, his Vardar offensive,
launched in September, shattered the weak
Bulgarian defences; the Germans had been
transferred to France. A sustained advance
began that ended on the Danube, with the
Central Powers collapsing. It was a stunning
victory that reinforced "Desperate Frankie's"
reputation as one of the best generals of the war.

Salonika was a difficult theatre in which to
fight. Logistic challenges were compounded
by an unhealthy environment. It could be
very hot – up to 46°C (115°F). Malaria was
prevalent: 10th (Irish) Division recorded
7,000 cases in August 1916. All this, and the
lack of achievement until the very end of the
war, had prompted many to ask whether the
forces would have better deployed elsewhere,
as Douglas Haig and others believed.

ABOVE: General Franchet d'Esperey landing at
Constantinople on 8 February 1919.

RIGHT: A section of Spahis (French colonial cavalry from
Morocco) on parade in Salonika.

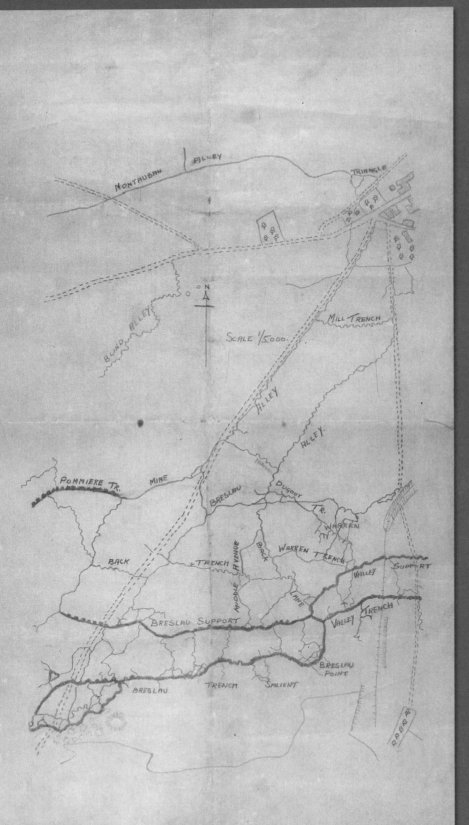

East Surrey objectives map

A hand-drawn map of
the East Surrey Regiment's
1 July objectives near
Montauban.

THE BATTLE OF VERDUN

OPERATION GERICHT

EVEN BY THE STANDARDS OF THE FIRST WORLD WAR, VERDUN HAS AN
EVIL REPUTATION AS A BATTLE OF PURE ATTRITION. IN HIS DECEMBER
1915 "CHRISTMAS MEMORANDUM", FALKENHAYN IDENTIFIED BRITAIN
AS GERMANY'S MOST DANGEROUS ENEMY. AT THAT STAGE THE
GERMAN HIGH COMMAND HAD LITTLE REGARD FOR THE BRITISH ARMY,
AND FALKENHAYN SAW THE FRENCH ARMY AS "ENGLAND'S BEST
SWORD" WITHOUT WHICH BRITAIN WOULD BE NEUTRALIZED.

1916

The final plan – Operation Gericht, or "Law Court" – pitted the German forces against Verdun, a fortress-city which represented the strength and spirit of France, a place with enormous symbolic as well as strategic importance. Historians still argue about Falkenhayn's true aims, but it is probable that, believing a clean breakthrough was impossible, he intended to grind the French down in a series of attritional battles that would force France to come to terms. Historian Jehuda Wallach described this calculated use of attrition as "the degeneration of the art of war". It certainly involved the application of total, ruthless methods to achieve a limited aim – to force France to come to a separate peace and thus destroy the cohesion of the Allied coalition.

"The forces of France will bleed to death"
FALKENHAYN
DECEMBER 1915

The city of Verdun had for many years been an important frontier position which had been fortified by the great engineer and siege-master Sébastien Le Prestre, Seigneur de Vauban in the seventeenth century. After the Franco-Prussian War, Verdun became a key part of the French defences against Germany, blocking the way to the Champagne region and, ultimately, Paris. In 1916, the main fortifications of Verdun consisted of a belt of forts some miles from the city. The French population may have believed that Verdun was a mighty fortress, but the truth was different. Much of its artillery had been removed and sent elsewhere on the Western Front to feed the insatiable demands of the field armies for guns, and the infantry garrison was thinly spread.

Falkenhayn entrusted the attack to Fifth Army, commanded by the Kaiser's eldest son, Crown Prince Wilhelm, with General von Knobelsdorf, as his chief-of-staff and the army's military brain. The offensive began on 21 February 1916. At 07:15, a nine-hour artillery bombardment was heralded by a shell from a heavy naval gun that overshot its target and landed near the Bishop's Palace in Verdun. The guns were able to rain shells onto the Verdun salient from three sides, creating the heaviest bombardment of the war so far, and the defenders suffered terribly. At 17:00, the German infantry began to push forward cautiously, probing for weak spots in the French positions. The plan was for the main infantry attack to begin on

CROWN PRINCE WILHELM
(1882–1951)

The eldest son of the Kaiser, Wilhelm held two important commands on the Western Front. As commander of Fifth Army, he was a central figure in the Verdun campaign. From September 1916, he led Army Group Crown Prince. His greatest success was the Aisne offensive of May 1918. Wilhelm showed a surprising streak of realism in his make up, recognizing the futility of Falkenhayn's Verdun strategy. He went into exile at the end of the war, but returned to Germany in 1923.

OPPOSITE: French infantry undergo a German bombardment. Artillery fire turned battlefields such as Verdun into cratered moonscapes.

ABOVE: Colonel Emile Driant in the Bois des Caures. His doomed defence of the position is one of the tragic stories of the battle.

ABOVE: The German stick grenade was known to the British as the "potato masher" because of its shape.

THE LÉGION D'HONNEUR

The Légion d'honneur is a decoration dating back to Napoleon I. Over 50,000 were awarded during the First World War.

Major Sylvain-Eugene Raynal was awarded the Légion d'honneur after he volunteered to defend Fort Vaux although he realized it meant almost certain death.

the following day, when it was hoped that the French defences would be thoroughly weakened. In the event, the Germans were overly wary, and a major assault might have paid off. General von Zwehl's VII Reserve Corps, which had ignored the instructions for caution and attacked in greater strength than the other two corps, captured the Bois d'Haumont and thus made a significant dent in the French lines.

As it was, the French put up strong resistance. In the Bois des Caures, Colonel Emile Driant's Chasseurs (light infantry) – who were virtually destroyed in the first days of the battle – succeeded in holding up the attacks of German XVIII Corps. Ironically,

Driant, a member of the French Chamber of Deputies, had previously raised the issue of the weakness of Verdun's defences, much to Joffre's fury. He was killed on 22 February.

By the following day, the French were reaching crisis point. Divisions were simply crumbling under the German pressure, having taken huge losses, and the French second position was falling into enemy hands. General Langle de Cary, Central Army Group commander, decided to abandon the right bank of the Meuse. While this was a sensible military decision, he was overruled by Noel de Castelnau, Joffre's chief-of-staff, acting on his superior's behalf, who saw the potentially disastrous political impact of

Fort Douaumont

The fall of Fort Douaumont on 25 February 1916 came as a major shock to the French and was greeted with delight in Germany. Initially the credit for the capture was given to Lieutenant von Brandis, even though he entered the fort after Sergeant Kunze and two other officers, Captain Haupt and Lieutenant Radtke. Kunze's role was not recognized until the 1930s, by which time he was back in civilian life as a policeman. In lieu of a medal, he was given accelerated promotion to inspector.

such a retreat. Instead, Pétain was placed in command of Second Army and began his dogged defence of Verdun.

Recognizing the central place of artillery on the modern battlefield, Pétain brought up additional guns and located them west of the Meuse to help counter the weight of German firepower. He also paid careful attention to logistics. The Verdun sector was supplied by a narrow gauge railway and by the minor road to Bar-le-Duc, the Voie Sacrée, (the "Sacred Way"). Pétain, offered solid, unflashy leadership, understood the poilu (the ordinary French soldier), who in return trusted him. His appointment was a turning point in the battle.

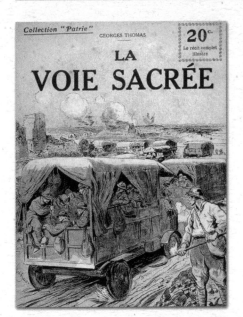

Collection "Patrie"

GEORGES THOMAS

20c.
Le récit complet illustré

LA VOIE SACRÉE

ABOVE RIGHT: Fort Douaumont early in the battle for Verdun. The fort is already showing signs of damage from artillery fire.

ABOVE LEFT: A French military band marching along La Voie Sacrée, the road that ran from Bar-le-Duc to Verdun.

LEFT: The cover of a wartime book showing troops going to the front along the "Sacred Way". A pioneer is repairing the road.

1916

II° ARMEE

Etat-Major

3° Bureau

Au Q.G.A., le 10 Avril 1916.

ORDRE

-:-:-:-

Le 9 Avril est une journée glorieuse pour nos armes. Les assauts furieux des soldats du Kronprinz ont été partout brisés. Fantassins, artilleurs, sapeurs, aviateurs de la II° Armée ont rivalisé d'héroïsme. Honneur à tous !

Les Allemands attaqueront sans doute encore. Que chacun travaille et veille pour obtenir le même succès qu'hier. Courage. On les aura.

Pétain

Pétain's "On les aura" message

Pétain's order of the day of 10 April 1916, which contains the phrase that passed into history – "On les aura" – "We'll get 'em!"

Translation

The 9th of April is a glorious day for our armies. The furious assaults of the Crown Prince's soldiers were overcome everywhere. Foot soldiers, artillery, sappers and aviators of the 2nd Army rivalled for heroism. Honour to all!

The Germans will doubtless attack again. Everyone must work and ensure that the same success as yesterday is achieved. Take courage. We'll get them.

[*signature*] Pétain

N°	JOUR	HEURE	NOMBRE et MARQUES des pigeons lâchés
15	4-6-16	11h.30	787-15

Nous tenons toujours mais nous subissons une attaque, par les gaz et les fumées très dangereuse

Il y a urgence à nous dégager - Faites nous donner de suite communication optique par Souville qui ne répond pas à nos appels.

C'est mon dernier pigeon

Raynal

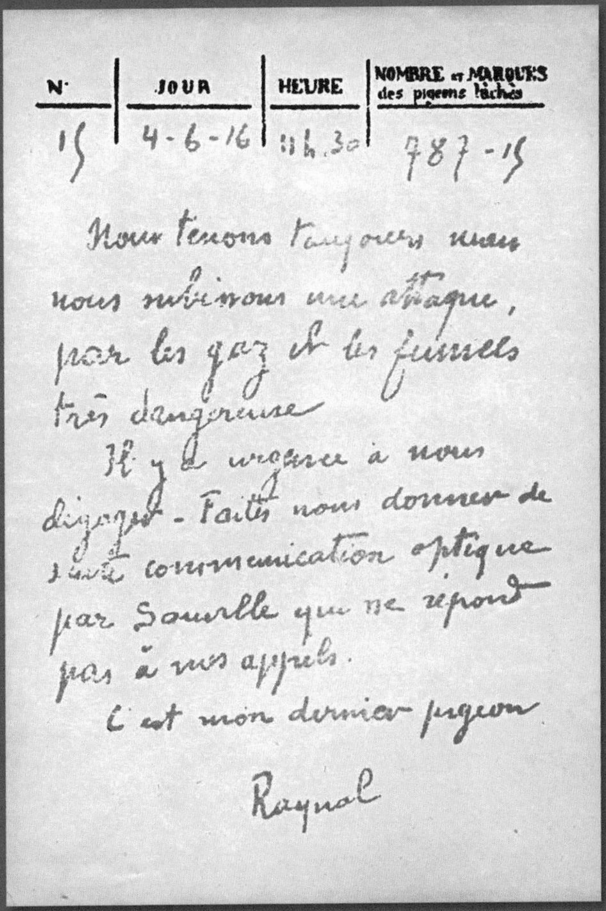

Fort Vaux message

Major Raynal's last message, which was sent by carrier pigeon from Fort Vaux on 4th June 1916.

Translation

We are still holding on, but we are coming under attack from gas and dangerous fumes.

We urgently need to disengage – send me an immediate visual communication via Souville, which isn't responding to my calls. This is my last pigeon

Raynal

THE BATTLE OF VERDUN

THEY SHALL NOT PASS

THE FACT THAT THE GERMANS NEVER MADE A SERIOUS ATTEMPT TO
CUT THE VOIE SACRÉE, ADDED TO THE LIMITED NUMBERS OF TROOPS
COMMITTED TO THE BATTLE AND THAT THE GERMANS ATTACKED ONLY ON
THE RIGHT BANK OF THE MEUSE, PROVIDES STRONG CIRCUMSTANTIAL
EVIDENCE THAT FALKENHAYN HAD INDEED ALWAYS INTENDED TO FIGHT
AN ATTRITIONAL BATTLE RATHER THAN TO CAPTURE VERDUN.

1916

THE VERDUN MEDAL

An unofficial Verdun Medal issued to combatants by the city itself. It could not be worn on military uniform.

If the Germans had put the supply route out of use, the effect on the French Army would have been catastrophic. At the height of the battle, 50,000 tons of supplies and 90,000 troops travelled to Verdun every week along the Voie Sacrée, while trucks took wounded and troops heading out of the line in the opposite direction. This was dubbed the "noria" system, after the word for a bucket water-wheel.

On the day Pétain arrived to take command, the Germans seized one of the key fortifications, Fort Douaumont. Its capture was largely because of a bizarre accident whereby the fort had been left almost defenceless. The Germans seemed on the verge of victory, but Pétain's arrival and massed French artillery fire helped to retard the German advance. Now attention switched to Le Mort Homme ("the Dead Man"), a French-held hill on the left bank of the Meuse from which guns wreaked havoc among the Germans.

By attacking at Verdun, Falkenhayn disrupted Anglo-French preparations for their offensive on the Somme and forced the Allies to dance to his tune. Yet Falkenhayn in turn was about to lose his tenuous grip on events. He sanctioned an attack on the left bank of the Meuse, which not only expanded the geographical scope of the battle, but undermined the whole concept of a limited battle as it played into the hands of Falkenhayn's critics, who sought an outright victory. The fresh attack brought the Germans some territorial gains, but the defenders clung tenaciously to the Mort

OPPOSITE: Crown Prince Wilhelm speaks to a stretcher-bearer at Verdun. To the British, "Little Willie" was a figure of fun.

ABOVE: Bodies in a trench at Le Mort Homme, April 1916. The Germans saw the capture of this position as an essential step.

CONSTANTIN SCHMIDT VON KNOBELSDORF
(1860–1936)

General von Knobelsdorf was Chief-of-Staff of Crown Prince Wilhelm's German Fifth Army during Verdun. The Kaiser, who told his son "Whatever he advises you, you must do", personally approved his appointment. Knobelsdorf and the Crown Prince's relationship became uneasy during the battle, as they came to have very different views on its conduct. In August 1916, at the Crown Prince's prompting, Knobelsdorf was removed from his position and sent to the Eastern Front.

FORT VAUX

Vaux was one of the smaller forts in the Verdun complex, but its week-long defence became one of the most famous episodes in the whole battle. The garrison commander, Major Sylvain-Eugene Raynal, was taken prisoner and brought to the Crown Prince. As a mark of respect, when Wilhelm saw that Raynal was without his sword, he presented him with another. A carrier pigeon that Raynal sent out from Fort Vaux delivered its message, but then died of gas poisoning. It was decorated for bravery.

ABOVE: A German soldier aims his rifle while lying beside a dead French soldier in the vicinity of Fort Vaux.

RIGHT: One of the most famous French posters of the War, advertising a war loan, featuring an enthusiastic poilu repeating Pétain's famous slogan: "we'll get 'em!".

1916

Homme. A new phase of the battle began on 9 April when the Germans attacked simultaneously on both banks of the Meuse, but the battle remained, in the Crown Prince's words, a "stubborn to-and-fro contest for every foot of ground". By the end of April, he had came to believe that "a decisive success at Verdun could only be assured at the price of heavy casualties, out of all proportion to the desired gains". Von Knobelsdorf disagreed, and for the moment the Germans continued their attacks. The Mort Homme and the neighbouring Hill 304 fell at last in May, after a huge and concentrated bombardment.

Pétain was promoted to command Central Army Group, and was replaced at Verdun by Robert Nivelle, whose aggressive subordinate Charles Mangin attempted, unsuccessfully, to retake Douaumont in late May. A fresh German push, Operation "May Cup", opened on the right bank on 1 June. Fort Vaux was captured after an epic, seven-day long defence led by Major Raynal, who was forced to surrender as his men were running out of water. The Ouvrage de Thiaumont, one of the last fortifications blocking the way to Verdun city, was captured by the Germans on 8 June. It was promptly retaken, and then captured and retaken another 15 times in the course of the battle. The Germans now went all out to take Fort Souville, 4 km (2.5 miles) from Verdun. On 23 June, after saturating the defenders with new phosgene gas, the German attack broke against the fort, which remained tantalizingly just beyond their reach. One last effort, on 11 July, also failed and the Germans went on to the defensive.

By then, the Allies had regained the strategic offensive. The Russian Brusilov offensive, launched on 4 June, forced Falkenhayn to detach divisions to the Eastern Front, and on 1 July the British and French attacked on the Somme, beginning the offensive that Joffre had been demanding for months. The pressure on the French at Verdun eased, but the fighting continued. The failure at Verdun contributed to Falkenhayn's replacement by Hindenburg and Ludendorff at the end of August, and von Knobelsdorf was posted to the Eastern Front. Nivelle, employing massed guns and sophisticated artillery tactics to fight limited battles, retook the Ouvrage de Thiaumont and Douaumont in late October. Fort Vaux fell on 2 November and in one last spasm of action, bemoaned by the Crown Prince as "this black day", on 15 December the French advanced 3 km (2 miles) past Douaumont. The battle was over. It had cost 377,000 French and 337,000 German casualties.

BELOW: The cheerful crew of a French 105mm gun pause to have their photograph taken, Verdun area, 1916. Their ragged appearance gives a realistic impression of campaign dress, which was often far removed from official uniforms.

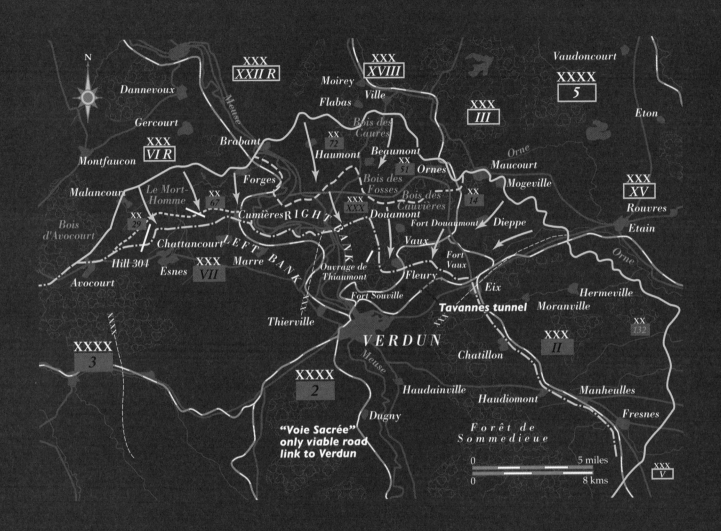

N

Dannevoux

Gercourt

Montfaucon

Malancourt

Bois
d'Avocourt

Hill 304

Avocourt

Meuse

Brabant

Forges

Le Mort-
Homme

XX
29

Chattancourt

Esnes

Marre

XXX
VI R

XXX
XXII R

Moirey

Flabas

Ville

Bois des
Caures

Haumont

XX
72

Beaumont

XXX
XVIII

XXX
III

Ornes

XX
51

Bois des
Fosses

XXX

XX
67

Cumières

R I G H T

L E F T

B A N K

B A N K

Douaumont

Bois des
Cauvières

XX
14

Fort Douaumont

Dieppe

Vaux

Ouvrage de
Thiaumont

Fort
Vaux

Fleury

Fort Souville

Thierville

V E R D U N

Tavannes tunnel

Eix

Meuse

XXX
VII

XXXX
3

XXXX
2

"Voie Sacrée"
only viable road
link to Verdun

Dugny

Haudainville

Chatillon

Chattillon

Haudiomont

Orne

Maucourt

Mogeville

Vaudoncourt

XXXX
5

Eton

XXX
XV

Rouvres

Etain

Orne

Hermeville

Moranville

XX
132

Manheulles

Fresnes

II
XXX

Forêt de
Sommedieue

0   5 miles

0   8 kms

XXX
V

THE BATTLE OF VERDUN: February–December 1916

Front lines

—— 21 February

– – – 24 February

------ 10 March

–·–·– 8 August

—— Allied positions, October–December

⟶ German advances

Soldier's postcard from côte 304

A 22 April postcard from E. Didelot of the 90th Infantry
Division to his "Godmother" or "Marraine de Guerre".
He describes the hell of fighting on côte 304 as a
"terrible bombardment on a grand scale".

PARTIE RÉSERVÉE À LA CORRESPONDANCE.

Chère Marraine   Le 22 Avril 1915

Je vous envoie ces quelques mots pour vous
recepion à votre mandat carte que je viens de recevoir auquel
je m'empresse de vous en remercier, escusez moi si je ne
vous fais qu'une simple carte je suis au pontuleix et moi
nous sommes il n'y a rien d'interressant l'on subit des bom-
bardements terrible avec de gros calibre et l'on a un temps
imployable de l'eau on est se toucher tellement que l'on est
sale et plein de boue enfin il faut prendre comme arsitot
que l'on en peux sortir si j'en ai le bonheur je vous ferai
une lettre avec des détails, j'espère que ma carte vous trouve
en bonne santé bien des compliments à votre famille de ma part
et dans l'attente de recevoir de vos nouvelles qui me fera plaisir
remerciements & ... Recevez chère Marraine mes plus sincères salutations et

IRELAND
THE EASTER UPRISING

IN AUGUST 1914, CIVIL WAR IN IRELAND SEEMED IMMINENT. SINCE 1910, THE BRITISH LIBERAL GOVERNMENT HAD RELIED ON THE MAINLY CATHOLIC IRISH NATIONALIST PARTY TO KEEP IT IN POWER, AND AS PART OF THE DEAL TRIED TO INTRODUCE HOME RULE – DEVOLVED GOVERNMENT THAT FELL WELL SHORT OF COMPLETE INDEPENDENCE.

1916

MICHAEL COLLINS

Michael Collins (1890–1922), a prominent Irish Republican leader, took part in the 1916 Easter Rebellion, fighting in the General Post Office in Dublin. Taken prisoner, Collins was fortunate to avoid execution. Subsequently a hero of the guerrilla war against the British, Collins played a prominent role in the negotiations in 1921 with the British that ended the Anglo-Irish War, earning the respect of Winston Churchill. However a minority refused to accept the Treaty which partitioned Ireland between the UK and the Irish Free State. Civil war broke out and Collins was ambushed and killed in a gun battle with anti-Treaty insurgents in August 1922.

ABOVE: Members of the Ulster Volunteer Force march through Belfast shortly before the outbreak of war.

OPPOSITE ABOVE LEFT: John Redmond speaking in support of Home Rule, 11 April 1912.

OPPOSITE ABOVE RIGHT: An artist's impression of how Sergeant O'Leary won a Victoria Cross, and became a national hero.

OPPOSITE BELOW LEFT: Members of the Irish delegation at the signing of the Irish Free State Treaty between Great Britain and Ireland, 6 December 1921.

OPPOSITE BELOW RIGHT: The issue of Home Rule provoked vehement public division, as this defiant poster illustrates.

This was fiercely opposed by Ulster Protestants led by Sir Edward Carson, who demanded that at least part of the north of Ireland should be excluded from the measure. By contrast more radical nationalists such as the Irish Republican Brotherhood (IRB) wanted complete independence and were prepared to fight for it. The situation deteriorated rapidly, with private armies – the Ulster Volunteer Force (UVF) and the Irish Volunteers – being set up. The Buckingham Palace conference in July 1914 failed to bring about agreement, and tensions were high, when, faced with war in Europe, an uneasy truce began.

In September, the Home Rule Act was passed but it was promptly shelved until the war was over. John Redmond, the leader of the constitutional Irish nationalists, believed that enthusiastic participation in the British war effort would help Home Rule to become a reality. The Catholic, nationalist 16th (Irish) Division was formed, alongside 36th (Ulster) Division, which was recruited from the UVF. In 1914–15 there was some enthusiasm for the war in Ireland. Some 200,000 volunteers from Ireland served in the army during the war. Sergeant O'Leary of the Irish Guards won the Victoria Cross and became a national hero.

On Easter Monday, 24 April 1916, a small group of IRB radicals led by Patrick Pearse staged an uprising in Dublin. Standing on the steps of the General Post Office, Pearse announced the birth of an Irish republic. In

a few days the British crushed the rebellion, which had little popular support. Four hundred and fifty people were killed. Of these 64 of were insurgents, 116 British military, 16 police, 254 civilians. What happened next helped to radicalize the population. Fifteen captured ringleaders were executed, the shootings being dragged out over a period of days. The rebels became martyrs, and support for Redmond's constitutional nationalists – and their policy of supporting the British – began to drain away. The British politician David Lloyd George tried and failed to stitch together a deal which was in retrospect the Home Rulers' last chance of success, but by the end of July it had failed.

The radical nationalist Sinn Féin (SF) party began to overtake the Redmondites in popularity, and British authority in Ireland began to crumble. In the 1918 election, Redmond's party was smashed as an electoral force, and the victorious SF set up a separate Dáil (parliament) in Dublin. A bloody guerrilla war began, and the British attempted to regain control. The Anglo-Irish Treaty of 1921 gave independence to 26 of the Irish counties, while six counties remained within the UK as Northern Ireland. Despite the troubles at home, Irish units in the British army had continued to fight well, although recruiting from Ireland had become increasingly difficult.

CAMPAIGNS IN MESOPOTAMIA

THE ESCALATION OF MILITARY OPERATIONS

"MISSION CREEP" IS A WELL KNOWN PHENOMENON BY WHICH MILITARY OPERATIONS GROW STEADILY MORE AMBITIOUS, ABSORB EVER MORE RESOURCES, AND LAST FAR LONGER THAN ANYONE HAD INITIALLY ENVISAGED. THE TERM IS A MODERN ONE, BUT THE IDEA IS NOT.

1914
1918

The British Empire's campaign in the Ottoman province of Mesopotamia (modern day Iraq) in 1914–18 was a classic example of this tendency. It began in November 1914, when an expedition sent from British India arrived at the head of the Persian Gulf. This was a sensible and limited operation to secure Britain's supplies of oil – particularly important given that the Royal Navy's reliance on it for fuel. But the temptation was to advance further inland. Basra, 32 kilometres (20 miles) away, was soon taken, and another advance of 90 kilometres (55 miles) brought the British and Indian troops to the confluence of the two great rivers in the region, the Euphrates and the Tigris on 9 December 1914.

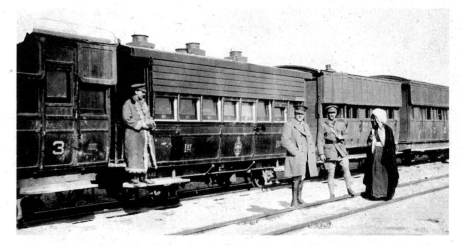

Lulled into a false sense of security by feeble Turkish resistance, the British sent out substantial reinforcements and a new Commander-in-Chief, General Sir John Nixon. Then, in spring 1915, twin pushes were launched along the two rivers. A riverine expedition – Major-General Townshend's "Regatta" – captured Amara on the Tigris (3 June) and Major-General Gorringe took Nasiriya on the Euphrates at the end of the following month.

Nixon then ordered Townshend to improve the strategic position by taking Kut, further up the Tigris. He did so in late September, and then pursued the beaten Turkish forces to Ctesiphon. Here the Ottoman army inflicted a defeat on Townshend, who on 25 November 1915 was forced to retreat to Kut. Exhausted, the British-Indian force halted and on 7 December was besieged by the advancing Turks. The siege was to last for five long months. More Imperial reinforcements reached Mesopotamia, but attempts to relieve

the Kut garrison failed. On 29 April 1916, Townshend surrendered his 13,000 strong force. It was the greatest humiliation suffered by the forces of the British Empire in the entire war.

This was not the end of the Mesopotamia campaign, however. In December 1916, the British once more took the offensive with extra forces under a new Commander-in-Chief, Lieutenant-General Sir Stanley Maude, and with much work having been carried out

DUNSTERFORCE

The Russian Revolution brought chaos to the Caucasus, and in 1918 "Dunsterforce" under Major-General L.C. Dunsterville (1865–1946) was despatched to keep the key town of Baku from enemy hands. It was lost in September 1918 and only retaken in mid-November, after the war was over. Just as the entire Mesopotamian campaign was ultimately concerned with the security of the British Empire, so was its off-shoot in Baku. Highly appropriately, Dunsterville was a school friend of Rudyard Kipling, Britain's greatest novelist and poet of the Empire. In Kipling's famous school story Stalky and Co. the eponymous hero is based on Dunsterville.

improving logistics and rebuilding morale. Maude's careful planning paid off: having steadily driven back the Turks, in March 1917 he captured Baghdad, where in November he died of cholera. His successor was Lieutenant-General Sir William Marshall, who began a major drive on the oil-rich area of Mosul in October 1918, to take advantage of the disaster suffered by the Turks in Palestine. In a week of fighting the British Mesopotamian forces won a significant victory over the Ottoman Sixth Army, which was forced to surrender on 30 October.

The extreme heat and inhospitable conditions made Mesopotamia a nightmarish place for an army to fight in. A tough and resourceful enemy and the logistic difficulties of the theatres were twin challenges that British forces eventually overcame – but a limited strategy that avoided mission creep would probably have been preferable.

OPPOSITE: A troop train on the military railway between Basra and Nasiriya in 1917.

ABOVE TOP: "Dunsterforce" gunners help the crew of an Armenian field gun in the caucasus.

ABOVE CENTRE: An artist's impression of British troops near the Ctesiphon Arch in Mesopotamia, in November 1915.

ABOVE: British troops marching through Mesopotamia during the First World War, circa 1916.

LEFT: A portrait of Lieutenant-General Sir William Marshall, seated and wearing full uniform.

THE ITALIAN FRONT

ATTRITIONAL FIGHTING AT ISONZO

"ATTRITION" IS A TERM USUALLY ASSOCIATED WITH KILLING GROUNDS
SUCH AS PASSCHENDAELE AND VERDUN ON THE WESTERN FRONT.
BUT SOME OF THE WORST ATTRITIONAL FIGHTING TOOK PLACE
ON THE ITALIAN FRONT.

1915
1916

ABOVE: Italian soldiers crossing the River Isonzo by ferry, during a series of battles between Italian and Austrian forces, June 1915.

OPPOSITE ABOVE: Illustration showing Italian troops, taking cover in doorways and behind chairs, engaged in a street fight against occupying Austrian forces in Asiago, Italy, 10 August 1916.

In the course of 1915, having carried out four offensives over much the same ground against the Austro-Hungarians, the senior Italian commander, General Luigi Cadorna, had made minimal gains, but sustained massive losses.

Since 1882, Italy had been an ally of Austria and Germany, but Rome chose to stay neutral on the outbreak of war. Many believed that the formation of the Kingdom of Italy in the nineteenth century was unfinished business.

Territory inhabited (at least in part) by Italian speakers was still part of the Austro-Hungarian Empire, including the Adriatic port of Trieste, and the Trentino, or southern Tyrol. Italy's foreign policy was described in a memorable phrase by Prime Minister Antonio Salandra as "sacred egoism", which not only indicates that Italy, like all other states, put its national interests first, but hints at the passions inherent in nationalism.

With Europe at war, the position of neutral Italy was of interest to both sides. Vienna refused to pay a bribe of territory to keep Rome neutral. By contrast, the Entente powers, in the secret Treaty of London (26 April 1915) traded away Austrian land in the event of victory. On 23 May, Italy declared war on Austria-Hungary, and a month later the First Battle of the Isonzo commenced.

This was an attack by Italian Third Army (Duke of Aosta) and Second Army (Frugoni) into the highland, stone-strewn wilderness

ALPINE WARFARE

Although overshadowed by the Isonzo front, the Dolomite mountains were the scene of fierce fighting. H. G. Wells, who visited the Alpine front in 1916, described the "grim and wicked" mountains; nonetheless, men contrived to fight there, battling at high altitudes over rocky outcrops and mountain ledges, often in the snow. The logistical challenges were truly formidable, and the dangers included avalanches – "white death" – which killed thousands.

of the Carso, which aimed for Gorizia and ultimately Trieste. The tactical conditions of the Western Front were replicated and magnified. The Austrian defenders held trenches cut out of the rock, making the job of the attacker even less enviable than in Flanders. There was a short break from 7 July, in which more artillery was deployed, and then the Second Battle of the Isonzo began on 18 July. Still hampered by insufficient artillery, the Italian assault ended on 3 August. Another pause followed, and then Cadorna began Third Isonzo (18 October– 4 November). The final attack of the year was the Fourth Battle of Isonzo (10 November– 2 December).

At the end of the year's efforts, the Italians had edged forward, but at the cost of 250,000 men. To take one example, the 48th Regiment lost around 2,300 men in four months of fighting. The Austrians fought stubbornly,

lost heavily and switched 12 divisions from the Eastern Front, but contained the Italian offensives with relative ease.

At first, 1916 saw more of the same: Fifth Isonzo was conducted in terrible weather during 11–15 March. The attention then switched to the Trentino front, to which the Austrians had moved divisions from the Isonzo. From 15–20 May, the Austrians advanced 8 kilometres (5 miles), but then halted in response to developments on the Russian front, and eventually pulled back. With the Austrian defenders on the Isonzo being weakened, the Italians made some real progress in the Sixth Battle (6–7 August), capturing the town of Gorizia and establishing a bridgehead on the Isonzo River itself. Fleetingly, a major breakthrough seemed possible, and Italian morale was high. But the high hopes of August were to be disappointed. The Seventh, Eighth and Ninth

Battles of the Isonzo, fought by stages from September to November, saw attempts to build on the success at Gorizia. The Austrians had been defeated but not destroyed, and their new positions were very strong. Consequently, Italian gains were slight, and once again, casualties were immense. As on the Western Front, 1916 ended in stalemate in Italy.

ABOVE: German machine gunners defend a position near the frontier with Austria-Hungary during the Isonzo Campaign, 1917.

OPPOSITE: Troops scaling Mount Nero on the Karst plateau during the Second Battle of the Isonzo.

THE EASTERN FRONT

THE BRUSILOV OFFENSIVE AND ROMANIAN CAMPAIGN

FOLLOWING THEIR VICTORY IN THE GORLICE-TARNÓW CAMPAIGN IN MAY–JUNE 1915, THE AUSTRO-GERMAN FORCES PUSHED ON INTO RUSSIA. WHEN THE OFFENSIVE CAME TO A HALT IN LATE SEPTEMBER, THERE HAD BEEN AN ADVANCE OF SOME 240 KILOMETRES (150 MILES). HAVING LOST ABOUT A THIRD OF A MILLION SOLDIERS AS PRISONERS OF WAR, AND SEEN OVER 3,000 GUNS CAPTURED BY THE ENEMY, RUSSIA SEEMED ON THE EDGE OF DEFEAT.

1916

Remarkably, the Russians were able to bounce back in the following year, launching their own offensives, one of which brought dazzling success.

At the end of 1915 Britain, France and Russia agreed to coordinate their offensives during the following year. Despite their problems, the Russians remained loyal to their allies, beginning in March 1916 an ultimately stalemated struggle around Lake Naroch to try to relieve pressure on the French at Verdun. The main offensive of the year was to begin in late May when three "Fronts" (Army Groups) were to attack. In the event, on 14 May, the Italians appealed to their Russian allies for help after they were attacked by the Austrians. The only force ready to assault was General Alexei's Southwestern Front, consisting of four armies. Brusilov would attack on 4 June, and General Evert's Northwestern Front would join in 10 days later.

Brusilov kept the Austrians guessing as to where he would attack by defying conventional military wisdom that forces should be massed at the decisive point. In spite of having only a small margin of numerical superiority (600,000 men to 500,000), Brusilov decided to attack simultaneously all along the line. Such bold methods might not have worked against German troops, but he faced five Austrian armies, all of which were suffering from morale problems. The artillery bombardment came crashing down at

OPPOSITE: Russian artillery brigades' dugouts on the emplacement in Litsevichy village, winter, 1915.

ABOVE: Tsar Nicholas II and General Brusilov surveying the Galician front, 1916.

RIGHT: A cigarette card featuring General Evert, part of the "Allied Army Leaders" series issued in 1917.

WILLS'S CIGARETTES.

GENERAL EVERT.

ROMANIAN CAMPAIGN 1916

Romania declared war on Germany and Austria-Hungary on 27 August 1916 and then invaded Hungarian Transylvania with three armies. The reaction of the Central Powers was swift. In September, led by the experienced German generals Falkenhayn and Mackensen, German, Austrian and Bulgarian forces counter-attacked on several fronts. Transylvania was quickly retaken and Romania itself was conquered in a brilliant campaign, the capital Bucharest falling on 6 December. The Anglo-French force at Salonika was unable to help the Romanians. Once again, the German army had demonstrated how effectively it could conduct mobile operations in the relatively open conditions of the Eastern Front.

4 a.m. on 4 June and some preliminary infantry assaults went in that morning. The defenders suffered badly from the shelling, but the main attack was still to come. The storm broke in the early hours of 5 June, and threw the Austrians into confusion. As the Russians pushed forward, some of the defenders were ordered to retreat, but thousands simply surrendered – eventually half a million prisoners were captured. The Austrians suffered a cataclysmic defeat. On 16 June, the Germans mounted a counter-offensive, but this did little to arrest to Russian advance.

But it could have been even worse for the Central Powers. The Russians did not build on their initial success. Reserves were not made available in sufficient numbers or in a timely fashion, and the iron chain of logistics brought Brusilov's advance to a halt by late June. Fighting continued into October, but for the Central Powers the crisis had passed. In the early summer, faced with Brusilov's offensive, the British-led attack on the Somme, and fighting at Verdun and in Italy, the forces of the Central Powers were under immense strain. Conceivably, had Romania joined the Allies in early summer, rather than late August (see box), the Austro-German line might have given way somewhere.

ABOVE: German troops marching through the streets of Bucharest after its capture, 6 December 1916.

1916

ABOVE: Austrian soldiers on the eastern front preparing to use a flamethrower, 1916.

THE BATTLE OF JUTLAND

A STRATEGIC VICTORY FOR THE BRITISH

FOR YEARS BEFORE 1914, THERE HAD BEEN EXPECTATIONS OF A "NEW TRAFALGAR", A DECISIVE CLASH IN THE NORTH SEA BETWEEN THE BRITISH AND GERMAN BATTLEFLEETS. IN REALITY, ALTHOUGH BOTH NAVIES WANTED BATTLE, BOTH BEHAVED WITH CAUTION. ADMIRAL SIR JOHN JELLICOE, THE COMMANDER-IN-CHIEF OF THE BRITISH GRAND FLEET, WAS, IN CHURCHILL'S LATER WORDS, "THE ONLY MAN ON EITHER SIDE WHO COULD LOSE THE WAR IN AN AFTERNOON".

1916

The British had the upper hand in the surface war, and to retain it merely needed to keep the Fleet intact so that it could blockade Germany and bottle up the German navy. However, it was also hoped to ambush the German High Seas Fleet and thus bring on a battle with the odds stacked in the Royal Navy's favour.

The Germans, with fewer ships, had a very similar strategy, of seeking to defeat fragments of the British fleet and gradually wear down its strength. Neither side was prepared to risk its precious dreadnoughts in a major fleet action.

Nearly two years of the two fleets tiptoeing around each other and engaging in minor clashes came to an end on 31 May 1916. Vice-Admiral Reinhard Scheer, appointed in early 1916, continued with the basic strategy, but brought more vigour to the German campaign. He sent out Vice-Admiral Hipper's battlecruisers (ships that were as heavily armed as battleships, but faster, having less armoured protection) towards the Skagerrak, the straits separating Norway from Denmark. The plan was to lure the British into action by offering up an apparently unsupported target, but then to bring his battleships into action.

ABOVE: The British fleet before the Battle of Jutland.

JELLICOE AND BEATTY

Naval historian Andrew Gordon has characterized Beatty as an aggressive "ratcatcher", prepared to take risks, and decentralize authority to subordinates who had to use their initiative, and Jellicoe as a "regulator"; a risk-averse, bureaucratic, micro-managing commander, the product of a pre-war culture of complacency. After Jutland, Jellicoe (above) moved up to become First Sea Lord, the professional head of the Royal Navy. Beatty replaced him in command of the Grand Fleet.

ABOVE TOP: The British battle cruiser HMS *Queen Mary* explodes, after the chamber of the ship is hit.

ABOVE: Admiral Reinhard Scheer.

ABOVE: Commander of the cruiser squadron, Vice-Admiral Franz Ritter von Hipper.

1916

Room 40, the British Admiralty's decoding section, was able to read German signal traffic, and thus warned, the Grand Fleet set sail four hours before Scheer. However, a mistake resulted in Jellicoe being led to believe that the main German fleet was still in harbour at 12.30 p.m. As a result, he failed to make haste.

Vice-Admiral David Beatty's Battlecruiser Fleet of six battlecruisers made contact with the destroyers supporting Hipper's fleet of five battlecruisers at 2.20 p.m. The German battlecruisers manoeuvred to the south-east and headed towards Scheer's battlefleet, followed by Beatty. The British got much the worse of the subsequent action. HMS *Indefatigable* and HMS *Queen Mary* both exploded and sank, and three other ships were damaged. Although pummelled by British guns (Von der Tann had two turrets put out of action), none of Hipper's ships were sunk. Had not an error delayed four fast British battleships into coming into action, the result could have been very different. Around 4.30 p.m., Scheer's battleships

came in sight and Beatty disengaged, with the Germans following up. Unexpectedly, Scheer found Jellicoe's battleships waiting for him. Although a third British battlecruiser, *Invincible*, was sunk, it was the Germans' turn to disengage, only to turn back, and run the gauntlet of British fire. The second withdrawal was covered by a salvo of torpedoes fired by light vessels. Controversially, Jellicoe ordered the fleet to turn away from the torpedoes, thus allowing the German ships to escape.

Tactically, the Germans were more successful at Jutland, as the British called the battle: for the loss of one battlecruiser (*Lützow*), one old battleship, four light cruisers and five destroyers, they had inflicted losses of three battlecruisers, four armoured cruisers and eight destroyers. In morale terms, the Germans felt victorious and the British were disappointed. But strategically, which is what mattered, the British were the clear victors. The Germans had failed to inflict a decisive defeat on the Grand Fleet; the German navy was as securely bottled up in the North Sea as before; and Jellicoe's fleet remained substantially intact, the ultimate guarantor of the security of the British Isles.

OPPOSITE ABOVE: "Situation in the morning, 9.17 hrs." A contemporary painting by Claus Bergen, showing the sea battle at Skagerrak.

OPPOSITE BELOW: A German warship firing.

ABOVE: Admiral Beatty's battle cruiser squadron regarded themselves as the élite of the Royal Navy, but had mixed fortunes at the Battle of Jutland.

CAMPAIGNS IN PALESTINE

T. E. LAWRENCE AND THE ARAB REVOLT

ONE OF THE MOST ROMANTIC FIGURES TO EMERGE FROM THE
FIRST WORLD WAR WAS COLONEL T. E. LAWRENCE – "LAWRENCE OF
ARABIA". A COMPLEX, TROUBLED FIGURE, LAWRENCE WAS WORKING
AS AN ARCHAEOLOGIST IN THE MIDDLE EAST WHEN HE WAS GIVEN A
TEMPORARY COMMISSION IN THE BRITISH ARMY.

1917
1918

In late 1916, he was appointed as liaison officer to Faisal bin Hussein, one of the leaders of the Arab Revolt against the Ottoman Empire. Although his exact role is controversial, Lawrence played a role as one of the leaders of the Revolt. This campaign of hit-and-run raids and attacks on railways posed a significant and growing threat to the Turks at the same time that British Empire Forces were invading Ottoman Palestine.

Under the command of General Sir Archibald Murray, the British Empire Forces put the logistic infrastructure in place across the Sinai desert that made an advance on Palestine possible. The first objective was

Gaza City, on the route into Palestine, which was defended by a force that included some German elements. Murray attacked on 25 March 1917. In a confused battle the EEF, which included the Anzac Mounted Division, made some progress, but the battle ended in fiasco with a communications breakdown leading to an undignified retreat. Murray unwisely informed London that he had won a significant victory, and was promptly ordered to renew the offensive. "Second Gaza" was launched on 19 April and was a failure. Murray was sacked and replaced by General Sir Edmund Allenby.

Allenby had a point to prove. He had been

removed from command of Third Army after a lacklustre performance at Arras in April 1917. The Prime Minister wanted Jerusalem to be captured as a Christmas present for the British people, and provided Allenby with significant reinforcements. Allenby brought with him knowledge of the most recent tactics and techniques in use on the

OPPOSITE: The Bikaner Camel Corps in the Sinai desert during the guerrilla warfare campaigns in 1917.

ABOVE LEFT: Faisal bin Hussein photographed at the Paris Peace Conference after the war.

ABOVE RIGHT: General Sir Archibald James Murray.

ABOVE: General Allenby (centre) making his speech on the steps
of the Citadel after the capture of Jersualem, December 1917.

Lawrence of Arabia

It is very difficult to separate fact from fiction when trying to assess the role of T. E. Lawrence in the Arab Revolt. His book *The Seven Pillars of Wisdom* was hailed as a masterpiece, and an abridged version, *Revolt in the Desert* was a popular success. In it, he cleverly constructs the myth of "Lawrence of Arabia", a brilliant guerrilla leader who used his understanding and sympathy for Arabs and their culture to forge a highly effective striking force. This picture contains some truth, perhaps a great deal, but he has been accused of exaggerating his own importance. The historical jury is still out.

Western Front, and his army was to put this knowledge to good use. Aided by imaginative deception methods, "Third Gaza" (31 October) was a smashing victory. The pursuit carried Allenby to Jerusalem, which surrendered on 9 December.

As a result of the great German offensives, in 1918 Allenby had to send British divisions to France and received Indian troops in return. Although he carried out some indecisive operations in Transjordan in March and April 1918, he waited until 19 September before mounting a major attack, the Battle of Megiddo. It was a brilliant example of manoeuvre warfare in which infantry, cavalry, artillery, aircraft and even armoured cars combined to rout the

Turks, commanded by the German Gallipoli veteran, Liman von Sanders. Seventy-five thousand prisoners were captured, 40,000 being taken in the first five days of fighting. Allenby's advance coincided with an upsurge of Arab guerrilla activity in Palestine. Damascus was captured by British and Arab forces on 1 October, by which time the Ottoman army was in a state of collapse. The seizure of Aleppo on 26 October marked the effective end of the Palestine campaign. Four days later, Turkey surrendered.

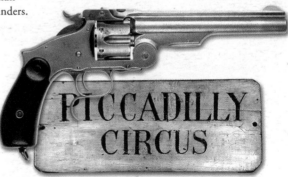

ABOVE: A .44 inch Smith & Wesson "Russian" revolver captured by the British at Gaza with a name, date and place of capture scratched on the butt, and a wooden sign from the British defensive trench system at Gaza.

BATTLES IN ITALY

ISONZO, CAPORETTO AND VITTORIO VENETO

THE ITALIAN CONTRIBUTION TO THE COMBINED ALLIED STRATEGY FOR 1917 WAS YET ANOTHER BATTLE OF THE ISONZO (THE TENTH), WHICH COMMENCED ON 12 MAY, HARD ON THE HEELS OF THE BRITISH AND FRENCH OFFENSIVES ON THE WESTERN FRONT IN APRIL. THE ITALIANS HAD CLAWED SOME GROUND FROM THE AUSTRIANS BY THE TIME THE OFFENSIVE WAS CLOSED DOWN IN MID-JUNE.

1917
1918

ABOVE: An observation post of an Austro-Hungarian infantry battalion in the front line near Vertojba on the Isonzo Front.

OPPOSITE RIGHT: General Boroevic, commander of the Austro-Hungarian Fifth Army on the Isonzo Front.

This offensive was followed by the Eleventh Battle in August. Reinforced with French and British heavy artillery and fresh divisions, the attack was timed to coincide with the Allied Passchendaele offensive. Following a preliminary bombardment, the infantry was unleashed. Although the Austrians, commanded by General Boroevic, held against the attacks of Italian Third Army, General Luigi Capello's Second Army drove through the defensive positions and finally reached open ground beyond. Pursuit rapidly ran into logistical problems, and Second Army paused to regroup, planning to renew the attack shortly. Ironically, this modest success was to contribute to the worst Italian debacle of the war.

Once again, Germany sent troops to bail out its allies. Italian intelligence warned that

War and Politics

The Battle of Vittorio Veneto is a good example of the military philosopher Carl von Clausewitz's famous saying that "War is the continuation of politics by other means". In 1918, General Diaz was reluctant to take the offensive, but Baron Sidney Sonnino, the Italian Foreign Minister urged him on. Military victory, he believed, would enhance Italy's credibility with the Allies and thus strengthen his hand in post-war negotiations. Although Diaz duly delivered victory, albeit with substantial Allied help, Italy's subsequent territorial gains at the Paris Peace Conference fell well short of Sonnino's ambitions. Many Italians were left with a lasting sense of grievance.

a major enemy offensive was in the offing. Cadorna gave orders to go on the defensive and pull back artillery to defensible positions, but the headstrong Capello ignored them. At the Battle of Caporetto, launched on 23 October 1917, 35 Central Powers divisions faced 41 Italian. Following a hurricane bombardment, and using advanced infiltration infantry tactics, the Austrian and German forces tore into the defenders. Italian Second Army collapsed, its soldiers' morale worn down by the ceaseless attrition of the previous years; some 90 per cent of Italian casualties were prisoners of war. Third and Fourth Armies, by contrast, fell back in reasonable order. By 10 November, the Italians had stabilized a line along the River Piave, a mere 40 kilometres (25 miles) from Venice.

This was the high-water mark of the Central Powers' success in Italy. Fresh offensives were mounted on the Trentino and Piave fronts in June 1918, but neither achieved much. Neither were the Italians keen to renew

effort. In addition to Italian Eighth Army, Twelfth Army was commanded by General Graziani, a Frenchman, and included French 23rd Division. Tenth Army, led by British General Lord Cavan, included the British 7th and 23rd Divisions. The three armies forced a crossing of the Piave, with the Austrians putting up a stiff resistance in places. On 30 October, the town of Vittorio Veneto fell, and the Austrian defenders collapsed. Elsewhere, on the Trentino Front, Italian, British and French attacked near Asiago on 1 November, and drove on until the Armistice came into effect on 4 November: Austria-Hungary had disintegrated, and the war in Italy was over.

the struggle. Although French and British reinforcements had arrived from the Western Front, General Armando Diaz, who replaced the discredited Cadorna in November 1917, was in no hurry to take the offensive. But on 24 October 1918, with the tide running strongly in the Allies' favour, he launched the Battle of Vittorio Veneto. It was an Allied

ABOVE LEFT: Some of the many Italian prisoners of war after the Battle of Caporetto, October 1917.

ABOVE TOP: Italian infrantymen in a trench along the defensive line of the lower Piave River, 1917.

ABOVE: Italian general Armando Diaz, who eventually led the Italian forces to victory at the Battle of Vittorio Veneto, featured on the front page of a French publication, 9 December 1917.

WAR IN THE ATLANTIC
THE U-BOAT MENACE

THE SINKING OF THE FRENCH BATTLESHIP *JEAN BART* IN
THE MEDITERRANEAN ON 21 DECEMBER 1914 WAS A PORTENT.
FOR THIS VESSEL WAS NOT DESTROYED BY THE GUNNERY OF AN
ENEMY CAPITAL SHIP: IT FELL VICTIM TO AN AUSTRIAN SUBMARINE,
A MIGHTY AND EXPENSIVE WARSHIP SUNK BY A SMALLER AND MUCH
CHEAPER WEAPON. AND IT WAS TO SUBMARINES (KNOWN AS
U-BOATS) THAT THE AUSTRIANS' GERMAN ALLIES WERE EVENTUALLY
TO TURN TO TRY TO WIN THE WAR AT SEA.

1914
1918

At the outbreak of war, the Allied (principally British) navies rapidly bottled up the German battle-fleet in home waters, mopped up stray German ships across the globe, and enforced a blockade of the Central Powers. In response, on 4 February 1915 Berlin announced that any merchant ships found in the waters around the British Isles, including neutrals, would be attacked. As a result, American ships were targeted. This unrestricted submarine warfare provoked furious American protests – famously after the British liner *Lusitania* was sunk by a U-Boat in May and 128 Americans were among the dead – and the strength of these forced the Germans, on 1 September 1915, to call off the strategy. Even so, the submarine campaign was a trump card that Berlin was to play again, once the U-Boat fleet had grown in numbers and experience.

The U-Boat war was far from over. It was vital for the Allies to keep open the Atlantic sea-lanes over which merchant ships carried munitions from North American factories and food-stuffs from farms. Cut this life-line

ABOVE: The loss of French battleship *Jean Bart* to an Austrian submarine in December 1914 symbolized a new era of naval warfare.

OPPOSITE ABOVE: A British standard-built merchant ship in dazzle camouflage.

OPPOSITE BELOW RIGHT: The controversial sinking of the *Lusitania* in 1915 by a German U-Boat was used by the British government as an emotive and powerful enlistment tool.

THE ZEEBRUGGE RAID

On the night of 22–23 April 1918 Rear-Admiral Roger Keyes led a daring attempt to block the German-held port of Zeebrugge. HMS *Vindictive* sailed up the Zeebrugge mole and put men ashore who tried to destroy it, while blockships were sunk to prevent the harbour being used by U-boats. The Germans fought back fiercely, and the raid achieved only limited success. However, it was a propaganda triumph for the British, with the Royal Navy living up to the tradition of Drake and Nelson, and it boosted home front morale at a time of crisis on the Western Front.

REMEMBER THE
LUSITANIA

THE JURY'S VERDICT SAYS:
"We find that the said deceased died from their prolonged immersion and exhaustion in the sea eight miles south south-west of the Old Head of Kinsale on Friday, May 7th. 1915, owing to the sinking of the R.M.S. Lusitania by a torpedo fired without warning from a German submarine."

"That this appalling crime was contrary to international law and the conventions of all civilized nations, and we therefore charge the officers of the said submarine, the Emperor and Government of Germany, under whose orders they acted, with the crime of wilful and wholesale murder before the tribunal of the civilized world."

IT IS YOUR DUTY TO TAKE UP THE SWORD OF JUSTICE TO AVENGE THIS DEVIL'S WORK.

ENLIST TO-DAY

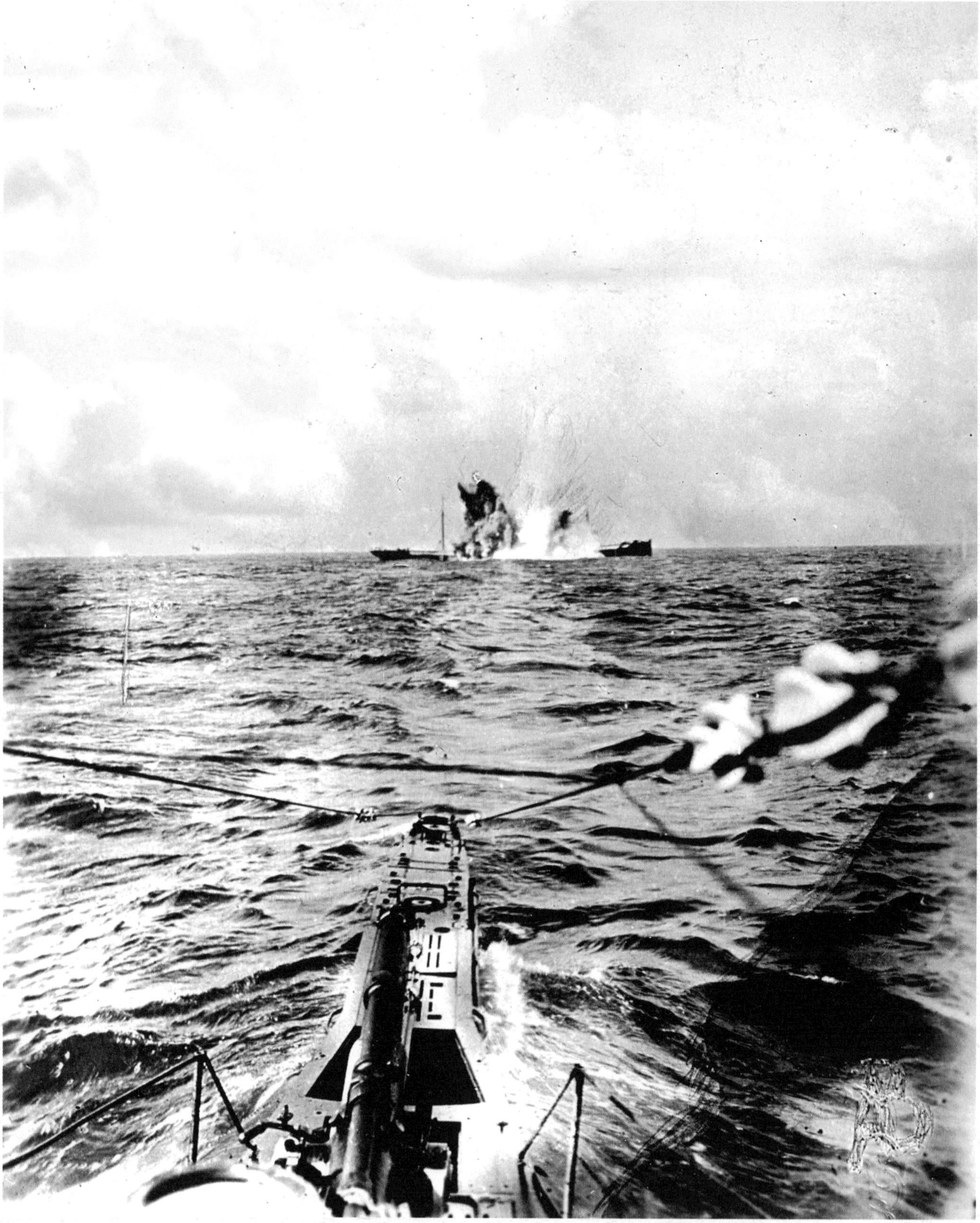

OPPOSITE: A surfaced U-Boat torpedoes a merchant steamer, scoring a direct hit.

ABOVE: The "Q" ship HMS *Underwing*, at anchor with guns exposed and striped dazzle camouflage.

and Britain would starve. Extensive belts of anti-submarine nets were laid in the Channel. Some merchant ships were equipped with guns. Then there were Q-ships, fitted with concealed guns; these were intended to lure U-Boats towards a supposedly helpless victim, at which they would open fire. After the Battle of Jutland in 1916, the Germans increasingly concentrated on the undersea war. In October 1916, British shipping losses amounted to a record 176,000 tons, with the combined loss of neutrals and Allied shipping amounting to a similar total.

Following the Battle of the Somme in 1916, the Germans turned again return to unrestricted submarine warfare. It promised a great reward – starving Britain out of the war – but the risk of making an enemy of the United States was high. Initially, the sink-

on-sight approach that began in February 1917 was highly successful. The tonnage of vessels sunk in British waters in January was about 300,000. That increased to more than 500,000 tons in February, 560,000 in March, and a frightening 860,000 tons in April. In the end, salvation for the Allies came in the form of the introduction of a convoy system. British naval authorities had resisted this course, urged by Lloyd George and others. Senior sailors had feared that convoys would simply present golden targets for U-Boats, but in fact it proved much easier for warships to protect merchantmen in a group. Losses declined; the numbers of U-Boats sunk increased; and the crisis was over – but the Germans had come very close to victory. The U-Boat proved to be a far greater menace to the Allies than the Kaiser's treasured battleships.

EMPIRES AT WAR

FIGHTING FOR "HOME"

BOTH BRITAIN AND FRANCE WERE GREAT IMPERIAL POWERS IN 1914,
ABLE TO DRAW ON THE VAST HUMAN RESOURCES OF THEIR EMPIRES.
IN AUGUST 1914, GEORGE V DECLARED WAR ON BEHALF OF THE
WHOLE BRITISH EMPIRE. THE AUSTRALIAN STATESMAN ANDREW FISHER
PROMPTLY PLEDGED TO SUPPORT BRITAIN "TO THE LAST MAN AND LAST
SHILLING", AND THIS REFLECTED A GENERAL MOOD IN AUSTRALIA,
NEW ZEALAND AND ANGLOPHONE SOUTH AFRICA AND CANADA.

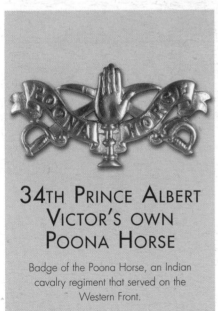

34TH PRINCE ALBERT VICTOR'S OWN POONA HORSE

Badge of the Poona Horse, an Indian cavalry regiment that served on the Western Front.

Imperial ties were still strong, there was much loyalty to the monarch and many still considered Britain as "home". A large number of the men who enlisted had been born in Britain, or were the sons of British migrants. In South Africa, where many Afrikaners had fought against the British only 12 years before, some of them revolted, and others were reluctant to support Britain. Other Afrikaners did rally to the Empire. Jan Christian Smuts, who had fought against the British in the South African War, became a leading member of the War Cabinet. The French-Canadian community were also notably less enthusiastic about fighting for Britain than English-speaking Canadians.

OPPOSITE: Zulus of the South African Native Labour Corps prepare to perform a war dance in June 1917. South Africa also provided white combat troops for Western Front service.

ABOVE: A dressing station in Tikrit, Mesopotamia in 1917. a Royal Army Medical Corps officer, helped by Indian medical orderlies, tends wounded Turks.

RIGHT: French Spahis (native light cavalry recruited from North Africa) at rest, Coudun camp, Oise, 22 June 1916.

THE FRENCH ARMY IN 1914

Like the rest of the French army, units from the Empire suffered terrible casualties. In a few days fighting in the battle of the Frontiers in 1914, 3rd Colonial Division lost 11,000 out of 16,000 men, including the divisional commander. By the end of the war, 36,000 Algerians, 10,000 Tunisians and 29,000 Africans were dead, although not all on the Western Front. It has been estimated that the Zouaves and the infantry of La Coloniale sustained some of the heaviest losses of any units in the French army.

The Australians and New Zealanders earned reputations as good fighting troops in 1915 at Gallipoli. They arrived in France in early 1916, where over the next two years the Anzacs won the respect of friends and enemies alike. The five-division Australian Corps was created in November 1917, and along with the New Zealand Division under General Sir Andrew Russell, played key roles in the Allied victories. The Canadians followed a similar path, first fighting at Second Ypres in April 1915. The four-division Canadian Corps was formed in 1916 and acted as a spearhead formation during 1918. Indian troops (all volunteers) fought in France in 1914–15 as part of the Indian Corps, which included British troops; they were a timely reinforcement to the BEF. Subsequently, the Indian infantry were sent to the Middle East, with the cavalry remaining in France. In all, about 210,000 Canadians, 180,000 Australians, 47,000 New Zealanders and 25,000 Indians were killed or wounded on the Western Front.

Not all the men from the Empire that went to France were fighting soldiers. Chinese from Weiheiwei and Black and Coloured South African labourers did valuable and sometimes dangerous work behind the lines.

One of the strategic problems France faced before the war was that it had a smaller population than its rival Germany: 35 million to 65 million. In a war of mass armies, this put the French at an obvious disadvantage. In La Force Noire, the then Colonel Charles Mangin advocated drawing upon the population of France's sub-Saharan colonies to boost its armies. This controversial suggestion earned him notoriety long before the Nivelle offensive (see pages 162–163). In the event, France did make extensive use of colonial manpower on the Western Front, in Italy, Salonika and at Gallipoli, as well as in colonial campaigns in North Africa. A small such force also fought

with the British in Palestine and Syria. A total of 150,000 soldiers from Algeria, 39,000 from Tunisia and 14,000 Moroccans served in the European theatre, in addition to 135,000 Black Africans, 34,000 from Madagascar and 143,000 from Indochina.

Under French law, conscripts from mainland France could normally not serve outside its borders. Control of the Empire was therefore the responsibility of two forces: the Armée d'Afrique and La Coloniale. Both provided units to reinforce the Western Front. They included troops of European origin, such as the élite Coloniale Blanche and the white Chasseurs d'Afrique (African Light Cavalry) and Zouaves (white troops who wore North African-style uniforms). In a class of its own was the Foreign Legion. One of its members was a British colonel, disgraced in 1914 for attempting prematurely to surrender his battalion on the retreat from Mons. He joined the Legion, fought bravely, and was eventually reinstated in the British Army. Black and North African units were often used as storm troops.

The French made far more use of its colonial troops in Europe than the British did of the Indian Army. Indeed, without their help, it is difficult to see the French home army could have coped with the stresses of war. I Colonial Division, fighting alongside the British on the Somme in 1916, made a favourable impression on their allies, as did the Moroccans operating on the flank of 2nd US Division during Second Marne. Probably most impressed of all were the Germans who had to face them across No Man's Land – they paid them a backhanded compliment by being reluctant to take Black and Arab troops prisoner.

OPPOSITE: Tirailleur Annamite, French colonial troops from Indochina, at rest in a military camp near Salonika, May 1916.

ABOVE: France's Force Noir on the march: Senegalese light infantry in a French town, 1914.

RIGHT: Men of a New Zealand regiment wearing gas masks during a rifle drill in March 1918.

ANZAC

The initials of the Australian and New Zealand Army Corps gave rise to the word "Anzac". It came to be applied, not merely to the military formation, but to the landing beach at Gallipoli and to Australian and New Zealand soldiers generally. The word is now deeply associated with Australian and New Zealand national identity, as is the idea that Gallipoli witnessed the birth of two independent nations. From late 1917, Australian Gallipoli veterans serving on the Western Front wore a small "A" (for "Anzac") badge on their uniforms.

THE ROLE OF WOMEN IN WAR

CHANGES AT HOME AND WORK

IN A TOTAL WAR SUCH AS THE FIRST WORLD WAR, THE MAXIMUM
AND EFFECTIVE USE OF MANPOWER CAN MAKE THE DIFFERENCE
BETWEEN VICTORY AND DEFEAT. THE INSATIABLE APPETITE OF ARMIES
FOR YOUNG MEN MEANT THAT THEY WERE INCREASINGLY REPLACED
IN THE JOBS ON THE HOME FRONT BY OLDER MEN –
AND BY WOMEN.

1914
1918

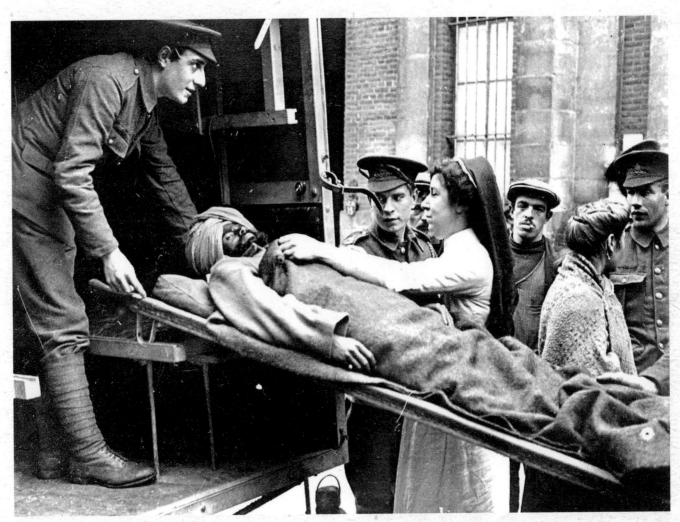

At one level, the novelty of women in the work place should not be exaggerated. For millions of working-class females across the developed world before the war, it was a case of work or starve, and so they were already present in the workforce, labouring in factories, as domestic servants or on farms. The option of staying decoratively at home was open only to the higher social classes.

But what was new after 1914 was the vast numbers of women who worked for the war effort in occupations previously the sole preserve of men, as was the redefinition of the boundaries of what was regarded as acceptable feminine behaviour. Social conservatives in many countries feared that the outcome would be destruction of traditional values and morals, with deep suspicion of the sexual liberation supposedly enjoyed by "new" women. A "League of Decency and Honour" founded in Britain to promote morality among women at home provoked an angry response from three women war workers, who wrote to criticize the "wicked insult to us girls".

In Germany, the Hindenburg Programme, an attempt to mobilize the resources of the state, attempted to tap the reservoir of female workers, but it failed to achieve its ambitious

OPPOSITE: Members of the Voluntary Aid Detachment (VAD) at work in Sister Barbier's office in Boulogne, France.

ABOVE: A nurse tends to a wounded Indian soldier, as he is placed into a motor ambulance in October 1914.

RIGHT: A 1916 poster aimed at recruiting female munitions workers.

ON HER THEIR LIVES DEPEND

WOMEN MUNITION WORKERS

Enrol at once

SOCIAL ADVANCES

The extent to which women made social gains as a result of the Great War is controversial. In France, many women worked during the war in traditionally male jobs, but were still not allowed to vote, only being enfranchised in 1944. Britain gave the vote to women in 1918 and the United States did so in 1920, but this was not purely a response to wartime developments. In both cases, there had been a long running campaign for female suffrage that predated the war. Generally, demobilization returned men to the civilian workforce and women lost their jobs. If women had advanced two steps during the war, they retreated one afterwards; but in the end they had still advanced a step.

goals. In Britain, by mid-1916, 750,000 women had replaced men in clerical and other jobs, with perhaps another 350,000 working in newly established war-related jobs such as in munitions factories. To take one example, female conductors became a common sight on London buses for the first time.

For many women, the double burden of carrying out traditional roles of wife and mother, while also working for a living, intensified during wartime. Often women, separated from their husbands, had to take on unfamiliar roles as head of households. An all too familiar female experience was of long hours queuing for food, which was often in short supply, and repairing clothes that could not easily be replaced. In addition,

there was the heavy psychological burden of dreading the arrival of bad news about a soldier or sailor husband, lover or son. In Britain, the arrival of a telegram could bring either joy – "I'm coming home on leave" – or despair – official notification of the death or wounding of a loved one. The heavy death toll left a generation of war widows and of young women whose potential husbands had perished in the war. While the demographic impact can be exaggerated, the perception of a cohort of "surplus" women was very real.

There was a close connection between home fronts and the battle fronts. For most major belligerents, there was a regular mail service and military morale could be affected by news from home. In 1918, the willingness of

German soldiers to fight was undermined by news of the sufferings of their womenfolk and children, hit by the double blows of the Allied "starvation blockade" and the near collapse of food distribution at home.

The effective mobilization of women was one factor, and not an insignificant one, in the eventual Allied victory.

OPPOSITE: Female workers pose with trolleys laden with sacks of flour in Birkenhead, Cheshire, September 1918.

ABOVE TOP: Poor German women sift through rubbish looking for food in post-war Germany, 1918.

ABOVE LEFT: A munitions girl works an automatic cartridge machine at the Inspection Buildings, Park Royal.

LITERARY INFLUENCES

THE MEMOIRS, NOVELS, POEMS AND FILMS OF THE FIRST WORLD WAR

WAR STIMULATES LITERARY CREATIVITY, AND THE 1914–18 CONFLICT PRODUCED SOME OF THE MOST FAMOUS WAR LITERATURE IN HISTORY. GERMAN VETERAN ERICH MARIA REMARQUE'S 1929 NOVEL *ALL QUIET ON THE WESTERN FRONT*, AN EXPRESSION OF THE SUPPOSED FUTILITY OF THE WAR, WAS A SENSATION. TRANSLATED INTO ENGLISH, IT HELPED TO STIMULATE WHAT HAS BEEN TERMED "THE GREAT WAR BOOKS BOOM", AN EXPLOSION OF WRITINGS ABOUT THE WAR THAT CONTINUED WELL INTO THE 1930S.

The cinema experienced a similar phenomenon. The Hollywood film of *All Quiet* (1930) evoked great sympathy for the former enemy in the English-speaking world. Some books and films, like the French director Jean Renoir's 1937 film *La Grande Illusion*, the American e.e. cummings's *The Enormous Room* (1922) and the English writer Siegfried Sassoon's semi-autobiographical "George Sherston" trilogy of novels showed disenchantment with the war. But it would be a mistake to see all the works of the time in this light. R. C. Sherriff, the author of the most famous British war play, *Journey's End* (1928), remained proud of his regiment, the East Surreys, to the end of his life, and the play displays ambiguous attitudes to the war. However, the producer of the initial production was a pacifist and thus *Journey's End* came across as an anti-war statement. Ex-German stormtrooper Ernst Junger's memoir *Storm of Steel* (1929) was a celebration of combat, as was Englishman A. O. Pollard's now almost completely forgotten memoir *Fire-Eater* (1932), his account of winning the Victoria Cross.

RIGHT: R. C. Sherriff, author of the play *Journey's End*, photographed at the Savoy Theatre 2 February 1929.

To some extent, the great war books boom was a reaction against the patriotic propaganda that had appeared during the conflict, produced by journalists and even some established writers, such as Rudyard Kipling and Anatole France. To be sure, there had been other writers who went against the grain while the war was going on: Henri Barbusse's *Under Fire* (1916) was an unflinching portrait of a French infantry squad in battle. Wilfred Owen, perhaps the greatest of British war poets, wrote of "the pity of war", although his work only became widely known once it was over (Owen himself was killed in 1918). Today, popular views of the First World War in Britain are heavily influenced by the poetry of Owen and a handful of others such as Sassoon, although they were not in any way representative of the average soldier, either in terms of their experiences or their attitudes to the war.

The First World War continues to be a rich seam of inspiration for writers and film makers. Recent French treatments of the subject include the film *A Very Long Engagement* (Jean-Pierre Jeunet, 2004). Peter Weir's 1981 film *Gallipoli* was an assertion of Australian nationalism, albeit one that was in many ways historically inaccurate. The British novelist Pat Barker achieved huge success in the 1990s with her *Regeneration* trilogy, which included Owen and Sassoon as characters. More recently, the War and its aftermath formed the backdrop for the hugely successful British costume drama *Downton Abbey*. The centenary of the war will undoubtedly stimulate writers and film-makers afresh.

ABOVE LEFT: A poster for Jean Renoir's 1937 film representing a move away from the glorification of war.

ABOVE RIGHT: The 1929 front cover for the first US edition of Erich Maria Remarque's novel *All Quiet on the Western Front*.

RIGHT: The celebrated English poet and author Siegfried Sassoon, wearing his army uniform, circa 1920.

From a place you may never have heard of...
a story you'll never forget.

A Peter Weir Film

GALLIPOLI

A

ROBERT STIGWOOD-RUPERT MURDOCH FOR ASSOCIATED "GALLIPOLI" MEL GIBSON Executive FRANCIS O'BRIEN Screenplay DAVID WILLIAMSON
R & R FILMS PTY LTD. PRESENT A PETER WEIR FILM MARK LEE Producer by

Based on PETER WEIR Produced ROBERT STIGWOOD and PATRICIA LOVELL Directed PETER WEIR
a Story by by by

Copyright © MCMLXXXI by Paramount Pictures Corporation A PARAMOUNT PICTURE DISTRIBUTED BY CINEMA INTERNATIONAL CORPORATION
All Rights Reserved

OPPOSITE: The stark poster design for Peter Weir's 1981 film *Gallipoli*.

RIGHT: The successful French novelist, poet and journalist Anatole France.

BELOW: A scene from Richard Attenborough's 1968 film *Oh! What a Lovely War*, based on a stage musical and emphasizing black humour and the grim reality of war.

OH! WHAT A LOVELY WAR

The musical *Oh! What a Lovely War* is one of the most powerful pieces of anti-war drama ever produced. First put on by Joan Littlewood's Theatre Workshop in 1963, it depicts the events of the First World War as an Edwardian pierrot show. A savage attack on British generalship in the war, it was filmed in 1969 and remains hugely influential. However, like many literary portrayals of the war, it is historically highly inaccurate. It tells us more about the Cold War mentalities of the early 1960s than those of the Great War, but all too often it is treated as sober history.

THE DIPLOMACY OF WAR
THE FAILURE OF A COMPROMISE PEACE

SOME 80 YEARS BEFORE THE FIRST WORLD WAR, THE FRENCH
WRITER ALEXIS DE TOCQUEVILLE HAD ARGUED THAT, ONCE THEY
WERE PROVOKED, DEMOCRACIES COULD WAGE WARS WITH THE
SAME PASSION AS THEY HAD CLUNG TO PEACE. THE EVENTS OF
1914 TO 1918 WERE TO SHOW THAT HE WAS CORRECT.

1914
1918

One of the principal reasons why, despite the deadlock, and despite the slaughter, the First World War was fought to the bitter end, was that France, Britain and the United States proved just as dogged in the pursuit of their war aims as the Central Powers were in theirs. A compromise peace was all but impossible as long as the

two sides clung to irreconcilable objectives. Without one side or the other's making a major concession, attempts at a diplomatic settlement were doomed to failure.

The fundamental problem was that at the beginning of the war, Germany succeeded in seizing large tracts of enemy land. The

captured territory included most of Belgium, a small but highly industrialized state; some economically important areas of eastern France; and, in 1915, much of Poland. One possible strategy would have been to use these as bargaining chips at a peace conference, but having conquered this ground, the Germans were loath to give it up. The secret

GERMANY'S MISSED OPPORTUNITY

An opportunity for a peace settlement came at the end of 1917. With Russia in revolution and effectively out of the war, Germany could have opened serious negotiations with the western Allies by offering to return captured territory. The Germans were carving out a vast empire in eastern Europe, and the exchange of Belgium for the Ukraine would still have left Germany in a much more powerful situation than before the war. Clever diplomacy might have split the Allies. Instead, Berlin gambled everything on a massive attack in France, which led eventually to Germany's collapse. The conference table would certainly have served Germany better than the sword.

> It will be our wish and purpose that the processes of peace, when they are begun, shall be absolutely open and that they shall involve and permit henceforth no secret understandings of any kind. The day of conquest and aggrandizement is gone by; so is also the day of secret covenants entered into in the interest of particular governments and likely at some unlooked-for moment to upset the peace of the world. It is this happy fact, now clear to the view of every public man whose thoughts do not still linger in an age that is dead and gone, which makes it possible for every nation whose purposes are consistent with justice and the peace of the world to avow now or at any other time the objects it has in view.

IN FLANDERS FIELDS

"In Flanders Fields", a poem written in 1915 by a Canadian medical officer, John McCrae, is still popular in Britain and is regarded by many as a statement of pacifism. In reality, the second verse argues that the dead buried on the battlefields would be betrayed by a compromise peace.

Take up our quarrel with the foe...
If ye break faith with us who die
We shall not sleep, though poppies grow
In Flanders fields.

Such sentiments, also heard in France, Germany and other belligerent states, help to explain why a compromise peace was never likely to happen.

1914 "September Programme" declared that the war was being fought for the "security of the German Reich in west and east for all imaginable time". Not until 1917 did Berlin begin to show some flexibility, and then it was a case of too little, too late.

So various peace efforts, some more serious than others, all failed. In December 1916, the German "Peace Note" was couched in confrontational language, which the Allies rejected. In the same month, the President of the still-neutral United States, Woodrow Wilson, tried to move things along by asking the belligerents to give their war aims. The Allies replied with far-reaching proposals that the Central Powers would never accept. In January 1918, Wilson, by now leader of a belligerent nation, issued his famous Fourteen Points. This was a utopian programme for a peace settlement, but not until military defeat was inevitable did the German government accept it, long after the train had left the station.

Home front morale, with the exception of Russia, proved remarkably resilient. This meant that heavy casualties made a compromise peace less rather than more likely. Having sacrificed so much, to settle for anything other than out-and-out victory became unthinkable, a betrayal of the dead. The French would not stop until they had, at a minimum, recovered the occupied territory lost in 1914. The British sought security by freeing Belgium and destroying "Prussian militarism". In Germany, the civil population was told that it was fighting a defensive war and, until late in 1918, lived on a diet of victory. Thus, when the truth that Germany was on the verge of military defeat suddenly became clear, the disillusionment and collapse of morale that ensued was catastrophic. Total war left little room for a compromise peace.

OPPOSITE: German infantry advancing across open country during the occupation of Belgium in August 1914.

ABOVE TOP LEFT: German soldiers on the Romanian front load a Howitzer gun during the advance on Bereth in January 1917.

ABOVE LEFT: The Canadian poet, artist, physician and soldier, John Alexander McCrae.

ABOVE: An extract from Woodrow Wilson's Fourteen Points.

Report on the recent operation
of the
2/ The GORDON HIGHLANDERS.

At 9.25 p.m. on 30ᵗʰ June 1916 the battalion marched from the BOIS des TAILLES to take up their positions in the trenches prior to the assault.

The strength of the battalion was: Off. 24   Other ranks. 783

The battalion was in position by 1 a.m. on 1ˢᵗ July. Ladders and bridges were placed in position and the men received a sandwich and a tot of rum.

The assault was timed to take place at 7.30 a.m. 1ˢᵗ July.

At 6.25 a.m. a bombardment of the enemy's trenches commenced which was kept up till zero hour (7.30 a.m.)

The battalion assaulted in 4 lines - 100 yards between lines.

The frontage for the battalion was about 400 yards.

The objective of the battalion was the village of MAMETZ. Three distinct lines of trenches had to be crossed before the assault on the village was possible.

The 1/S. STAFFORD REGT. was on our right, whose objective was the E. side of MAMETZ VILLAGE and the 9ᵗʰ DEVON Regt on our LEFT, who were to prolong the line to the WEST of MAMETZ.

At 7.30 a.m. the assault was launched. The lines advanced steadily under a v. heavy machine gun fire and rifle fire and high explosive shrapnel. The casualties were heavy but the lines pushed on.

The Left Company (D) were held up by wire and suffered very considerably.

The road immediately in front of MAMETZ was occupied at 7.55 a.m.

The 1ˢᵗ message received - Timed 7.55 a.m. from O.C. 'A' Coy.

"Am rallying in sunken road N. of CEMETRY TRENCH preparatory to rushing MAMETZ"

2ⁿᵈ message received - Timed 9 a.m. from O.C. 'A' Coy.

"Am in touch with party of 50 1/S. STAFFORD on right. They are in SHRINE ALLEY. Cannot get any touch on my left which is at present in the air." MAMETZ being heavily shelled. Reinforcements badly needed.

3ʳᵈ message received. Timed 9.30 a.m. from O.C. 'A' Coy.

"Situation more normal - MAMETZ still being heavily shelled - LEFT FLANK still in the air and valley WEST of SHRINE held by enemy machine guns. No Officer or N.C.O. with party of S. Staffords on my right.

4ᵗʰ message received. Timed 11.5 a.m. from O.C. 'A' Coy.

"My Left flank on SHRINE still in the air. Patrols cannot gain touch with D or C. Coys (these two companies advanced in the low ground were held up by the wire) and have met with serious opposition from enemy's machine guns in valley W. of SHRINE. Am occupying from SHRINE to point F.11.a.7.9. along bank of road - Propose to advance to objective when Devons and Borders on LEFT get in line -

A reply to the 4ᵗʰ message was sent from R.H.Q. at 11.30 a.m. saying that "reinforcements were an coming up but to hold on at all costs in your present position until you are re-inforced" (This message was never delivered, both runners being wounded). O.C. 2/Gordons

5ᵗʰ message received - Timed 1.45 p.m. from O.C. 'A' Coy.

"Situation grave - being bombed by large parties at SHRINE - Reinforcements absolutely necessary."

A reply to 5ᵗʰ message was sent as follows at 2.40 p.m.

"Two companies 2/Warwicks are coming up to in support of you at once." O.C. 2/Gordons.

The two companies of 2/Warwicks advanced in 4 lines at 4 p.m. and met with little opposition the enemy having surrendered (about 600) prior to the

2nd Battalion, the Gordon Highlanders' report

A handwritten report on the successful 1 July attack on Mametz by 2nd Battalion, the Gordon Highlanders. The casualty rate for the battalion from 1 to 4 July was 56.9 per cent.

2 more

second line of 2/Warwicks manning the SUNKEN ROAD.
At 4.5 p.m MAMETZ VILLAGE was captured & A force
At 4.30 p.m
consisting of 2/Warwicks, 2/Gordons 8/Devons and 3
machine gun sections went forward to the N. side of
MAMETZ VILLAGE to consolidate the position.
The distribution was as follows.

    2 Coys 2/Warwicks held the line from the LEFT of the
        1/S. Staffords linking up with the 2/Gordon
        Highlanders who linked up with the 8/Devons
        on the left.

The position was consolidated. 3 strong points made
and a machine gun section placed in each strong
point.
At 10 p.m 2 Coys 2/Warwicks came up and were
formed a close support. R.H.Q. being in SHRINE
ALLEY.
The 95 Coy R.E worked throughout the night in
assisting in consolidating the position.
During the night a good deal many high explosive
shells burst over MAMETZ VILLAGE but little
damage was done.
The whole of July 2nd the position remained unaltered
and on July 3rd about 11 p.m orders were
received for the 8 Devons to take over the
line occupied by the troops (distribution above)
& the 2/Warwicks and ourselves withdrew.
We marched back to the CITADEL about 3 miles
arriving at 3 a.m on 4th July.
The casualties amounted to :-

	Killed	Wounded	Missing	x Trench mortar officer
Officers	7	9 x		
Other ranks	119	265	39	Total Off - 16 Other ranks 443.

4

The battalion captured 600 prisoners, one machine gun
and trench mortar, one anti air craft machine gun.
The prisoners captured comprised the 110th & 109 R.R. also
23rd R.R. & 18 M. Gun Corps.
A signal station was established at S.W. corner of
MAMETZ VILLAGE at 10 a.m and communication was
established with 91st Brigade.

                BGR. Gordon Lt Colonel
6-7-16.   commanding 2/ The Gordon Highlanders.

      At 4.0 p.m
P.S. A party under 2/Lieut. Lawrenson bombed all the day onto up the HALT
      accounting for many casualties and prisoners.

THE BATTLE OF THE SOMME

THE BIG PUSH

THE BATTLE OF THE SOMME WAS A PRODUCT OF COALITION WARFARE,
AN OFFENSIVE FOUGHT IN THE SECTOR WHERE THE BOUNDARY
BETWEEN THE BRITISH AND FRENCH FORCES LAY. HAIG'S AIMS AT
THE BEGINNING OF THE BATTLE WERE MIXED. WHILE HE HOPED TO
BREAK THROUGH THE GERMAN LINES AND REOPEN MOBILE WARFARE,
HE RECOGNIZED THAT AN ATTRITIONAL, "WEARING-OUT BATTLE"
MIGHT BE ALL HIS ARMY COULD ACHIEVE.

1916

By the end of 1 July 1916 – the first day of the Battle of the Somme – 57,470 men of the BEF had become casualties; 19,240 were killed. In the northern part of the battlefront, the British had taken very little ground. However, in their part of the battlefield the French army had taken comparatively light casualties in making significant gains. Alongside them, the British forces in the south had also done well, taking all of their objectives, albeit at a high cost in lives. What had gone wrong in the north?

For the seven days before 1 July, Allied guns had pounded the German positions. In retrospect, the British guns were given too many targets. Massed on a short length of front, artillery could be very effective. Spread out along many miles and given multiple targets, the effect was dissipated.

> "Without our superiority in guns where would we be?"
>
> CAPTAIN JC DUNN DSO MC AND BAR DCM MEDICAL OFFICER WITH THE 2ND ROYAL WELCH FUSILIERS

This mistake reflected a further problem in the British plan. Haig sought a breakthrough battle, while Rawlinson, Fourth Army commander and Haig's principal lieutenant on 1 July, wanted to fight a limited bite-and-hold affair. The eventual compromise was neither one thing nor another. To be added to this was the inexperience of the British soldiers – mainly wartime volunteers – and the fact that British war industries were still developing. In both respects, the French were ahead. While the British had only one heavy gun for every 52 m (57 yds) of trench, the French had one to every 18 m (20 yds).

North of the Albert-Bapaume road, there was a depressingly familiar story of troops suffering high casualties for little gain. 1st Newfoundland Regiment suffered losses of nearly 700 men at Beaumont-Hamel. In Sausage Valley, the 103rd (Tyneside Irish) Brigade was reduced to a mere 50 men. There were some exceptions. Near Thiepval,

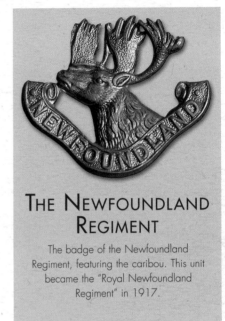

THE NEWFOUNDLAND REGIMENT

The badge of the Newfoundland Regiment, featuring the caribou. This unit became the "Royal Newfoundland Regiment" in 1917.

HENRY SEYMOUR RAWLINSON
(1864–1925)

General Rawlinson bore the primary operational responsibility for the first day on the Somme. An Eton-educated infantry officer, son of a noted Assyriologist, he saw service in the South African War (1899–1902). He was a reforming Commandant of the Staff College, Camberley and in the First World War he commanded consecutively IV Corps, First Army (temporarily) and the Fourth Army. His finest hour came as commander of Fourth Army in the Allied Advance to Victory in 1918. He died in 1925, when Commander-in-Chief, India

OPPOSITE: British infantry move up through wire, August 1916. By this stage the British were slowly gaining ground but at heavy cost.

ABOVE: A British officer's whistle. At 7.30 a.m. on 1 July, the blowing of whistles signalled the beginning of the infantry assault on the Somme.

BELOW: This German Maxim 1908 model machine gun is mounted on a tripod. Although manufactured in 1918, similar weapons were used on the Somme two years earlier.

36th (Ulster) Division advanced deep into German lines, only to be driven back. South of the road, the British did much better. The German positions were weaker, and the British benefited from the proximity of their Allies. On XIII Corps front, the German defences crumbled and, arguably, Rawlinson might have exploited this success to produce a victory of sorts out of defeat. For all that, on 1 July 1916 the BEF landed a heavy blow on the German army, which suffered greatly from British artillery fire and was dangerously stretched.

Fayolle's French Sixth Army did very well on 1 July, capturing all of their objectives and taking 4,000 prisoners. I Colonial Corps and XXXV Corps, positioned south of the Somme, deployed 84 heavy batteries; the Germans had only eight. Not surprisingly, Fayolle was frustrated by the inability of the British to push on. The French success on 1 July 1916 poses a fascinating allohistorical: what if, as originally planned, the French Army had taken the lead in the campaign, with the inexperienced BEF able to learn the ropes under relatively favourable conditions?

After 1 July, Haig switched the British main effort to the south of the main road, while the French continued to fight on the southern flank. Rawlinson launched a well-conducted limited attack on 14 July on Bazentin Ridge which briefly opened the possibility of a major advance. Otherwise, in the British sector, the months of July and August were marked by bloody and laborious struggles to wrest ground from determined defenders in places like Delville Wood, High Wood and Pozières, the latter being captured by the Australians on 23 July. The Germans, clinging to a doctrine of refusing to countenance the abandonment of territory, counter-attacked vigorously. Under increasing pressure on the Somme, by the end of July the Germans had been forced to go onto the defensive at Verdun.

1916

RIGHT: A sentry and sleeping soldiers in a front line trench at Ovilliers. These men are from 11th Cheshires, 25th Division.

Co-ordination between the BEF and the French Army was difficult, and often they appeared to be fighting parallel battles rather than making a combined effort. The French continued to push ahead, nearing Péronne on 2 July. A few days later, Joffre contemplated moving cavalry forward. But lacking sufficient reserves, and with the British failing to keep up and the German defenders recovering their balance, the chances of the French army breaking though diminished. The French continued to advance; for instance on 3 September Sixth Army captured 2,000 prisoners. Joffre pressured Haig to conduct another major offensive on a wide front, believing that the numerous small efforts being made by the BEF were inefficient and costly. By mid-September, the British were ready, and Haig made his second attempt at a break-through on the Somme.

ABOVE: The Somme typified the "war of the guns". Here British 8 inch howitzers of 39th Siege Battery Royal Garrison Artillery are in action in August 1916.

OPPOSITE: German dead in a shell hole, the victims of British XVIII Corps' successful attack at the beginning of the Somme Offensive.

MARIE ÉMILE FAYOLLE
(1858–1928)

At the beginning of the war, General Fayolle was in retirement, but was recalled to command an infantry division. A gunner by background, he earned Joffre's admiration and rose rapidly as less competent or fortunate commanders were sacked. He commanded French Sixth Army on the Somme in 1916, and in 1917 went on to command an army group. He played a key role in the battles of 1918. Fayolle was created a Marshal of France in 1921.

O.A.D. 90.

BJoAfol

366 **70**
3

S E C R E T

No 3 *copies made*
No 1 *dispatched*
No 2 *CIGS*
No 3 *Reserd BJO*

1st August, 1916.

The Chief of the
    Imperial General Staff.

      As requested by you, I submit the following summary of my views on the present situation for the information of the War Committee.

    1. The results of the Allied offensive on the west, which has now lasted just over a month, are as follows:-

    (a) The pressure on VERDUN has been relieved.

    The Germans have withdrawn* not less than six divisions, besides heavy guns, which had either been engaged, or were apparently intended to be used as reinforcements, at VERDUN. The attack on the left bank of the MEUSE has quite died down. The French are holding their own successfully on the right bank, and amongst other indications of the curtailment of the enemy's means of pressing his attack there has been a considerable lessening of his aerial activity in the VERDUN area. I am assured that the situation is no longer regarded with serious anxiety by the French military authorities. The moral effect of this on the French army and the French people has undoubtedly been considerable. If VERDUN had fallen - as the French military authorities told me must occur if the British offensive were delayed beyond the date finally chosen for it - the effect in France would have been very serious to the Allied cause.

    (b) The successes achieved by Russia during the last

month

*Vide attached statement marked I.a. 16408.

2.

367

month would almost certainly have been brought to a speedy termination had the Germans been free to reinforce their Eastern front considerably, as they certainly would have been but for the Allied offensive on the Western front.

    (c) The proof given to the world that the Allies are capable of making and maintaining a vigorous and combined offensive, and of driving from the strongest positions the enemy's best troops, has raised the belief of the armies in their own power to achieve victory and in the power of their Governments to organise it. There is evidence that it has shaken the faith of the Germans, of their friends, and of doubting neutrals in the invincibility of Germany; and that it has impressed on the world England's strength and determination, and the fighting power of the British race. The experience and increased self-confidence gained in the recent successful operations by our new armies, many of them until then untried in such fierce fighting, is also an asset of considerable value.

    (d) Our successes in the West have not only had the moral results claimed above, but they have inflicted very heavy material losses on the enemy. Exact figures cannot be given, but there is ocular demonstration that many thousands of German dead have been left on the ground which we are now in occupation of. Further statistics regarding the enemy's losses are given in the note annexed hereto*, to which I invite the careful attention of the War Committee.

    (e) In short, there can be no doubt that the moral and material results of the events of the last month have brought the Allies a considerable distance forward on the way to victory and that the maintenance of a steady offensive pressure on the enemy's main fronts will result eventually in his complete overthrow.

The

*I.a.16408.

Haig's 1 August report

Haig's secret 1 August report to Sir William Robertson on the progress of the Somme battle during July, including transcripts of messages from General Fritz von Below, commander of the German Second Army.

368.

The enemy still fights strongly, but evidence is not wanting that this is due rather to a realisation of the danger of defeat than to confidence in his power to win; and the conviction is apparent in the British Army, and, I believe, in all the Allied armies, that the enemy is already partially beaten and that all that is now required is unrelenting effort to turn the scale finally.   In this connection the attached copy (marked B) of a captured document, giving "Orders of the Day" issued by a highly-placed German commander, shows how seriously the SOMME operations are regarded by the Germans.   Moreover, the great moral and material effects on the enemy's troops of our artillery fire and of the vigour and determination of our attacks are fully established by other documents captured, as well as by the statements of prisoners, both officers and men.

2.   From the above, the principle on which we should continue to act is clear.   Under no circumstances would it be possible to relax our efforts in this battle without prejudicing, probably fatally, the offensive of our Allies and their hopes of victory.   We must, and we can, maintain our offensive, and it is essential that we should prove to our Allies, to our enemies, and to neutral Powers, our ability and our determination to do so.

Our losses in the last month's very heavy fighting - totalling to about 120,000 more than they would have been if we had not attacked - cannot be regarded as unduly heavy, or as sufficient to justify any anxiety as to our ability to continue the offensive.   Both the enemy and our Allies have borne far heavier losses than this without being turned from their purpose, and, moreover, our ranks have been filled up again and our troops are still in excellent heart.

It

4

369.

It is my intention -

(a)   To maintain a steady, methodical pressure, giving the enemy no rest and no respite from anxiety;

(b)   To push my attack strongly whenever and wherever the state of my preparations and the general situation make success sufficiently probable to justify me in doing so, but not otherwise;

(c)   To secure against counter-attack each advantage gained and prepare thoroughly for each fresh advance.

Proceeding thus I expect to be able to maintain the offensive well into the autumn and to inflict on the enemy material and moral losses which will amply recompense us for our own losses.

It would not be justifiable to calculate on the enemy's resistance being completely broken by these means without another campaign next year.   But, even if another campaign prove to be necessary, the enemy will certainly enter on the coming winter with little hope left of being able to continue his resistance successfully through next spring and summer, and I am confident that it will prove beyond his power to do so provided the Allies maintain their determination to fight on together, vigorously, to a successful conclusion.

Sd D Haig
General,
Commanding-in-Chief,
British Armies in France.

Ia/16408.

N O T E

o n

THE RESULTS OF THE BATTLE OF THE SOMME

DURING THE MONTH OF JULY.

****

1.   TROOPS EMPLOYED.-

The number of troops maintained by the Germans on the Western front has varied between 116 and 123 divisions during the past six months.   At present it stands at 120½.

At the commencement of the battle 8 of these divisions held the sector of the line attacked with 3 divisions in close reserve at CAMBRAI and ST. QUENTIN.

Up to the 31st July this number had increased to a total of 30 divisions employed by the Germans to resist the attack.   The extra divisions have had to be drawn from every part of the Western front.

This figure of 30 divisions employed during one month must be compared with the total number of divisions (viz. 39½) used by the Germans in the five months of the attack on VERDUN from February up to July.

It will be noted that in one month Germany has had to put in nearly as many divisions to resist our offensive as she employed herself during five months in her own effort to take VERDUN.

A diagram is attached showing the fluctuation in strength of the Germans along the whole of the Western

front

front during July.   It will be observed that the numbers of men per yard used by the enemy for the defence of the SOMME front is now greater than that employed at the commencement of the month on the VERDUN front, when the German attack was at its fiercest.

Six German divisions which had already fought and suffered very severely in the VERDUN area, and had been withdrawn to rest and reform, had to be again employed in the SOMME battle.   Allowing for this, 65½ divisions of the total German force of 120½ divisions on the Western front (i.e., approximately 53%) have been engaged, and have undoubtedly suffered severely in one or other of these great battles.

Assuming the wastage in divisions to continue at the same rate for another six weeks, then, theoretically, every German division on the Western front will have been employed, and the enemy's power of resistance on the Western front will have been weakened accordingly.

2.   CASUALTIES.-

The following data are available:-

(a)   Between the 1st and 27th July, not less than 166 hospital trains were observed to move from Belgium to Germany.   Allowing for unobserved hours, this represents at least 50,000 badly wounded men.

(b)   The total number of prisoners taken by the Allies now amounts to 26,500.

(c)   All evidence points to an exceptionally large number of German dead.

While

1916

144

While any estimate must be largely speculative,
it is not unduly sanguine to approximate the total
German casualties at certainly not less than 130,000.

3. GERMAN RESOURCES IN MEN.-

Accurate figures are not possible. It is,
however, established that the whole of the 1916 Class,
and a large proportion of the 1917 Class are already
at the front. To meet the drain of men up to the
end of the year, Germany can only rely on:-

The remainder of the 1917 Class, probably	= 200,000 men
Returned wounded, probably	= 100,000 men
TOTAL:	300,000 men

The 1917 Class have undergone training now for
about four months. It is estimated that the 1918
Class will not be ready to take the field before
January, 1917.

The figure of 300,000 has to be distributed
between the Eastern and Western fronts. On a
percentage of strength (viz. 50 divisions to 180
divisions), 200,000 will be available for the Western
front.

Under ordinary conditions on the Western front,
i.e., when no battle is in progress, the casualties
per month in a division of the German Army probably
amounts to about 800 per month, or a total of 67,000
for six weeks for the 90 divisions on the Western
front not employed in the SOMME battle.

Assuming that the battle on the SOMME is
continued for another 6 weeks with the same intensity
as during the past month, the German casualties in

this

---

this battle alone for these extra six weeks will
presumably not be less than 160,000. Adding this
to the 67,000 for the remainder of the divisions
during the six weeks, it will be seen that by the
middle of September the total available resources
in trained men of Germany for the Western front for
the remainder of the year will have been exceeded
by 27,000.

4. CO-OPERATION WITH OPERATIONS ON OTHER FRONTS.-

Both in 1914 and 1915, Germany, owing to her
central position, was enabled to move troops from
one front to the other, either to meet pressure exerted
by the Allies, or herself to exert pressure on one
or other front.

During the last month, the successes of the
Russians against the Austrians would have given the
Germans every reason to reinforce the Eastern front
by large bodies of troops drawn from the Western front,
if it had not been for the pressure exerted by the
battle of the SOMME.

The 19 divisions which have been thrown into the
SOMME battle to bring the 11 already there up to the
30 who are now opposing us, would obviously have been
available to reinforce the Eastern front. With
reinforcements up to this amount, it is more than
probable that the Russian offensive would have been
checked at its inception.

5. STRENGTH OF THE ALLIES AT PRESENT.-

At the present moment, Germany has on
the SOMME front an equivalent of 30

divisions

---

divisions. The allies on the same front have massed
considerably superior forces in men and guns, and they
can maintain their superiority.

SUMMARY.-

The effect of the offensive on Germany may, therefore,
be summed up as follows:-

(a) Germany has had to draw troops from the whole extent
of her Western front to meet the threat.

(b) She has been forced to employ defensively a
strength in men per yard exceeding that which
she was able to employ for the offensive
operations on the VERDUN front.

(c) In spite of such reinforcements it is proved possible
for the Allies to maintain a superiority of numbers
and of guns in the battle.

(d) Owing to the battle, Germany has been unable to
move troops to meet the Russian offensive
in the East. Had she been able to move
these troops, which calculations show would
amount to 19 divisions, it is more than
probable that the Russian offensive would have
been unable to make progress.

(e) The German offensive on the VERDUN front appears
to have been definitely postponed, if not
entirely abandoned.

(f) Germany has suffered losses far in excess of the
proportion of drafts which she can make available
for this front.

(g) If the battle is maintained for another 6 weeks
it appears probable that the German losses will
be more than she will be able to make good by
the end of the year.

(Annexe to G.H.Q. Summary of 30th July, 1916.)

Ia/16307.

ORDERS OF THE DAY by General von BELOW,

COMMANDING 2nd ARMY.

(1).

3rd July, 1916.

The decisive issue of the war depends on the victory
of the 2nd Army on the SOMME. We must win this battle in
spite of the enemy's temporary superiority in artillery and
infantry. The important ground lost in certain places will
be recaptured by our attack after the arrival of reinforcements. For the present, the important thing is to hold on
to our present positions at any cost and to improve them by
local counter-attacks.

I forbid the voluntary evacuation of trenches. The
will to stand firm must be impressed on every man in the Army.
I hold Commanding Officers responsible for this. The enemy
should have to carve his way over heaps of corpses. Every
available means must be utilized to push forward the construction of the front line, of intermediate lines behind the
principal salients, and of defensive lines in rear.

These rear lines of defence must be constructed on
the reverse slopes, in order that their position and the details
of their final construction may be concealed from the enemy's
view.

I require Commanding Officers to devote their utmost
energies to the establishment of order behind the front.

(Sgd) v. B e l o w .

(2).

16th July, 1916.

His Majesty the Emperor and King, in the course of
his visit to-day to Army Head-Quarters, has been pleased to
express his great satisfaction with the heroic resistance
offered by the 2nd Army to an enemy greatly superior in
numbers.

His Majesty is fully convinced that his glorious
troops will continue to stand firm and that they will master
the enemy's assaults by irresistible dash in the attack, by
immovable tenacity in the defence.

Officers and men may be proud of the unshaken confidence placed in them by their Supreme Chief. Let each one
in his sphere continue to merit that confidence.

This order will be circulated to all units of the
Army.

(Sgd) v. B e l o w .

THE BATTLE OF THE SOMME

ENTER THE TANKS

FOR HIS SECOND "BIG PUSH" ON THE SOMME, ON 15 SEPTEMBER 1916, HAIG WAS ABLE TO DEPLOY 32 TANKS, A NEW AND SECRET WEAPON, ALTHOUGH ONLY 24 TOOK PART IN THE ACTION ON THAT DAY. THEIR IMPACT WAS MODEST, ALTHOUGH THEY MADE A BIG IMPRESSION ON THE GERMAN TROOPS WHO WERE CONFRONTED BY THEM. ASSISTED BY TANKS, 41ST DIVISION CAPTURED THE VILLAGE OF FLERS.

1916

ABOVE: British troops leave their trenches near Ginchy during the Battle of Morval, September 1916. This battle achieved some local success.

OPPOSITE ABOVE: "Clan Leslie", a Mark I tank on 15 September 1916, the day of the first tank action in history.

Many other British divisions also did well, as did the Canadians and New Zealanders. In all, the line advanced about 2.5 km (1.5 miles). By the standards of trench warfare, this was creditable enough, but the Battle of Flers-Courcelette fell a long way short of a breakthrough.

Ten days later, at Morval, a more limited attack on a narrow front did achieve considerable success. Simultaneously, the French army made important gains in the nearby Rancourt sector. On the following day, 26 September, the fortress of Thiepval, which was supposed to have fallen on 1 July, was captured by 18th Division in a well-planned and executed attack. These two attacks, in which British troops had demonstrated that they were absorbing the hard-won tactical lessons of the Somme, pointed the way towards a more successful way of fighting. Unfortunately, Haig misread the message of these limited battles, believing that German resistance was crumbling, and hence he ordered ambitious attacks rather than further bite and hold battles. Subsequent offensives, such as the battle for the high ground around

PAUL VON HINDENBURG
(1847–1934)

Partly because of the extreme pressure on the German army on the Somme, Field Marshal von Hindenburg assumed supreme command in Germany on 29 August 1916. The hero of the Eastern Front in 1914–15, Hindenburg made a formidable team with Erich Ludendorff, and they became dictators of Germany in all but name. Although their policies contributed mightily to Germany losing the war, Hindenburg retained his prestige. He played an important role in the politics of the post-war Weimar Republic (which replaced the German Empire), serving as President of Germany from 1925 to 1934.

Le Transloy in October, demonstrated that Haig's optimism was misplaced. Although he can be criticized for this, in truth Haig had no alternative but to continue the battle as he was under pressure from Joffre. As autumn arrived the weather deteriorated, with sticky Somme mud adding to the troops' woes.

During this time, the French continued to attack on the Somme, committing Micheler's

Tenth Army to the fighting in September. However, co-operation with the BEF, already poor during Flers-Courcelette, broke down. In later offensives the French, like the British, tended to neglect large-scale well co-ordinated battles in favour of smaller, disjointed actions. The French suffered heavily in engagements such as those at Sailly-Saillisel, St Pierre-Vaast, and in the Rancourt sector. "On the 16th, 18th, 21st and 22nd of October," Joffre

THE BATTLE OF THE SOMME: 1 July–18 November 1916

| Front lines | — Morning 1 July | – – 26 September | → British advances |
| | ···· Evening 1 July | –·–· 18 November | → French advances |

ABOVE: Ludendorff. His strategy was ultimately disastrous for Germany.

candidly admitted in his memoirs, "a series of small attacks followed one another without great results." One problem was that that the "fragmentary ... attacks" of the French played into the hands of the Germans. Under the new team of Hindenburg and Ludendorff, who replaced Falkenhayn at the end of August, new tactics had been introduced. Gone were rigid trench lines. Now German positions had depth, with machine guns in shell-holes to break up enemy attacks. The British, too, experienced problems in dealing with these new defensive methods.

The final phase of the Somme returned the focus of the action to the northern extremity of the battlefield, which had seen relatively little action since the early stages of the offensive. On 13 November, General Sir Hubert Gough, commander of British Fifth Army, launched the Battle of the Ancre. Gough applied many of the lessons of the previous months. His plan was reasonably limited; there was a sufficient number of guns, including 282 heavies; the field guns fired a "creeping barrage", a relatively flexible curtain of shells that moved ahead of the infantry (the failure to use such methods on 1 July had been a contributory factor to the British setbacks); and staff work showed a distinct improvement over the earlier months of the battle. While not completely successful, the Fifth Army took most of its objectives, including Beaumont-Hamel and Beaucourt villages.

FIFTH ARMY

General Sir Hubert Gough's Reserve Army, which was renamed Fifth Army in late 1916, was responsible for operations in the northern part of the Somme battlefield. "Goughie", strongly supported by Haig, was the youngest of the senior British generals. He earned an unenviable reputation as a "thruster", intolerant of criticism. The fighting was attritional, with heavy casualties sustained in attacks such as those at Pozières and Mouquet Farm, where the Australians lost more men in six weeks than they had in eight months at Gallipoli.

Losses on the Somme were shockingly high. The British suffered 420,000; the French 200,000. German losses were probably in the region of 450,000 to 600,000. The battle is customarily portrayed as a British defeat. It was not. While not a victory in the conventional sense of the word, the attrition was in favour of the Allies, and the BEF's bloody apprenticeship meant that it ended the year as a more effective army than it had been at the beginning. The German High Command was well aware of the serious consequences of the Somme; it had discounted the British army, but now realized that it was a major force that stacked the odds against a German victory on land. Instead, 1917 was to see an attempt to use the U-boat fleet to starve Britain out of the war. This failed, and served to bring the USA into the war instead. British generalship and tactics were often poor on the Somme, but the overall result was a success for Allied arms.

ABOVE TOP: On 25 September at the Battle of Morval supporting troops go over the top.

ABOVE: The Mills Bomb was the classic pineapple-shaped hand grenade, the first safe and reliable time-fused grenade issued to the British Army.

Instructions regarding War Diaries and Intelligence Summaries are contained in F. S. Regs., Part II. and the Staff Manual respectively. Title Pages will be prepared in manuscript.

Place	Date	Hour	Summary of Events and Information			Remarks and references to Appendices
Green Dump	15/9/16		Below will be found a small tabulated report on the work of the D Coy Tanks.			

NAME of COMMANDER	UNIT TO WHICH ATTACHED TO	TANK No.	ORDERS RECEIVED	HOW ORDERS WERE CARRIED OUT	CASUALTIES
Capt. H.W. MORTIMORE	14th Div. 15th Corps	D 1.	To proceed to S.E. corner of DELVILLE WOOD and at 5·30 A.M. on Sept. 15th to attack and clear HOP ALLEY. Then endeavour to overtake advancing Infantry and proceed with them to further objectives.	Cleared HOP ALLEY and had caught up and passed Infantry when Tank was hit by shell in rear starboard sprocket & put out of action.	NIL
LT. H.R. BELL	15th Corps 41st Div. on Sept 15 3rd Corps 23rd Div. Oct 7th	D 2	Did not go into action on Sept.15 Oct. 7th To proceed from M.22.c.7.1. to LE SARS via THE TANGLE & SUNKEN Road M.16.c.7.1.	On Sept. 15 When going up to starting line car became ditched & took no part in action. Car was eventually dug out. Carried out all orders till E edge of Le SARS, where car was hit by H.E. & caught fire	Sept. 15th 1 Officer wounded (at duty) H.E. Splinters outside TANK Oct. 7th 3 O/R wounded At ly H.E. & Shrapnel after car had been abandoned & crew were returning to trenches.

2449 Wt. W14957/M90 750,000 1/16 J.B.C. & A. Form/C.2118/12.

Instructions regarding War Diaries and Intelligence Summaries are contained in F. S. Regs., Part II. and the Staff Manual respectively. Title Pages will be prepared in manuscript.

Place	Date	Hour	Summary of Events and Information	Remarks and references to Appendices
Sept	13/9/16		Major Summers attended a conference at XV Corps. Captain Mann was detailed to command Tanks of III Corps & he attended a conference at III Corps H.Q.	
	13/9/16	4 pm	Preliminary bombardment commenced. Tanks moved from LOOP to Position of Assembly GREEN DUMP arriving at midnight. LT Colle returned on foot to the Loop reporting that he had a broken track New car was supplied	
GREEN DUMP	14/9/16		Our bombardment grew more intense. Crew skippers reconnoitred route up to the trenches, & found the ground cut up very badly by shell holes. Communication trenches etc. To move Tanks over this ground in the dark would mean heavy work & careful manipulation, & this was fully realized by Crew skippers.	
do		3 pm	Major Summers left Loop & arrived at Green Dump at 3 pm. From this hour until 8 pm the C.O. was occupied with his skippers issuing operation orders & explaining same	
do		8.30 pm	Tanks moved off to starting line	
	15/9/16		Z day Zero time 6·20 A.M. Tanks to advance before infantry. Reports came through that Tanks had passed through Flers at 8·30 A.M. Large numbers of prisoners passed Green Dump on their way to cages At about 4 pm our own wounded officers & men commenced to arrive at Green Dump	

2449 Wt. W14957/M90 750,000 1/16 J.B.C. & A. Form/C.2118/12.

4th Battalion, the Tank Corps war diary

A handwritten official war diary of 4th Battalion, the Tank Corps, describing the unit's build-up to the 15 September attack, then, tank-by-tank, D Company's actions and casualties.

Instructions regarding War Diaries and Intelligence
Summaries are contained in F. S. Regs., Part II.
and the Staff Manual respectively. Title Pages
will be prepared in manuscript.

Place	Date	Hour	Summary of Events and Information		Remarks and references to Appendices
NAME OF COMMANDER	UNIT TO WHICH ALLOTTED	TANK No.	ORDERS RECEIVED	HOW ORDERS WERE CARRIED OUT	CASUALTIES
2nd Lt H.G. PEARSALL	N.Z. Div. 15th Corps	D 11.	Same orders as for D10 (Lt Darby) but did not stop on CREST TRENCH.	When this Tank reached FLERS and failed to find any Germans the officer reported to a N.Z. Officer who asked that Tank might protect his flank. Lt Pearsall took up this position & remained there till 7·45 P.M. Tank was then asked to go forward to meet expected counter attack and remained forward till 6 A.M. next day (16th Sept). Tank advanced with infantry at 9 A.M. & carried on till hit by H.E. shell which burst under belly of car blowing in the gear box. Lt Pearsall remained on Tank for some while using his Vickers guns on enemy & also took one Vickers gun into the trenches when he had to abandon Tank.	3 O/R Wounded Caused by H.E. bursting under Tank blowing gear box to pieces.
CAPT. G. NIXON	N.Z. Div. 15th Corps.	D 12	Same orders as for D11 Tank (Lt Pearsall)	Orders were carried out as given till Tank advanced through FLERS, where in village Tank was hit putting tail out of action. Capt. Nixon decided under these circumstances to withdraw. In withdrawing Tank became ditched at M36 D.9·9. & during digging operations Tank was again hit & caught fire. Crew brought back to camp with 1 man missing.	1 O/R Missing. Last traces of this man when returning to cover after having abandoned Tank.

2449 Wt. W14957/M90 750,000 1/16 J.B.C. & A. Forms/C.2118/12.

WAR DIARY

Army Form C. 2118.

INTELLIGENCE SUMMARY

(Erase heading not required.)

Instructions regarding War Diaries and Intelligence
Summaries are contained in F. S. Regs., Part II.
and the Staff Manual respectively. Title Pages
will be prepared in manuscript.

Place	Date	Hour	Summary of Events and Information		Remarks and references to Appendices
NAME OF COMMANDER	UNIT TO WHICH ALLOTTED	TANK No.	ORDERS RECEIVED	HOW ORDERS WERE CARRIED OUT	CASUALTIES
2nd Lt. W.H. SAMPSON	47th Div. III Corps	D 13	To proceed from HIGH ALLEY S4.c.6.2. to FLERS LANE N29 d.6·6 via HIGH WOOD	Advanced with Infantry through HIGH WOOD and when on far side Tank was hit by shell & Tank caught fire. Crew were ordered to abandon Tank. Crew remained in trenches with infantry and worked machine guns	2 O/R Wounded In Tank. 1 O/R wounded by German infantry man shooting through loop hole. Germans crept up & opened loophole shot Gunner in leg. Other eyes burnt when tank caught fire.
2nd Lt. G.F. COURT	41st Div	D 14	To proceed from starting line at 5·45 ahead of infantry to TEA SUPPORT, then to 1st objective SWITCH TRENCH. Thence to FLERS AVENUE on to FLERS VILLAGE and on from there to GIRD TRENCH, GIRD SUPPORT to GUEUDECOURT	The Tank advanced from behind FLERS Village on Sept 16th. The Tank has been reported blown up at point N 26.B. No news whatever has since been received. Tank has since been visited and is now absolutely blown to bits.	1 Officer 7 O/R Missing cause not known.

2449 Wt. W14957/M90 750,000 1/16 J.B.C. & A. Forms/C.2118/12.

2

No 3 Southern Gen Hosp.
Oxford England
24/10/16

My Dear Mr Beach

I suppose you will be
suprised to hear from me but
no dought you will be looking
foward for a letter from some
of us boys to hear of poor old
Heald my mate. I suppose
you will know long before
this letter reaches you that
Heald died of wounds on
the Somme. He got hit the
first morning we went over
the top & he lay out all that
day & the next night. The
strecherbearers found him next
morning at dawn. It was

imposial to get at the wounded
in the daylight & they were
very hard to find at night
as all the land was new
to the bearers. They could
only find the wounded by
their groan & some of the
poor fellows were never found
intill it was to late & they
were either dead & or would
die as soon as they moved them
just the same as in Healds
case. I never seen Heald while
he was conious after he got
hit, but I think he must have
known that he was done, as
when they brought him to the
dressing station he asked for
me if I was still alive & if he

Private W. M. Innes' letter

A letter from Private W. M. Innes to the father of his close
friend, Private Harold Beach, who was killed with the New
Zealand Division on the Somme on 16 September 1916. In his
letter, Innes left nothing to the imagination.

1916

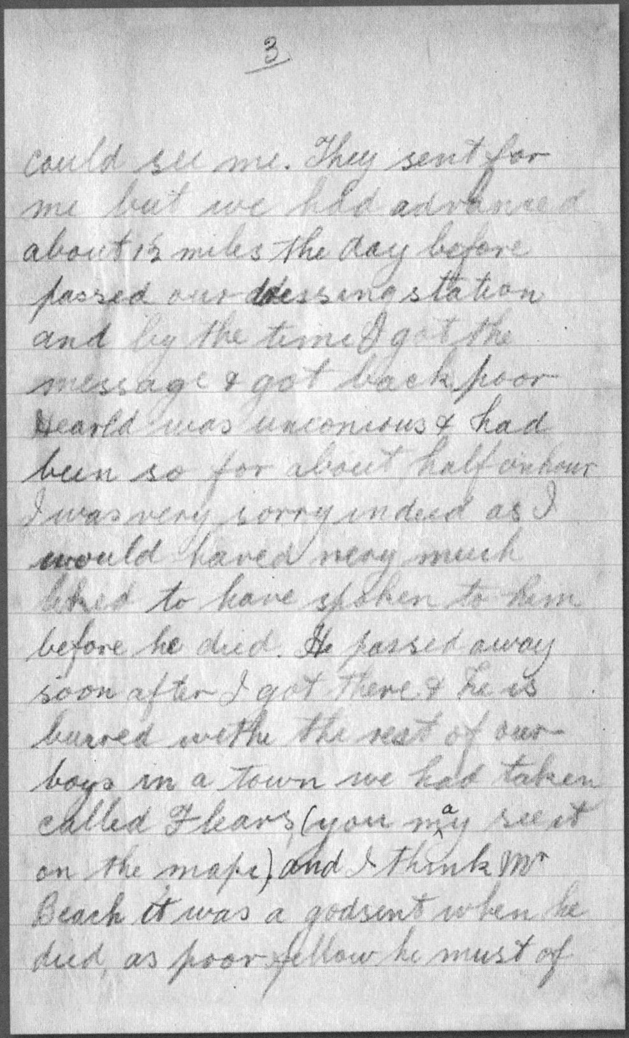

could see me. They sent for
me but we had advanced
about 1½ miles the day before
passed our dressing station
and by the time I got the
message & got back poor
Heald was unconious & had
been so for about half anhour
I was very sorry indeed as I
would haved very much
liked to have spoken to him
before he died. He passed away
soon after I got there & he is
buried with the rest of our
boys in a town we had taken
called Flears (you may see it
on the maps) and I think Mr
Beach it was a godsent when he
died, as poor fellow he must of

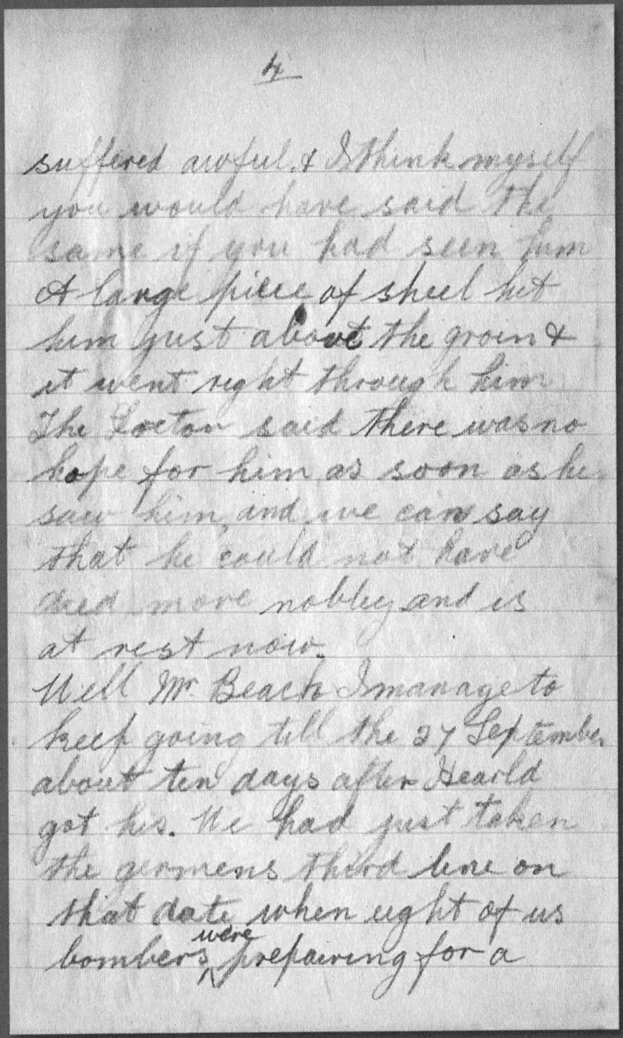

suffered awful. & I think myself
you would have said the
same if you had seen him
A large piece of sheel hit
him just about the groin &
it went right though him
The Doctor said there was no
hope for him as soon as he
saw him, and we can say
that he could not have
died more nobley and is
at rest now.
Well Mr Beach I manage to
keep going till the 27 September
about ten days after Heald
got his. We had just taken
the germens third line on
that date when eght of us
bombers were preparing for a

FRENCH CHANGE
OF COMMAND

THE APPOINTMENT OF NIVELLE

BY THE END OF NOVEMBER 1916, ACTIVITY DIED DOWN ON THE
WESTERN FRONT, AND THE GENERALS PREPARED TO RENEW THE
OFFENSIVE IN THE NEW YEAR. HAIG AND JOFFRE CONSULTED ON
PLANS BUT IN MID-DECEMBER JOFFRE, THE MAN WHO HAD SACKED
SO MANY GENERALS, WAS HIMSELF DISMISSED.

He was still popular, so his sacking was dressed up as a promotion to strategic adviser to the government and he was elevated to Marshal of France. But in reality Joffre's power was at an end, and he was reduced to a ceremonial role for the rest of the war. The enormous moral capital Joffre had amassed through his steady, calm generalship in 1914 had been eroded by the huge casualties and the continuing deadlock. Despite the sanguinary efforts of 1915, despite Verdun, despite the Somme, the invading Germans were still firmly camped on French soil, at their closest only 65 km (40 miles) from Paris. The politicians had had enough. It was time for a change.

OPPOSITE: Georges Clemenceau greets British General Pinney, April 1918. Clemenceau's appointment as Premier in 1917 helped France to put the disasters of that year behind them.

ABOVE: Foreground, left to right: Albert Thomas (French Munitions Minister), Haig. Joffre and Lloyd George, 1916. By the end of the year, Joffre had been "kicked upstairs".

ROBERT GEORGE NIVELLE
(1856–1924)

Nivelle was a gunner by background. His career included service in North Africa, China and Indochina and was sound rather than distinguished. By 1914 Nivelle was a colonel. His skilful handling of artillery in the initial campaigns brought him promotion to general in October 1914, and his performance at Verdun led to his becoming Commander-in-Chief of the French armies at the end of 1916. The failure of the April 1917 offensive to which he gave his name (see pages 162–63) led to his dismissal and slide into obscurity.

Change took the form of General Robert Nivelle who was appointed as de facto French Commander-in-Chief on the Western Front. From the beginning he wielded a new broom. Articulate and persuasive in French and English (his mother was British), Nivelle had a very different personal style from Joffre. Initially, Haig, who had had a sometimes turbulent relationship with Joffre, thought Nivelle "a most straightforward and soldierly man". In the context of French military politics, where Catholic piety was a handicap, Nivelle had good credentials as a Protestant. Above all, he promised success. Nivelle had come to prominence as a result of his successes at Verdun, which had been based on the techniques of the set-piece attack. Massed artillery fire covered the advance of the infantry, who were set limited objectives. This had worked well in small-scale actions, but now he persuaded his superiors that the same methods could be used to achieve the elusive breakthrough on the Western Front

which would reopen mobile warfare and lead to a decisive victory. At his first meeting with Haig, Nivelle made it clear that he intended to disregard existing plans. Haig noted in his diary that the new French commander was "confident of breaking through the Enemy's front now that the Enemy's morale is weakened". The key was for the attack to achieve surprise "and go through in 24 hours".

Nivelle found a key supporter in London as well as in Paris. David Lloyd George, who had become Prime Minister in December 1916, distrusted Haig and Robertson and was opposed to a fresh British offensive on the Western Front. As the leader of a coalition government, however, he was too weak politically to move against the senior generals. He fell for Nivelle's eloquence, and so decided to push for the BEF to be placed directly under the French command: this would marginalize Haig and effectively reduce him to an administrative role. The

prospect of getting a firmer grip on their ally appealed to some senior French commanders, and Lloyd George conspired with Nivelle and others to present Haig with a fait accompli. This was duly delivered at a meeting at Calais on 26 February, ostensibly called to discuss transportation. Haig and Robertson were predictably furious that their own prime minister wanted to hand the BEF over to foreign generals. As one of the participants at the conference, the British liaison officer Brigadier General Edward Spiers (known after the war as Spears), later wrote, "Seldom in history can Englishmen have been asked to subscribe to such abject conditions … such as might be imposed on a vassal state."

Haig and Robertson fought back, and the end result was an uneasy compromise. Haig remained in operational control of the BEF but was placed under Nivelle's command for the forthcoming operation. Crucially, the British Commander-in-Chief was given the right of appeal to London if he objected to Nivelle's orders. This was a long way short of what Lloyd George and Nivelle had wanted, and came at a high price. The Calais plot destroyed what remained of the trust between Lloyd George and the two most important generals in the British army. Unity of command was certainly desirable, but a shotgun marriage was not the sensible way to achieve it. Haig did not know how deeply Nivelle had been involved in the conspiracy, and he remained correct in his dealings with him. The French change of command had avoided a major breach between the Allies, but had precipitated the worst clash between the British military and government of the entire war.

OPPOSITE: Paris at war: the sandbagged exterior of the Cathedral of Notre Dame, 1916.

RIGHT: Retreating German troops destroy a railway station and sidings during the withdrawal to the Hindenburg Line.

BELOW: France's transition to a total war economy from 1914 to 1918 was impressive. These factory workers are soldering the fins onto bombs.

RETREAT TO THE HINDENBURG LINE

In February and March 1917, the German army abandoned the positions they had defended so tenaciously on the Somme in 1916. The German troops fell back to a new, immensely strong fortified defensive system. Work on this position, called by the British "the Hindenburg Line", had begun in the middle of the Somme offensive. The retiring Germans carried out a scorched-earth policy, damaging towns such as Bapaume and Péronne. The retreat was a sensible move by the Germans, and badly disrupted Nivelle's offensive plans.

MONDAY, 9 APRIL 1917–WEDNESDAY, 16 MAY 1917

THE BATTLE OF ARRAS

ALLIED OFFENSIVE

THE 9 APRIL 1917 WAS THE MOST SUCCESSFUL DAY THAT THE BEF
HAD ENJOYED SINCE THE BEGINNING OF TRENCH WARFARE. THE BEF
COMMITTED TO BATTLE AS THE FIRST STAGE OF AN ANGLO-FRENCH
OPERATION, WITH THE FRENCH NIVELLE OFFENSIVE BEGINNING
ON 16 APRIL (SEE PAGES 162–163).

1917

THE CANADIANS

A Canadian cap badge which incorporates the maple leaf, the symbol of the Canadian nation.

JULIAN HEDWORTH GEORGE BYNG
(1862–1935)

General Byng, a British officer from a smart cavalry regiment (10th Hussars), was a great success in command of the Canadian Corps. The Corps was nicknamed "The Byng Boys" after a popular musical show. Vimy Ridge was his finest achievement, and he took the title of Viscount Byng of Vimy when he was ennobled. In late 1917, he was promoted to command Third Army, which he led with success until the end of the war. He became Governor-General of Canada in 1921.

After a heavy artillery bombardment, 14 British and Canadian divisions of General Sir Edmund Allenby's Third Army attacked on a 23,000-m (25,000-yd) front near Arras. For an army that on the Somme had become used to gains that were meagre at best, the results of the day's fighting were hugely encouraging. The Canadian Corps – which was commanded by a British officer, General Sir Julian Byng and included a number of British troops – captured the daunting high ground of Vimy Ridge, while further south British forces made some important gains. The 4th and 9th (Scottish) Divisions of XVII Corps pushed 5.5 km (3.5 miles) into the German positions and dug in on the German Third Line. This was the longest single advance achieved by a British formation under conditions of trench warfare. VI Corps pushed forward about 3.25 km (2 miles); Battery Valley, complete with German artillery, fell to 12th and 15th (Scottish) Divisions. The village of Neuville-Vitasse fell as VII Corps advanced 1,800 m (2,000 yds). Not surprisingly, on the afternoon of 9 April, Haig wrote to King George V on a note of triumph.

OPPOSITE: A ditched tank surrounded by curious British infantrymen, possibly of 4th Division, on the Fampoux Road, Battle of Arras, April 1917.

ABOVE: Following the success of the initial attack, Canadian troops advance on Vimy Ridge. Note the German prisoners in the foreground.

EDMUND HENRY HYNMAN ALLENBY
(1861–1936)

General Allenby was Haig's exact contemporary. Both were cavalrymen, and while there was never an open breach, the two never worked together entirely easily. After Arras, to his disgust, Allenby was sent to command the Egyptian Expeditionary Force. Ironically, the move away from trench stalemate to conditions of open warfare was the making of him. In 1917 and 1918, Allenby fought a series of successful battles against the Turks in Palestine, and today his popular reputation stands in stark contrast to that of Haig.

The first day of Arras was a successful example of a limited battle founded on careful planning and preparation. Twelve tunnels were dug under Vimy Ridge which allowed troops to move up to the front line safe from artillery fire. Light railways brought supplies and ammunition to the front line, and troops trained in the new tactics that had emerged from the Somme, were thoroughly rehearsed in the roles they were to play on 9 April. The artillery preparation lasted for five days – Allenby had wanted a shorter bombardment, but Haig overruled him – and was thorough and effective. The effectiveness of much

of the German artillery was sharply reduced by British fire, with many German gunners killed or forced to take shelter. At Vimy Ridge, the artillery fire plan was masterminded by a British gunner, Lieutenant Colonel Alan Brooke, who was to rise to become Churchill's principal military adviser in the Second World War.

The seizure of Vimy Ridge was a particularly impressive operation, where the infantry-artillery combination was highly successful, and four Victoria Crosses were awarded. Vimy Ridge has since become a symbol of the birth of Canadian nationhood, and

a beautiful memorial was inaugurated in 1936. It is sometimes said that the Canadians succeeded in capturing Vimy Ridge where the British had failed. This is inaccurate; since the British had taken over the sector, they had mounted no major operation against the Ridge. Despite the fact that the German defence-in-depth tactics did not work well here – the German commanders made mistakes and the terrain did not lend itself to these methods – in many places the Germans fought very effectively. The Canadian Corps emerged from Vimy with its reputation as an élite formation greatly enhanced.

The first day of the battle demonstrated that the BEF had matured greatly since July 1916, but it was unable to capitalize on its success. The weather was poor, and Allenby did not receive reconnaissance reports from Royal Flying Corps (RFC) aircraft. He wrongly believed that Third Army was facing a retreating enemy and ordered that "risks must be taken freely". In reality, German reserves were arriving on the battlefield as the Allied advance slowed down. The infantry were moving out of range of the field artillery, which was struggling to get forward over ground which had been cratered in the initial attack. This starkly revealed the problem

of artillery-driven limited offensives – it was very difficult to maintain operational tempo. The battle congealed, and although bloody actions continued for a month – the Australians had particularly gruelling fights in two actions at Bullecourt in April and May, and a general attack on 23 April gained over 2 km (more than a mile) – Allenby's optimism was proved to be chimerical.

Arras was the product of coalition politics, a battle that Haig never wanted to fight. Nevertheless, it demonstrated that the BEF was now capable of conducting an effective limited battle and that the German line could

be broken, knowledge which was to influence Haig and GHQ in their planning for Third Ypres later in 1917 (see pages 174–177). Arras was the shortest but most intense of the BEF's major offensives under Haig. The daily loss rate of 4,076 was higher than that at the Somme or Passchendaele. In all, 150,000 of the BEF's solders became casualties, along with over 100,000 Germans.

OPPOSITE: A group of German prisoners. The doctor is treating a man in a litter constructed from a groundsheet and a pole.

ABOVE: Australian infantry cleaning their rifles in a second-line trench near Bullecourt, May 1917, while serving in Gough's Fifth Army.

THE NIVELLE OFFENSIVE

BUILD UP TO A MUTINY

THE BATTLE LAUNCHED ON THE AISNE ON 16 APRIL 1917 IS KNOWN
TO HISTORY AS "THE NIVELLE OFFENSIVE". IT IS A MONUMENT TO ONE
MAN'S FOLLY. WHEN HE WAS BRIEFED ON NIVELLE'S PLANS, GENERAL
LYAUTEY, A VETERAN OF FRENCH COLONIAL CONFLICTS WHO WAS
SERVING AS MINISTER OF WAR, THOUGHT THEM RIDICULOUS.

1917

PUNISHING THE MUTINEERS

Of the tens of thousands of poilus affected
by the mutinies following the Nivelle
Offensive, only 554 were condemned to
death. Of these, most were not executed.
Historians' estimates of men actually shot
range from around 40 to 62 (in all about
600 men were executed during the entire
war for all offences). Pétain's strategy was
to mix reforms of the soldiers' conditions
with making examples of individuals to
reassert the authority of the army. The
latter policy had, he later wrote, "a
deterrent effect".

Likewise, Nivelle's principal
subordinates expressed reservations.
Nivelle planned to smash through
the enemy front by heavy artillery fire
followed by infantry attacks, which he
believed would lead to a decisive defeat of
the Germans. Moreover, he asserted that,
unlike battles of the past, this one would
be time limited. Nivelle promised that if,
by some mischance, the troops did not
break through, he would call off the battle
rather than allow it to become a lengthy
attritional struggle.

The initial objective of the offensive was the
ridge of the Chemin des Dames in Champagne,
an area that was no stranger to warfare. It
was a tough prospect for the attackers: the
Germans had taken maximum advantage of the
high ground and strengthened it to create an
immensely strong belt of trenches and strong-
points designed according to the principles of
elastic defence. To add to the problems of the
French army, the element of surprise was soon
lost. Nivelle himself was unbelievably indiscreet,
and before long rumours of the offensive were
being reported in the French press, which was
assiduously read by the Germans. In any case, a

set of preliminary "Instructions" for the attack
fell into German hands as early as 15 February.
All this merely confirmed the build-up they
could see with their own eyes. The Germans
reinforced the threatened sector, the number
of divisions there rising from 18 divisions in
January to 42 in March.

Micheler's Reserve Army Group, (Fifth, Sixth
and Tenth Armies under Mazel, Mangin and
Duchêne respectively) was entrusted with
the main attack, with Pétain's Central Army
Group playing a secondary role. Originally,
Franchet d'Espèrey's Northern Army Group

was to have attacked as well, but the planned German withdrawal to the Hindenburg Line in February-March 1917 had made this plan redundant. The British, of course, were to attack at Arras a week earlier. Morale among the troops was generally high, but curiously, as the date of the attack neared, Nivelle's confidence sagged, and thanks to a change of government, his political support waned.

On 16 April, the attack began. For days beforehand the French guns pounded the German defences. The French artillery observers were hampered by poor weather and enemy strength in the air; this was the period known to the British pilots as "Bloody April". The resulting bombardment was heavy – Micheler's artillery fired 11 million shells – but inaccurate and ineffective. Since Nivelle's method depended heavily on artillery blasting a way for the infantry through the German positions, this was a disastrous start to the attack. The French infantry struggled through the in-depth defences, finding wire uncut, machine-gun posts untouched, and the German reserves virtually unscathed. Even so, some of the French infantry did well. By 20 April, part of Sixth Army had pushed forward about 6.5 km (4 miles) and taken 5,300 prisoners. By the end of the battle, Nivelle's troops had taken 29,000 enemy prisoners and had carved out a salient 6.5 km (4 miles deep) and 26 km (16 miles) wide. Judged by the standards of 1917, this was a limited success. But the huge French losses – 134,000 casualties of which 30,000 were fatalities – incurred in a few days and the failure of Nivelle's ambitious plans to come even remotely close to achievement meant the attack was written off as a ghastly failure, and the Chemin des Dames gained the sinister reputation it holds in France to this day.

The morale and cohesion of the French army was badly shaken. Swathes of divisions were affected by "collective indiscipline", that is, by mutiny, which broke out almost as soon as the Nivelle Offensive began. Some acts of defiance were relatively minor, such as the shouting of slogans or smashing of windows. Others threatened the very disciplinary fabric of the French army. Troops refused to obey orders to return to the trenches and gathered in crowds to air their grievances and even express revolutionary sentiments. The failure of the Nivelle offensive was the trigger for the mutinies, but the causes were deeper, reaching back to the huge losses since 1914, to the soldiers' discontent with their conditions, and their lack of faith in their officers. The mutinies were at their worst in June, but over the next few months General Philippe Pétain, who replaced Nivelle, rebuilt the army's fragile cohesion. Fortunately for the Allies, the Germans did not take advantage of the French army's most traumatic period of the war.

HEALING THE ARMY

On being appointed Commander-in-Chief on 17 May, Pétain energetically addressed the bread-and-butter issues that underlay the soldiers' grievances. He introduced more frequent leave, better food and improved welfare facilities. He also mounted several small-scale operations, carefully planned and backed by massed artillery, to demonstrate that battlefield success was possible. Pétain, however, made it clear that his strategy had changed, announcing that he intended to "wait for the Americans and the tanks". The French Army would no longer bear the principal burden of the war on the Western Front.

OPPOSITE: Craonne, the scene of one of Napoleon's victories in 1814, also witnessed heavy fighting in the Nivelle Offensive 103 years later.

ABOVE LEFT: Although the French army's morale was in a delicate state after the Nivelle Offensive, nevertheless, here the 313 Infantry move up to the trenches on 7 June 1917.

ABOVE: King George V decorates General Philippe Pétain with the Order of the Bath on 12 July 1917.

LEFT: Scenes of carnage at Craonne, after the French attack of 16 April 1917.

RIGHT: A French F1 hand grenade.

1917

GRAND QUARTIER GÉNÉRAL
DES ARMÉES
du Nord et du Nord-Est

ÉTAT-MAJOR

1er BUREAU

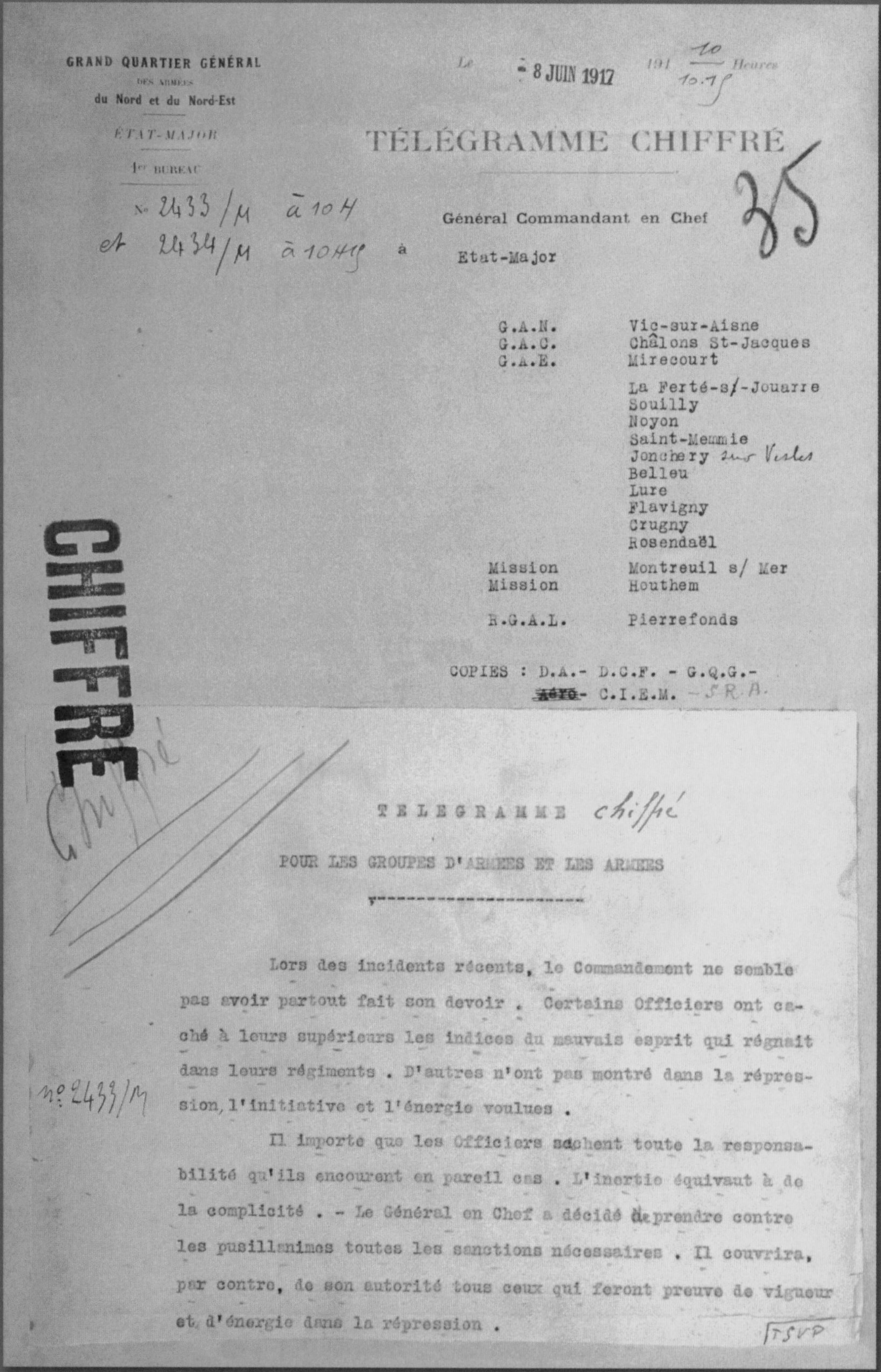

N° 2433/M à 10 H
et 2434/M à 10 H 15

Le - 8 JUIN 1917 191 10/10.15 Heures

TÉLÉGRAMME CHIFFRÉ

25

Général Commandant en Chef

à

Etat-Major

G.A.N.	Vic-sur-Aisne
G.A.C.	Châlons St-Jacques
G.A.E.	Mirecourt
	La Ferté-s/-Jouarre
	Souilly
	Noyon
	Saint-Memmie
	Jonchery sur Vesles
	Belleu
	Lure
	Flavigny
	Crugny
	Rosendaël
Mission	Montreuil s/ Mer
Mission	Houthem
R.G.A.L.	Pierrefonds

COPIES : D.A.- D.C.F. - G.Q.G.-
~~Aéro~~- C.I.E.M. - S.R.A.

CHIFFRE

Chiffré

T E L E G R A M M E chiffré

POUR LES GROUPES D'ARMEES ET LES ARMEES

n° 2433/M

Lors des incidents récents, le Commandement ne semble pas avoir partout fait son devoir . Certains Officiers ont caché à leurs supérieurs les indices du mauvais esprit qui régnait dans leurs régiments . D'autres n'ont pas montré dans la répression, l'initiative et l'énergie voulues .

Il importe que les Officiers sachent toute la responsabilité qu'ils encourent en pareil cas . L'inertie équivaut à de la complicité . - Le Général en Chef a décidé de prendre contre les pusillanimes toutes les sanctions nécessaires . Il couvrira, par contre, de son autorité tous ceux qui feront preuve de vigueur et d'énergie dans la répression .

TSVP

Pétain's telegram

Pétain's policy for dealing with mutinies was set out in this telegram to Army Groups and Armies.

Translation
CODED TELEGRAM
FOR THE ARMY TEAMS AND ARMIES

During the recent incidents, it seems to me that the Commandant was not entirely doing his duty. Certain Officers hid the clues from their superiors about the bad spirit that reigned within their regiments. Others did not show the required initiative and energy in repression.

It is important that the Officers should be aware of the entire responsibility incumbent upon them in such cases. Inertia is equivalent to complicity. The General in Chief has decided to take all necessary sanctions against the pusillanimous. On the other hand, he will shield with his authority all those that prove their vigour and energy in repression.

Certain officers or NCOs are entrenching, not having accomplished their orders; there is a general feature behind this move and it is difficult to unmask the ringleaders. Any other reason is not logical. Indeed, it is always possible to turn a general action into an individual one. It's enough to give the order for some men (beginning with the unruly ones) to be executed. In the case of a rejection, these men are arrested immediately and passed to the authorities who must follow the due course as quickly as possible.
[signature] Pétain

n° 2434/m

Certains Officiers ou gradés se retranchent, pour ne pas accomplir leur devoir, derrière ce fait, que les mouvements ayant un caractère collectif, il leur est difficile de démasquer les meneurs . Une pareille raison n'est pas valable . Il est toujours possible, en effet, de transformer un acte collectif en un acte individuel . Il suffit de donner à quelques hommes (en commençant par les mauvaises têtes) l'ordre d'exécution . En cas de refus, ces hommes sont arrêtés immédiatement et remis entre les mains de la Justice qui devra suivre son cours le plus rapide .

[signature]

CHIFFRE

THE BATTLE OF MESSINES

MINE WARFARE COMES OF AGE

EVER SINCE HE BECAME COMMANDER-IN-CHIEF, DOUGLAS HAIG HAD WANTED TO FIGHT A MAJOR BATTLE IN THE YPRES AREA. UNLIKE ON THE SOMME, HERE THERE WERE IMPORTANT STRATEGIC OBJECTIVES. A RELATIVELY SHORT ADVANCE WOULD THREATEN THE MAJOR GERMAN COMMUNICATIONS CENTRE AT ROULERS.

1917

This would open the enticing prospect of reducing the threat to the Channel ports, on which the BEF depended for supplies. It also would allow the BEF to threaten the German-held Belgian coast. The Admiralty were extremely worried about the risk posed by German U-Boats and surface warships. While capturing the ports such as Ostend would not eliminate the German naval threat, it would certainly help to reduce it.

The first stage of the offensive was an attack against Messines Ridge. This key position had been lost to the Germans in 1914, and General Sir Herbert Plumer's Second Army was given the task of winning it back. He formed an effective team with General Sir "Tim" Harington, his Chief of Staff, who described Plumer's methods as being underpinned by three Ts: "Trust, Training and Thoroughness". Plumer was popular with his men, who gave him the nickname "Daddy". His methodical approach and his insistence on extensive training for operations were very evident in his preparations for Messines. For months, a series of mines

had been dug under Messines Ridge. Each consisted of a tunnel, laboriously bored under No Man's Land by specialized mining companies, packed with explosive. It was, even by the standards of the Western Front, dangerous work. Aside from the normal perils of working deep beneath the ground, miners faced the continuous fear that the enemy might explode a small charge in the mine shaft and bury them alive. Alternatively, German miners, engaged in their own tunnelling, might break into a British working party, in which case a hand-to-hand struggle would take place beneath the ground. In the event, 24 mines were excavated. On average, each mine contained about 21 tons of high explosive, but the largest charge was roughly double that size. No wonder that on the eve of the battle

OPPOSITE: Wytschaete village (known as "Whitesheet" to the British), captured on 7 June 1917 and photographed a day later.

ABOVE: In 1917 the Germans often used "flexible" defensive tactics in which outlying parties were deployed in shell holes to break up attacks.

SIR HERBERT PLUMER
(1857–1932)

General Plumer (left) was the ultimate safe pair of hands on the Western Front. He commanded in the ever-dangerous Ypres Salient from 1915, except when he was sent to take command of British forces in Italy for a period in late 1917 to early 1918. His methodical approach to offensive operations paid dividends at Messines and in the middle phase of Passchendaele, albeit at a heavy cost in the lives of British and Empire soldiers. His reputation remains high among historians.

Harington said "I do not know whether we will change history tomorrow, but we shall certainly alter the geography."

Nine divisions were to be used for the initial assault. These included the Catholic, Nationalist 16th (Irish) Division and the Protestant, Unionist 36th (Ulster) Division, fighting alongside each other for the first time. As at Arras, the preliminary artillery bombardment was highly successful. The British had twice as many heavy guns as the Germans, and had a five-to-one advantage in other guns. British artillery fired 3.5 million shells between 26 May and 6 June. The German artillery suffered badly even before the mines were detonated, meaning that when the British and Anzac infantry attacked, they did so under highly favourable conditions. The commander of German XIX Corps contributed to the defenders' problems when he rejected a solution to pull out of the Messines sector.

Nineteen of the mines were detonated at 03:10 on 7 June 1917. The force of the explosion was tremendous, leaving many of those defenders that survived the blast shocked and easy targets for the Allied infantry that advanced under an accurate barrage. The attackers rapidly captured their objectives: Messines village fell to the New Zealanders; and the Wytschaete area was occupied by 16th and 36th Divisions. In the fighting, the BEF demonstrated how proficient they had become at combined arms tactics, with 72 tanks accompanying the infantry. The battle was effectively won on that first day, although the fighting continued spasmodically for a week. The Germans mounted a number of counterattacks from 8 June to 14 June, but none succeeded in dislodging the British. Ironically, the worst loss of life for the BEF came not in the initial assault but on subsequent days, when the Germans shelled British troops crowded onto the newly captured ridge, causing heavy casualties.

Messines was Plumer's masterpiece, and it is not surprising that when he was ennobled after the war, he took as his title Plumer of Messines. The battle showed that, by June 1917, the BEF had become highly proficient at limited, set-piece battles. However, Haig controversially judged that Plumer was not the right man to command the next stage of the Flanders offensive. Haig believed a breakthrough was possible and placed Hubert Gough, renowned as a "thruster", in charge of the push. Logistic problems and the time needed for Anthione's French First Army to arrive meant that six weeks elapsed between Messines and the beginning of the Third Battle of Ypres.

1917

LEFT: Engineers (sappers), such as these Australians, and tunnellers played a crucial role in the preparation and execution of the Battle of Messines.

OPPOSITE: Lancashire Fusiliers in a trench opposite Messines clean a Lewis light machine gun. Note the gas alarm horn and sandbags.

WILLIAM "WILLIE" REDMOND

(1861–1917)

Major William Redmond (left) was in his 50s when he was killed at Messines. Brother of John, the leader of the constitutional Irish National Party, Willie was one of some 210,000 Irishmen who served in the British Army in the First World War. Given the level of Irish involvement in the battle, fittingly, Messines was many years later chosen as the site of an Irish "Peace Tower". Curiously it was erected in the sector over which the New Zealand Division attacked in June 1917.

BELOW: Plunging the handle generated an electrical charge down the wires connected to the two knobs on the box and set off an electric detonator in the explosive.

REVOLUTION IN RUSSIA

KERENSKY, LENIN AND CIVIL WAR

THE REIGN OF NICHOLAS II, TSAR OF ALL THE RUSSIAS, CAME TO AN ABRUPT END ON 15 MARCH 1917. THREE DAYS EARLIER, THE IMPERIAL REGIME WAS STRUCK A DEATH BLOW WHEN SOLDIERS JOINED PROTESTERS IN PETROGRAD (FORMERLY ST PETERSBURG) AND A "SOVIET", OR COUNCIL, OF DISAFFECTED WORKERS, SOLDIERS AND SOCIALISTS GATHERED.

1917

Lenin's regime consolidated its power in the new Soviet Union ruthlessly. Non-Bolshevik political parties were suppressed and persecuted, and a mutiny by the fleet at Kronstadt in 1921 was crushed mercilessly. A local Soviet had the Tsar and his family murdered in July 1918 at Ekaterinburg, where they were being held. Lenin, who died in 1924, was ruthless enough, but he was outshone by his successor Josef Stalin. Under Stalin's rule, the country underwent political purges, enforced industrialization and the collectivization of agriculture, at the cost of millions of deaths. Similarly, his labour camps were filled with opponents, real or imagined.

Members of the Duma, the toothless Russian parliament established after the troubles of 1905, joined with the Soviet in setting up a Provisional government. The Tsar's abdication and arrest followed. A revolution which had seemed initially to be a bourgeois affair had been captured by far more extreme revolutionary forces.

Russia had been on the verge of revolution 12 years earlier. In 1905, frustration and resentment at the autocratic rule of the Tsars boiled over, triggered by defeat at the hands of Japan in the Far East. Some of the middle classes resented being excluded from the political process. The peasantry (among whom serfdom had only been abolished in 1861) wanted land to farm. In the cities, rapid industrialization produced a growing working class, often living and working in terrible conditions. Violent clashes between protesters and troops, and mutinies in the navy, led some to fear – or hope – that full-scale revolution was about to break

out. In the end, a mixture of repression and concessions brought Russia back from the brink. Crucially, the army remained loyal.

The fragile national unity of August 1914 soon came under strain. The problems that underpinned the 1905 uprisings had worsened. Food shortages, defeats and heavy losses among the conscript army (even successful campaigns like the 1916 Brusilov Offensive came with a large "butcher's bill") caused discontent to grow. Nicholas II committed a bad error in assuming nominal personal command of the army in September 1915. Now he was seen as personally responsible for the disasters.

In March 1917, the Provisional Government vowed to continue the war. However, the July offensive named after the War Minister, Alexander Kerensky, was a failure, and damaged the credibility of the new regime. In September, a German offensive took the key Baltic city of Riga, almost 500 kilometres (300 miles) distant from Petrograd. Worse,

OPPOSITE: People demonstrating on the streets of Moscow at the start of the Russian Revolution in March 1917.

ABOVE LEFT: Alexander Fyodorovich Kerensky, leader of the Russian Provisional Government.

a new threat had appeared in the shape of the veteran Marxist revolutionary Vladimir Ilyich Lenin. He had been in exile in Switzerland, but was conveyed back to Russia by the Germans in a cynical attempt to undermine the stability of the country. Already reeling from an abortive coup by a disaffected general, the government – now led by Kerensky – was overthrown by Lenin's

Bolsheviks on 7 November (25 October in the old Russian calendar).

Lenin's coup ushered in a Communist regime bent on exporting revolution, but it also found itself in a bitter civil war in which the "Reds" fought the "Whites" – who were supported by foreign armies – that only ended in 1921. The Germans forced the

Bolsheviks to accept the harsh Peace of Brest-Litovsk (March 1918) and carved out a huge empire in the East. Germany was the victor in the first part of the Great War, but threw away the fruits by gambling on an all-or-nothing offensive in the West.

OPPOSITE: A line of Austro-Hungarian riflemen in the Nida River area during the Brusilov Offensive in 1916.

LEFT: Lenin addressing a crowd of people at a rally in Moscow at the start of the revolution, 1917.

BELOW: The diplomats and officers of Central Powers and Russia signing the Treaty of Brest-Litovsk ratifying the exit of Russia from the war, 3 March 1918.

THE THIRD BATTLE OF YPRES

ATTEMPTING THE BREAKTHROUGH

HAIG HOPED THAT THE THIRD BATTLE OF YPRES WOULD PROVE
DECISIVE. THE BEF WOULD BREAK OUT OF THE SALIENT, AND TRIGGER
A LANDING ON THE BELGIAN COAST BY BRITISH 1ST DIVISION, WHICH
HAD BEEN SECRETLY TRAINING FOR THE OPERATION. GIVEN THE
GRAND SCALE OF HIS PLANS, IT IS NOT SURPRISING THAT HAIG CHOSE
GOUGH OVER THE MORE CAUTIOUS PLUMER FOR THE COMMAND.

1917

On 17 July, the Allied guns began a preliminary bombardment of the German positions. Haig had 3,091 guns at his disposal, and nine infantry divisions of Gough's Fifth Army were to be committed to the first phase of the campaign, officially known as the Battle of Pilckem Ridge. Just as in the First and Second Battles of Ypres, British and French troops were to fight alongside each other. General François Anthoine's French First Army of six divisions (and more than 900 guns) was slotted into the line on the British left flank. Plumer's Second Army guarded Gough's other flank.

On the other side of No Man's Land, the troops of German Fourth Army were deployed in a very strong defensive system based around a series of miniature fortresses, known to the British as "pillboxes". The essence of German defensive tactics was flexibility. The front line was defended lightly, with pillboxes used to slow the enemy advance, while counter-attack troops would hit the attackers as they became over-extended and vulnerable. In spite of some sensible suggestions from GHQ for a more limited approach, Gough believed that his Fifth

Army could rapidly overcome the German defences and so planned for an ambitious advance of up to 5,500 m (6,000 yds). This was to reach the German Third Position, after which further fighting would carry Fifth Army out of the Salient altogether.

The infantry attack began at 03:50 on 31 July, as the artillery fire reached a crescendo. The assault was supported by tanks, and thanks to a major aerial offensive commenced on 11 July, British and French aircraft had superiority in the air. Initially, the attack made progress. Anthoine's infantry had been carefully trained for the operation, and were supported by a mass of heavy artillery; French First Army gained about 3,200 m (3,500 yds); the left-hand British formation, XIV Corps, advanced about the same distance. The Guards Division, which in a brilliant preliminary operation on 27 July at Boesinghe had crossed the Yser Canal and seized positions on the German bank, took 600 prisoners. The advance was reasonable in the circumstances, but still only about half what Gough had hoped to achieve. In the centre and on the right, the picture was much gloomier. Here, the German defensive tactics worked well. The advancing British

OPPOSITE: The armies of 1917 were heavily dependent on horses for transportation. Here, a British 18-pounder field gun moves up on the first day of Third Ypres, 31 July 1917.

ABOVE: German barbed wire obstacles. The introduction of advanced shell fuses in 1916–17 improved the ability of artillery to cut wire.

infantry were caught off balance by the German counter-attack units and forced back as much as 1,800 m (2,000 yds). Allied losses amounted to about 17,000. In spite of some modest success achieved, Gough's ambitious plan had failed.

In the early evening of 31 July, it began to rain. The ground, badly churned up by shelling, which had severely damaged the drainage system, turned to thick mud. The weather is an ever-present and unpredictable factor in military operations. Frequent statements by subsequent writers to the contrary, rain in these quantities could not have been predicted; Flanders was not regularly subject to a "monsoon" in August. Major operations had to be halted on 2 August, and were not recommenced until 16 August when the Battle of Langemarck began.

This phase of fighting lasted only two days and was a bigger failure than 31 July. Langemarck village itself was captured, but the Gheluvelt Plateau, the possession of which was critical if the BEF was to make a substantial advance, remained in German hands. Haig had made it clear that the ridge, which dominated the battlefield, had to be taken as a priority, but Gough had not made it his priority. The battle spluttered into a

1917

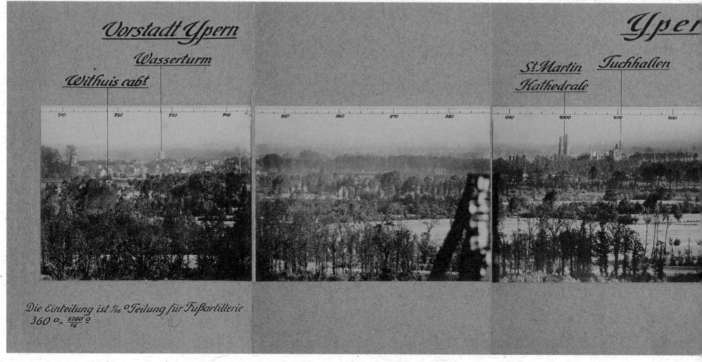

number of small-scale actions rather than being joined up into a coherent offensive. Fifth Army's progress was stymied by a combination of heavy German fire and tenacious defence, poor weather and difficult ground, and failure to concentrate artillery. It all seemed a far cry from the heady days of Messines, only two months earlier. The main operation was halted on 18 August, but smaller actions continued.

In London, the War Cabinet came close to ordering the halt of the entire offensive, but Haig won the day. Clearly, however, something had to change. Haig did not readily admit to making errors, but when in mid-August he relegated Gough to a supporting role and made Second Army the principal attacking force, he implicitly acknowledged his mistake.

OPPOSITE: In the conditions in the Ypres salient, pack mules came into their own, though many were killed by shell fire. This photograph was taken on 31 July 1917.

ABOVE: One of the iconic images of the Third Battle of Ypres: stretcher-bearers struggle in the mud near Boesinghe, 1 August 1917.

BELOW: A panoramic photograph of the Ypres battlefield, from the German perspective, used by German artillery.

CROWN PRINCE RUPPRECHT OF BAVARIA
(1869–1955)

The Ypres sector came under the Army Group of Crown Prince Rupprecht, son of the King of Bavaria. Under the German system, royal personages often received high military positions. Unlike some of his peers, Rupprecht was a highly effective commander and thoroughly merited his promotion to lead an army group. If history had turned out differently 200 years earlier, Rupprecht might have been commanding British forces. When his mother Queen Marie Theresa died shortly after the war in February 1919, he became the Jacobite Pretender to the British throne.

St Jakobkirche

inalbrücke
uiver cab.

St Peterskirche

St Jean

Ecole de bienfai-
sance de l'Etat.

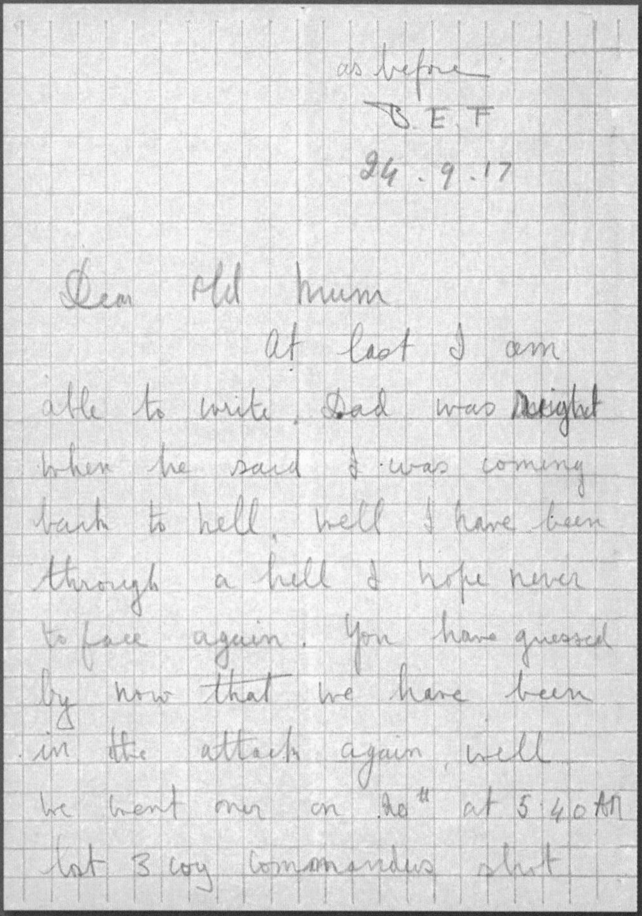

as before
B.E.F
24.9.17

Dear Old Mum
At last I am
able to write. Dad was right
when he said I was coming
back to hell. well I have been
through a hell I hope never
to face again. You have guessed
by now that we have been
in the attack again, well
we went over on 20th at 5.40AM
last 3 coy commanders shot

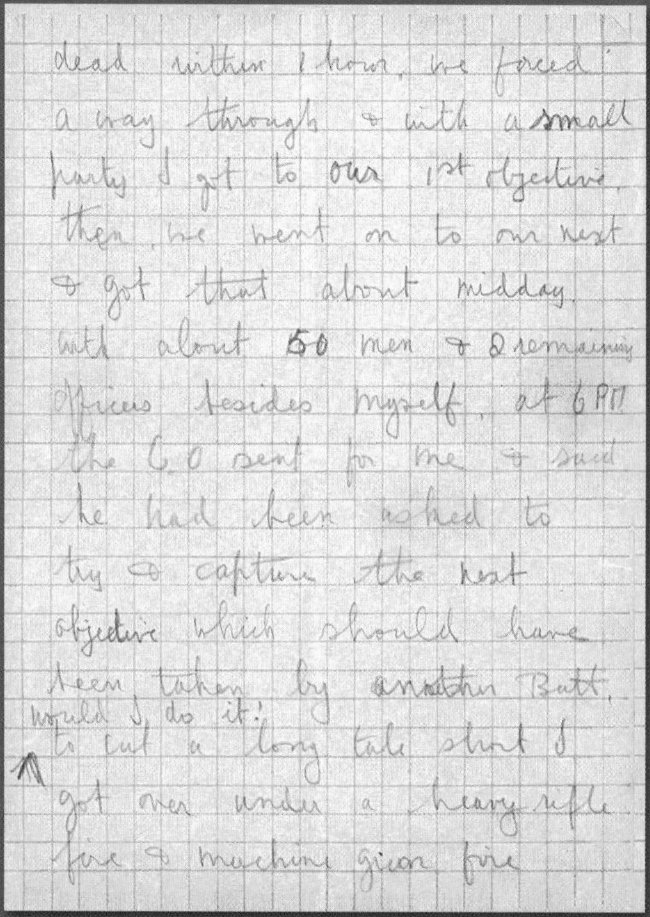

dead within 1 hour, we forced
a way through & with a small
party I got to our 1st objective,
then we went on to our next
& got that about midday,
with about 50 men & 2 remaining
Officers besides myself, at 6 P.M
the C.O sent for me & said
he had been asked to
try & capture the next
objective which should have
been taken by another Batt,
would I do it?
to cut a long tale short I
got over under a heavy rifle
fire & machine gun fire

2nd Lieutenant Moore's VC account

A letter from 2nd Lieutenant M. S. S. Moore of 15th
Hampshires describing the action for which he was awarded
the Victoria Cross. He won it on 20 September 1917 during
an action at "Tower Hamlets" in the Ypres salient.

1917

through TOWER HAMLETS & in his line with 4 men & 1 sergt, captured 8 prisoners 2 machine guns & 1 light field gun. well I stayed there until the rest of my men came up, dug-in & held off the Boche, that night he bombed us but we drove him off the next morning, our guns put a most deadly barrage on us, thinking we were all gone, it was a most awful time, finally I was left with 10 men

in the afternoon he counter attacked, but I spotted it & got the S.O.S. up, once again the guns opened & fairly pasted our dug-out. all that night 21-22 Sept first a Boche barrage & then ours my hat it was awful hell in the early morning mist I cleared out with my men, being absolutely useless staying there any longer, got back greatly to the astonishment of the General & the C.O. they

had given me up as dead long ago & fairly fell on my neck. well I got a hat for you a most beautiful pair of glasses worth £15 2 watches & several other odds & ends. Love to all I cannot explain the whole thing in writing but on my next leave you shall hear it all we are out now.

Much love
Monty

PASSCHENDAELE

TAKING THE RIDGE

WITH PLUMER IN CHARGE, BRITISH FORTUNES BEGAN TO IMPROVE.
HAIG PROVED AMENABLE TO PLUMER'S REQUEST FOR A THREE-WEEK
DELAY TO ENSURE EVERYTHING WAS READY. AT 05:40 ON
20 SEPTEMBER THE BATTLE OF THE MENIN ROAD BEGAN.

1917

Four divisions attacked, each on a narrow frontage, with further divisions guarding the flanks of the main assault. The infantry's objectives were limited, some 1,450 m (1,600 yds) away, and the attackers advanced behind a deep and complex artillery barrage. Pillboxes proved death traps to any German infantry caught in them, as by now the BEF had evolved sophisticated tactics for tackling defensive positions. German counter-attacks were negated by British firepower – the infantry did not advance out of artillery range – and special units held in reserve. Menin Road was a clear, if costly, victory for Plumer's British and Australian troops.

On 26 September, Plumer began the process all over again. The battle of Polygon Wood repeated the formula of the Menin Road. The pattern of massing combat power on a relatively narrow front, formidable artillery support, and limited advances was the epitome of the bite and hold operation. Ludendorff highlighted the acute problems that it posed the defenders: "We might be able to stand the loss of ground, but the reduction of our fighting strength was [on 26 September] again all the heavier… The depth of penetration was limited so as to secure immunity from our counterattacks, and the latter were then broken by the massed fire of artillery." The Germans tried different tactics, reinforcing the front lines, but with little success.

OPPOSITE: Heavy usage took its toll on artillery. The barrel of an 8-inch Howitzer is lowered into place, 26 September 1917.

ABOVE: A testament to the power of artillery to cause devastation: the Passchendaele battlefield, with shell holes, mud and shattered trees.

INSET: A potentially lethal sliver of metal from a shell.

Plumer's hammer swung for a third time on 4 October and delivered another smashing blow. In preparation for the Battle of Broodseinde, the guns were moved forward (Second Army fielded 796 heavy and medium guns, and over 1,500 field guns and howitzers). To avoid predictability, on this occasion there was no full-scale preliminary artillery bombardment. This time it was to be primarily an Anzac battle: 3rd Australian Division, the New Zealand Division and 1st and 2nd Australian Divisions were deployed side by side, with British formations protecting the flank. The Germans also planned a major attack on 4 October, and as the Anzac infantry assembled for the assault, they were caught in a German bombardment. However, the Germans suffered much more heavily from the British barrage that at 06:00 rained down on the defenders' positions. Packed into the front line and deployed for attack rather than defence, many Germans were killed or wounded either by the shelling or by Allied infantry advancing with fixed bayonets. Following the setback, Plumer's assault rapidly got back on track, and by the evening the Germans were counting the cost of what their official history referred to as a "black day". Their luck was about to turn, however. The weather had mostly been fine during the period of Plumer's attacks. On the night before Broodseinde it began to rain, and once again the ground was turned into a morass. Believing that the Germans were on the verge of defeat now that much of the Gheluvelt Ridge had been captured, Haig elected to fight on.

The next battle, Poelcappelle, was launched on 9 October. The moonscape created by shelling in previous battles, the rain and the mud hindered the preparations, which were incomplete when the infantry went

ARTHUR CURRIE
(1875–1933)

General Currie was a pre-war businessman and part-time Canadian Militia officer. He did well as a brigade and divisional commander, and in 1917 replaced Byng as the first Canadian at the head of the Canadian Corps. The hallmark of Currie's generalship was careful, meticulous preparation, and it helped turn his Corps into an exceptionally effective formation. When tasked by Haig with capturing Passchendaele Ridge, he stated that it could be done but at the cost of 16,000 casualties. He was right on both counts.

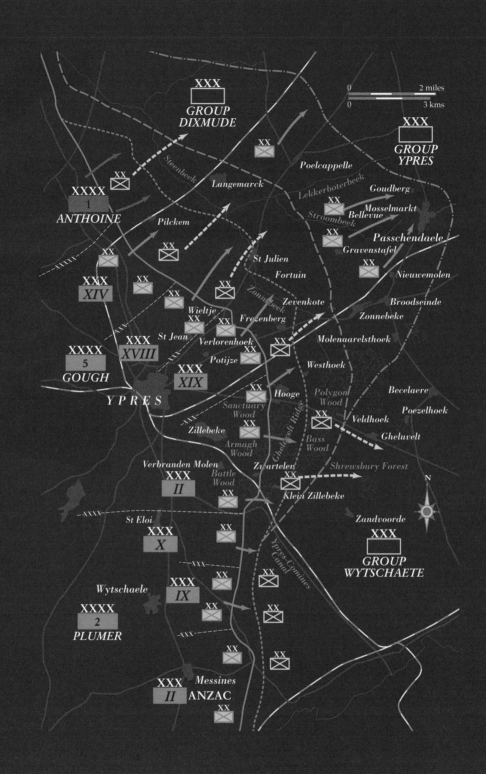

GROUP
DIXMUDE

GROUP
YPRES

0 ——— 2 miles
0 ——— 3 kms

Poelcappelle

Langemarck

Goudberg

XXXX
1
ANTHOINE

Pilckem

Lekkerboterbeek

Mosselmarkt
Bellevue

Stroombeek

Passchendaele

Gravenstafel

St Julien

Nieuwemolen

XXX
XIV

Fortuin

Broodseinde

Wieltje

Zevenkote

Zonnebeke

XXXX
5
GOUGH

XXX
XVIII

St Jean

Frezenberg

Zonnebeek

Verlorenhoek

Molenaarelsthoek

Potijze

Westhoek

YPRES

XXX
XIX

Hooge

Polygon
Wood

Becelaere

Sanctuary
Wood

Poezelhoek

Gheluvelt Ridge

Veldhoek

Zillebeke

Bass
Wood

Gheluvelt

Armagh
Wood

Zwartelen

Shrewsbury Forest

Verbranden Molen

Battle
Wood

N

XXX
II

Klein Zillebeke

Zandvoorde

St Eloi

XXX
X

GROUP
WYTSCHAETE

Wytschaele

Ypres-Comines Canal

XXX
IX

XXXX
2
PLUMER

Messines

XXX
II   ANZAC

THE THIRD BATTLE OF YPRES: July–December 1917

——— Morning, 31 July   - - - 20 September   → British advance

······· Evening, 31 July   -·-·- 7 December   ⇢ German retreat

182

over the top. The terrible conditions meant that many were exhausted by the time they reached British front line. The artillery bombardment was simply inadequate. Not surprisingly, the result was few gains for heavy losses. The same was true of the First Battle of Passchendaele (12 October). Haig's decision to push on was – and is – highly controversial, but he did not want to leave the Germans on the ridge at Passchendaele to dominate the battlefield over the winter. Writing to Pétain in October, General Anthoine stated that Haig had failed to admit the lack of success, and feared his own French First Army would suffer casualties in a fruitless battle. For the sake of the alliance, Pétain insisted that First Army fight on. The key objective of Passchendaele Ridge eventually fell to the Canadian Corps in the Second Battle of Passchendaele, which ended on 10 November. The bad conditions made Passchendaele (the name popularly given to the entire campaign) infamous. The losses were heavy – 245,000 British, 8,500 French, perhaps 230,000 German. Haig argued that the attritional effect on the Germans made the battle worthwhile. Under extreme pressure, the German High Command considered withdrawing from the Ypres salient, which would have been a significant strategic victory for Haig. A senior German general argued that the Allied Offensive at Ypres, had prevented the Germans from taking advantage of the poor state of the French army after Nivelle's unsuccessful offensive earlier in the year.

New Zealanders at Passchendaele

The First Battle of Passchendaele, 12 October 1917, was the bloodiest day in New Zealand's military history. The attack on Bellevue Spur by the New Zealand Division was a comprehensive setback. An undeniably élite formation, the NZ Division suffered from inadequate artillery support but returned to form in 1918. New Zealand's contribution to the British Empire's war effort was impressive. The population was a little over a million in 1914, yet more than 100,000 served in the military forces overseas. In all 18,500 New Zealanders died, 12,500 on the Western Front.

RIGHT: An example of the "iron harvest" of unexploded shells which still lie in fields in France and Belgium.

ABOVE TOP: Walking wounded of the New Zealand Division receiving hot drinks at a YMCA stall the day after the Battle of Broodseinde.

ABOVE: German soldiers surrender to British infantrymen in 1917.

TRENCH LIFE

A SOLDIER'S LIFE FOR ME

IT IS A POPULAR MYTH THAT THE SOLDIERS SPENT ALL THEIR TIME IN THE TRENCHES. ONE BRITISH REGIMENTAL INFANTRY OFFICER CALCULATED THAT IN 1916 HE WAS UNDER FIRE FOR 101 DAYS, SPENDING 65 DAYS IN THE FRONT LINE. THE REST OF HIS TIME WAS SPLIT BETWEEN PERIODS IN RESERVE, IN REAR AREAS, ON LEAVE, AND ON INSTRUCTIONAL COURSES.

He spent 12 separate periods in the trenches, and was involved in fighting four times, only one of which was a "direct attack". This pattern held true, with variations, for all armies, although some sectors of the Western Front were more dangerous than others. A French infantry unit at Verdun in May 1916 was likely to see more action than one holding positions near the Swiss frontier. The Ypres Salient was an active sector throughout the war, while for much of 1915 the Somme was generally quiet – although anywhere near the front line random death or wounding was an ever-present threat, whether from sniping, or from "marmites" (as a heavy German shell was known to the French; the British called it a "Jack Johnson", after a Black American boxer).

The trenches themselves evolved during the war. At the end of 1914, they were little more than a series of holes in the ground protected by a little barbed wire. The following years were to see the trench systems become much more elaborate. Duckboards were laid on trench floors, sandbags on the parapet, and barbed wire grew from a few strands festooned with tin cans (a crude early warning system) into dense belts. The men sheltered in "dugouts". In general, German trenches

FOOD AND DRINK

Food was either cooked on primitive stoves in the trenches, or brought up from the rear from mobile field kitchens. Staples of the British soldier's diet included Maconochie's stew (meat and vegetables) and bully beef. The French nicknamed their tinned meat "singe" ("monkey"). Favourites with German soldiers included sausages and other tinned meats, but as the British naval blockade took effect they often got "ersatz" ("substitute") materials such as acorn coffee and coarse black bread. Alcohol was an important morale booster. The British issued rum, the French wine and gniole spirit – rum or brandy from the French West Indies.

LEFT: German soldiers at a mobile ("Field") kitchen behind the lines on the Western Front, 1916.

OPPOSITE LEFT: A well developed trench in the Vimy sector, manned by French troops. This photograph was taken by British Liaison Officer Brigadier-General Spiers.

OPPOSITE RIGHT: French cigarettes. Tobacco was important for morale, but was also expensive. Given the soldiers' poor pay these were probably smoked by civilians.

ABOVE TOP: These German troops have elaborate electric trench digging machines. The use of a Mark 1 pick and shovel was more normal.

LEUR MARRAINE THEIRGODMOTHER

ATTAQUE BRUSQUEE   SUDDEN ATTACK

were more elaborate with deeper dugouts than their British or French equivalents. The Germans, sitting on occupied territory, were usually content to hold what they had, while the British and French saw the trenches as jumping-off points for offensives. By the time of the Somme in 1916, defensive systems usually consisted of three parts: fire, support and reserve trenches. Later this set-up was replaced by a much looser defensive system, with front-line posts held lightly, and the main defences further back.

When the troops were not involved in major operations, trench life was a matter of constant work parties, carrying out such tasks as repairing wire, observation, and – since much activity took place at night – trying to snatch naps. Soldiers fought a constant and losing battle against the lice that infested their clothes and the rats that inhabited the trenches. All armies carried out patrols and raids: to gather information; intimidate the enemy; and, supposedly, to inculcate fighting spirit in the troops. These could be highly dangerous. The British were probably the keenest on raiding, while the French had a more pragmatic approach.

Out of the line, soldiers trained, provided work parties that often involved heavy manual work, and had a limited amount of leisure time. Sport was popular, and in the BEF this ranged from simple football

kickarounds to elaborate Divisional Horse Shows with gambling (another popular, but illegal, pastime) on the side. Estaminets, a type of café-bar, were ever present. Over a simple meal and rough wine, men could relax, gossip, tell stories, or perhaps sing. For the soldier who simply wished to read or write a letter, organizations such as the YMCA provided some quiet rooms. Toc H, at Poperinghe, provided a Christian haven in which rank was ignored. At the other end of the scale, soldiers could go to brothels, some officially sanctioned, and visit prostitutes. Many French soldiers had a marraine de guerre – a sort of female pen-friend who provided a home for the soldier when on furlough.

The factors that maintained a soldier's morale under such terrible conditions were many and varied: tobacco and alcohol; belief

in the cause; pride in the unit; religious faith; superstition; paternal officers; mail from home; leave; baths; and periods away from the front line – all these things were important. The British army was particularly good at sustaining morale by enforcing a "bureaucracy of paternalism" – ensuring that officers inspected soldiers's feet for signs of trench-foot, and providing baths behind the lines, for example – while French morale suffered because of the lack of such a system, with near-disastrous results in 1917. German soldiers in 1918 were badly affected by news from home of the poor conditions being endured by their families. Trench life was hard for everyone, although officers generally had superior facilities. That the morale of soldiers survived so well under the circumstances is testimony to the astonishing ability of the human being to endure the most extreme conditions.

OPPOSITE LEFT: A suggestive French postcard. "Marraines" were women who adopted a soldier and provided him with letters and tobacco. "Attaque brusquee" was a military term, here being used as a double entendre!

OPPOSITE RIGHT: Canadian soldiers undertaking mundane but necessary tasks. Both are smoking the inevitable "gasper".

ABOVE: A British soldier using a trench periscope.

LIVE AND LET LIVE

Informal, tacit arrangements often sprung up between Allied troops and their German enemies with the aim of making trench life a little easier. Graham Greenwell, a British officer, noted "We go out at night in front of the trenches… The German working parties are also out, so it is not considered etiquette to fire." On other occasions troops would refrain from firing when food was being brought up, or ritualize aggression by firing at the same time every day. Such examples of "live and let live" were discouraged by High Command.

LEFT: Gas was an ever present threat for the infantryman, and survival depended upon the speed with which a gas mask could be donned. Here, a German soldier uses a frying pan as a gas alarm.

RIGHT: A bottle of patent foot powder as used by British soldiers. Many manufacturers cashed in on the war by producing goods designed for the military market.

BELOW: This tin contained compressed instant tea. The automatic reaction of British soldiers in a quiet moment was to have a "brew up".

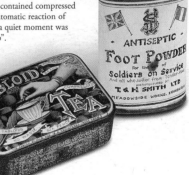

LOCAL ACTIONS

FROMELLES, HILL 70 AND LA MALMAISON

THE FIGHTING ON THE WESTERN FRONT ENCOMPASSED LOCAL AS WELL AS MAJOR ACTIONS, SOME OF WHICH HAD MAJOR CONSEQUENCES. OTHERS WERE FUTILE. THIS WAS TRUE OF THE AUSTRALIAN IMPERIAL FORCE (AIF)'S FIRST TASTE OF ACTION IN FRANCE AFTER ARRIVING FROM THE MIDDLE EAST IN MARCH 1916.

1916
1917

The Australians

The Rising Sun badge was worn by Australian soldiers in both world wars. Introduced in 1904, along with the slouch hat on which it was worn, it came to typify the "digger".

The newly created and inexperienced 5th Australian Division under Major-General J. W. McCay was initially sent to the quiet Armentières sector, known as "the nursery", to learn the ropes. But on 19 July 1916, 5th Australian Division and British 61st Division were committed to an ill-thought-out operation at the village of Fromelles, on ground fought over in 1915. This was a diversion intended to support the Somme offensive by pinning the Germans to their trenches, diverting German reserves, and making clear that the British would not be confining operations to the Somme area. While this was sensible in theory, in practice Fromelles was too obviously an isolated diversion, and had little impact on the German High Command.

Virtually every aspect of the execution of the attack was bungled. The ground which the Australians and British were sent to contest was terribly bare and dominated by the Sugar Loaf, a formidable German strongpoint. The preparations were rushed, the troops and many of the commanders involved were inexperienced and command blunders

OPPOSITE: During the Battle for Hill 70 in August 1917, a wounded soldier is brought in on a stretcher by German prisoners of war.

RIGHT: Action shot of the Battle for Hill 70, near Lens, taken by a Canadian official photographer. Note the bursting shells.

were made at various levels. In spite of some initial success, such as the capture of part of the German front line by the 2/7th Royal Warwicks, and much heroism, by the troops, Fromelles was a disaster, the only results the slaughter of troops and embitterment of Anglo-Australian relations.

Hill 70 was very different from Fromelles. During Third Ypres in 1917, the Canadian Corps were tasked with attacking this rise near Lens, partly as a diversion from the main operation, but also to seize a key position for future use. The original British plan for an assault on Lens itself was altered by General Arthur Currie, the Canadian Corps commander, to become an attack on the vital high ground to the north of the city. The battle lasted 10 days (15–25 August 1917), and cost the Canadians over 9,000 casualties. Currie prepared for the battle in his trademark meticulous fashion, using many of the methods that had proved successful in the capture of Vimy Ridge earlier that year: detailed planning; a creeping barrage; smoke screens; thoroughly rehearsed infantry. An essential element of his plan was to prepare for the inevitable German counter-attacks, and ensure that they were broken up by heavy Canadian fire. This was a sophisticated form of bite-and-hold.

Harold Edward "Pompey" Elliot
(1878–1931)

Brigadier-General Elliot commanded 15th Australian Brigade at Fromelles. Nicknamed "Pompey", Elliott was a brilliant leader of men and an inspired commander. A breakdown in communications led to one of his battalions attacking unsupported at Fromelles, with disastrous consequences. This only reinforced his fiercely anti-British feelings. In 1918, Pompey Elliott was passed over by his Australian superiors for promotion to command a division, a slight he resented for the rest of his life and which almost certainly contributed to his suicide in 1931.

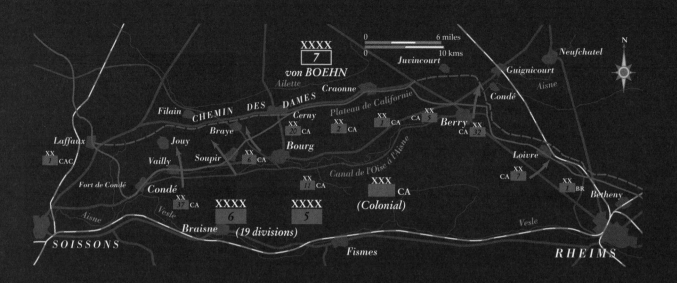

XXXX 7
von BOEHN
Ailette
Juvincourt
0   6 miles
0   10 kms
Neufchatel
Guignicourt
Aisne
Condé
Craonne
Plateau de Californie
Filain CHEMIN DES DAMES
Cerny XX 5
Braye XX 20 CA XX 2 CA 1 CA CA
Laffaux
Jouy
Berry XX CA XX 32
XX 1 CAC
Soupir XX 6 CA **Bourg**
Canal de l'Oise à l'Aisne
Vailly *Loivre*
Fort de Condé XX 11 CA CA XX 7
Condé XXX CA XX 1 BR
XX 37 CA (*Colonial*) *Betheny*
Aisne XXXX 6 XXXX 5
Vesle
Braisne (19 divisions)
SOISSONS *Vesle*
Fismes
RHEIMS

THE SECOND AISNE: Chemin des Dames, April–May 1917

——— Front line, 16 April   – – – Front line, 8 May   ➤ French advance

Three Canadian divisions attacked at dawn on 15 August, with a fourth in reserve. The attackers rapidly secured their objectives. At 09:00 the German counter-attacks began; in all there were 21 attempts to retake the hill. Although the Canadians suffered severely – including casualties from mustard gas – they held their ground. Hill 70 is rightly remembered as one of the Canadian Corps's finest feats of arms, with five German divisions that could otherwise have fought at Ypres being engaged and defeated. Several months later in 1917, the French army carried out a similarly successful minor operation at Fort La Malmaison, on the Chemin des Dames. This formed part of a series of "healing battles" ordered by Pétain to nurse the French Army back to health after the trauma of the Nivelle offensive and the Mutinies (see pages 162–163). Successful limited attacks had already been carried out at Verdun in mid-August 1917. As Ludendorff later noted, "The French Army was once more capable of the offensive. It had quickly overcome its depression."

The Malmaison attack was well planned, limited in scope and, above all, designed to reduce French losses to a minimum. Sixth Army, under General Maistre, was heavily reinforced with artillery, but Pétain refused to allow the infantry of Tenth Army to attack, in order to minimize the chance of casualties. The point of attack was selected in such a way that a relatively short advance would make a sizeable portion of the German defences untenable.

The preliminary bombardment began on 17 October, and the infantry attacked before dawn on 23 October, supported by tanks and aircraft. The crushing weight of artillery fire helped the French infantry on to their objectives. The infantry pushed forward to a maximum depth of 6 km (3.72 miles), and took 11,000 prisoners at a cost of some 12,000 French casualties. The Germans were forced to abandon the Chemin des Dames ridge, the scene of so much fighting in earlier battles (see pages 162–163). Like the Canadians at Hill 70, and Plumer at Ypres, Malmaison demonstrated how effective well-planned, artillery-heavy, limited offensives could be.

OPPOSITE: Canadian troops receiving drinks at a makeshift canteen close to the front line, before the assault on Hill 70.

ABOVE: French troops overlooking German positions during the Battle of Malmaison in 1917. Malmaison was an outstandingly successful attack.

PAUL ANDRÉ MARIE MAISTRE
(1858–1922)

Maistre, commander of Sixth Army at Malmaison, earned a reputation as a general with a safe pair of hands. He rose from a staff job to command XXI Corps in September 1914. Thereafter, he appeared stuck in this position, but was assigned to lead Sixth Army and rebuild its morale after the trauma of the April 1917 offensive. Thereafter, he commanded French Tenth Army in Italy, and in 1918, Central Army Group in which he fought alongside Pershing's Americans.

THE BATTLE OF CAMBRAI
THE FIRST MASSED TANK ASSAULT

IRONICALLY, THE BITTER SLOGGING MATCH AT PASSCHENDAELE, THE
EPITOME OF ATTRITION, WAS FOLLOWED BY THE RETURN OF MOBILE
WARFARE TO THE WESTERN FRONT. THE BATTLE OF CAMBRAI, WHICH
BEGAN ON 20 NOVEMBER 1917, WAS INITIALLY PLANNED AS
A LARGE-SCALE TANK RAID.

1917

With some notable exceptions, the performance of the tanks in the Third Battle of Ypres had been disappointing, which was unsurprising given the poor terrain and the weather. The commander of the Tank Corps, Brigadier General Hugh Elles, and his Chief-of-Staff, Colonel J. F. C. Fuller, believed that the country around Cambrai offered more scope to show what the tank could really do. As Third Ypres dragged on, the idea of

a fresh offensive away from Passchendaele grew more attractive to Haig and GHQ. The crushing defeat inflicted on the Italians at Caporetto in October 1917 provided further reasons for a new attack, as a major effort on the Western Front might divert German attention from the Italian front. The original idea of a raid, in which the capture of territory was unimportant, grew into a major offensive by General Sir Julian Byng's Third Army designed to break through the

Hindenburg Line (the extensive system of defensive fortifications built by the Germans in northeastern France in 1916–17) and take Cambrai itself. With this stage successfully completed, GHQ would judge the best way to exploit the victory – perhaps an advance on Douai.

There were two novel features about the attack. The attack would take place without a preliminary bombardment or even the

JOHN FREDERICK CHARLES FULLER
(1878–1966)

Colonel Fuller, as Chief of the Staff of the Tank Corps, was a major architect of the Cambrai plan. After the war he was an influential writer, lambasting British high command in the Great War (not always fairly) and making important contributions to the development of armoured warfare. A visionary military thinker, "Boney" Fuller was a man of extremes: at various times he embraced the occult and fascism. His views on tanks on the Western Front were partisan in the extreme.

TANK CORPS

A cap badge of the Tank Corps. This replaced the badge of the Machine Gun Corps, of which the first tank formations were technically a part.

guns firing preliminary shots to establish the range. The latter was a revolutionary suggestion, based on the fact that gunnery techniques were now sufficiently sophisticated to allow "shooting off the map". This meant that the tell-tale signs that an offensive was imminent would not be needed and surprise could return to the battlefield. The second novelty was the use of tanks, not thinly spread out in support of infantry formations, but concentrated to gain the maximum advantage from the shock of the assault. A total of 378 fighting tanks were deployed, accompanied by a further 98 for transporting supplies. Haig concentrated 19 infantry divisions on the Cambrai front, plus cavalry formations. Pétain sent three French infantry and two cavalry divisions to the area. If a major success did materialize there, the Allies would be hard pressed to exploit it, given the insufficient numbers of reserves available. The ravages of Passchendaele and the need to send reinforcements to Italy left precious few troops available for Cambrai.

The initial attack was highly successful. At 06:20 the tanks rumbled forward, accompanied by infantry, under the cover of a bombardment. The Germans were caught by surprise, and at first it seemed

that the attack was unstoppable. The tanks crushed barbed wire and dropped fascines (bundles of wood) into trenches to allow them across. Third Army broke through the Hindenburg Line and the possibilities seemed limitless. The cavalry passed through the gap and did relatively well, but given the shortness of daylight hours in late November, its effect was limited. Only on the left flank, on the front of 51st (Highland) Division, where the tanks got too far ahead of the infantry at the village of Flesquières, was there a major setback.

Tanks in the First World War were effectively a one-shot weapon. Mechanical failure and casualties from enemy action meant that the tank force was savagely reduced, and only 92 remained as "runners" three days after the beginning of the battle. With the Allies unable to reinforce the initial success, and with the Germans rushing reserves to the battlefield, the fighting became bogged down on the left flank in a seesaw struggle for Bourlon Wood. This was back to attritional slogging, the antithesis of mobile warfare. Worse was to come, because on 30 November General von der Marwitz's German Second Army launched a counter-attack, giving a taste of the tactics – stormtroopers, hurricane bombardments and low-flying aircraft – that were to be employed to great effect in the German's March 1918 offensive. The British reeled under the impact, and Haig sanctioned

OPPOSITE: A British tank at Cambrai. The rhomboid shape of the early tank is still featured on the badge of the Royal Tank Regiment.

BRIGADIER GENERAL HUGH JAMIESON ELLES
(1880–1945)

Aged 37, Elles (left) commanded the Tank Corps at Cambrai. He served as a staff officer from 1914, being wounded at Second Ypres in 1915. A Royal Engineer by profession, Elles's obvious competence attracted the patronage of both Haig and Robertson. At Cambrai, he personally led the attack in his Mark IV tank Hilda. This was a conscious return to old-style heroic leadership. Elles had a forceful personality and he made an outstanding contribution to the development of the Tank Corps.

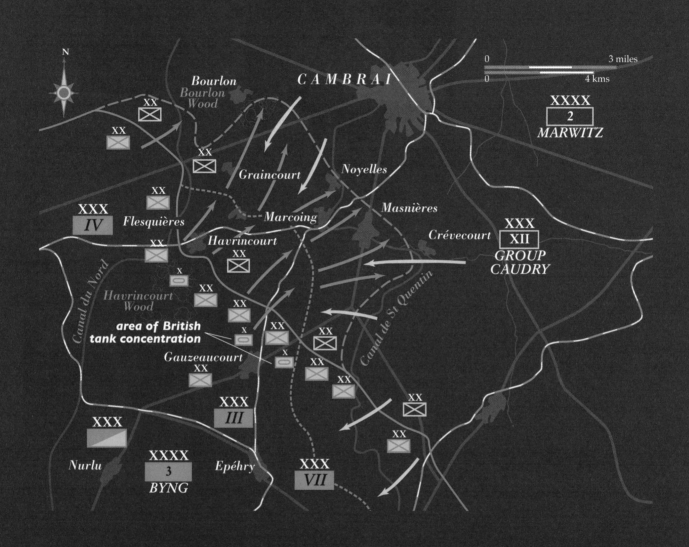

N

CAMBRAI

Bourlon
Bourlon
Wood

XX

XX

Graincourt

Noyelles

Masnières

Crévecourt

XXX
IV

Flesquières

Marcoing

XX

XXX
XII

**GROUP
CAUDRY**

XX

Havrincourt

XX

X

Havrincourt
Wood

XX

**area of British
tank concentration**

X

XX

XX

XX

Canal de St Quentin

Gauzeaucourt

X

XX

XX

XX

XX

XX

XXX
III

XX

XXX

Nurlu

XXXX
3
BYNG

Epéhry

XXX
VII

XX

Canal du Nord

0 ——————— 3 miles
0 ——————— 4 kms

XXXX
2
MARWITZ

THE BATTLE OF CAMBRAI: November–December 1917

———— Front line, 20 November ------ British withdrawal 5 December ⟶ British advance

- - - - Front line, 26 November ⟶ German counter-attack

a withdrawal – he could not afford another lengthy attritional battle. Some of the gains of 20 November were retained but most were lost. German casualties equalled British losses of about 45,000.

The ringing of the bells in England to celebrate a victory had been premature. Haig's credibility as a commander suffered more as a result of disappointed expectations at Cambrai than it did because of Passchendaele. For those who had eyes to see, Cambrai was a very significant battle. It indicated that the tactical advantage, which for so long had lain with the defender, now rested with the attacker. Trench warfare was on the verge of ending for good.

ABOVE: A crowded rear area scene, Battle of Cambrai, 22 November 1917, with cavalry, infantry, bicyclists and motorcyclists.

LEFT: A chainmail mask worn by tank crews to protect the face from metal fragments flying around the tank.

BELOW: The perils of "Hyacinth": infantrymen with a tank of H Battalion Tank Corps in a German trench near Ribécourt, 20 November 1917.

GERMAN SPRING OFFENSIVE

HOLDING OUT AGAINST
OPERATION MICHAEL

IF 1917 HAD BEEN A YEAR OF FRUSTRATION AND STALEMATE FOR THE
WESTERN ALLIES, FOR THE RUSSIANS IT HAD BEEN A YEAR OF DISASTER.
MILITARY SETBACKS ON THE EASTERN FRONT HAD HELPED TO TRIGGER
THE LIBERAL REVOLUTION IN MARCH 1917. BY THE END OF THE YEAR,
FURTHER DEFEATS AND THE BOLSHEVIK SEIZURE OF POWER ALL BUT
REMOVED RUSSIA FROM THE WAR.

1918

The British and French, suffering from manpower shortages, would be able to field only 156 divisions in early 1918 to the Germans' 192. From the perspective of the German High Command, this offered the chance to mass its forces in the West and seek a knockout blow before American troops could arrive in overwhelming numbers. In a meeting at Mons on 11 November 1917 (in retrospect, both the venue and date are richly ironic), the decision was taken to gamble on a strike in the West. Later, Ludendorff confirmed

OPPOSITE: The Allies in retreat, Omiecourt, March 24 1918: huts and stores are destroyed as gun teams move to recover their weapons.

ABOVE: German stormtroopers. Tactical developments on both sides of No Man's Land had produced a revolution in infantry tactics by 1918.

FERDINAND FOCH
(1851–1929)

If any one individual can be said to have been essential to the Allied victory in 1918, it was Foch. He successfully carried out the difficult job of holding together an international coalition in the face of many competing agendas, being prepared to overrule both Haig and his countryman, Pétain. Deservedly appointed a Marshal of France in August 1918, he said – truthfully – "I am conscious of having served England as I served my own country." He formed a good team with Haig in the final offensives.

"Holding out – Boche all around within fifty yards – can only see fifty yards, so it is difficult to kill the blighters"

MESSAGE FROM COMMANDER OF 7TH BATTALION ROYAL WEST KENTS, 21 MARCH 1918

LEFT: The Germans on the advance, March 1918: reserves move across the old Somme battlefield.

OPPOSITE: Two days before the fall of the town, German and British wounded are unloaded from a British hospital train near Bapaume.

1918

that the target would be the British Fifth and Third Armies. The codename for the attack was Operation Michael.

The Allies, aware that they had lost the strategic initiative, went on to the defensive. Haig was forced to reduce the size of British divisions from 12 battalions to nine. He was misled by German deception and, realizing he could not be strong everywhere, chose to keep the bulk of his forces in the north, defending the critical areas that led to the Channel ports. In the event, this was to prove to be the correct decision. In the short term, however, Gough's Fifth Army stationed at the southern extremity of the British line and which bore the brunt of the attack, was dangerously weak, with only 12 infantry divisions covering a 68-km (42-mile) front from south of Flesquières to La Fère.

At 04:40 on 21 March 1918, Michael began with a furious hurricane bombardment of British positions in the St-Quentin sector orchestrated by Colonel Bruchmüller. Overwhelmed by the fire of nearly 10,000 guns and trench mortars, five hours later waves of German stormtroopers from Second and Eighteenth Armies assaulted the British defences. The British, having spent most of the previous three years on the offensive, were unused to defending. They

misunderstood the principles of defence in depth, massing too many soldiers in the front positions which were supposed to be lightly held. Morale was poor in some units, and by the end of the day, Fifth Army was in serious trouble. Materially aided by thick fog, the Germans captured the British Forward Zone, taking some 500 guns and 21,000 prisoners. Worse, the stormtroopers got through III Corps's Battle Zone, where attackers were supposed to be stopped. However, in places Fifth Army fought well and the Germans did not reach all their objectives. To the north, British Third Army stubbornly held out south of Arras against German Seventeenth Army's attack.

The attack made further progress on 22 and 23 March as Gough's Fifth Army fell back. Ludendorff, frustrated that his plan was lagging behind schedule, gave Hutier's Eighteenth Army, which had made the most ground, the lead role, although it had been intended to act as a flank guard. Ludendorff's new plan dissipated the strength of his attack, although it threatened to separate the British from the French. It would have been better to continue to aim for the critical communications centres which, if captured, might have crippled the BEF's ability to fight on. Paradoxically, the severe threat forced the Allies to agree to unity of command,

a factor that was greatly to improve their command performance. Fearful that the French would give priority to defending Paris over maintaining contact with the BEF, on 26 March the British supported Foch's appointment as overall Allied commander.

Byng's British Third Army decisively defeated another major attack near Arras on 28 March. Operation Michael was slowing down; as the Allies recovered, French reserves arrived, and German infantry outran their artillery support. The German attempt to take the critical rail-hub of Amiens was halted on 4–5 April at Villers-Bretonneux, 16 km (10 miles) from the key city of Amiens, by Australian and British troops. Ludendorff, recognizing that Michael had run out of steam, halted the offensive. It had gained a great deal of ground, but the possession of a bulge into the Allied lines some 65-km (40-miles) deep proved difficult to defend and in the long run more trouble than it was worth. Haig's forces had suffered tactical defeat – Gough paid for it with his job – but the BEF was still very much in the fight. Moreover, Ludendorff had failed to break the link between the French and British armies. The trench deadlock had been broken, and open warfare restored. Who could best take advantage – the Germans or the Allies?

OSKAR VON HUTIER
(1857–1934)

General von Hutier, commander of German Eighteenth Army in 1918, came to prominence on the Eastern Front. At Riga, in September 1917, his Eighth Army had given an early demonstration of the methods that would be used in March 1918: a short bombardment without previously registering the guns, arranged by Bruchmüller; followed by the infantry using infiltration tactics (although the Russians put up little resistance). This approach became known as "Hutier tactics", although Hutier himself had little influence on their development.

GERMAN SPRING OFFENSIVE

OPERATION GEORGETTE
TO THE SECOND MARNE

THERE WAS LITTLE RESPITE BEFORE LUDENDORFF'S NEXT ATTACK
WAS LAUNCHED. OPERATION GEORGETTE (OR THE BATTLE OF THE
LYS) OPENED ON 9 APRIL WITH THE NOW-FAMILIAR HURRICANE
BOMBARDMENT, AND INFANTRY OF GERMAN SIXTH ARMY DROVE
INTO ALLIED POSITIONS SOUTH OF YPRES. THE OBJECTIVE WAS
HAZEBROUCK, A MAJOR COMMUNICATIONS CENTRE WHOSE
CAPTURE WOULD IMPERIL THE ENTIRE BRITISH SITUATION.

1918

ABOVE: The spring offensive saw fighting under conditions very different from the trench warfare of earlier years: British soldiers defend Bailleul, 15 April 1918.

This threat was, potentially, much more dangerous than that posed by Operation Michael, as it would put the Channel ports directly at risk.

A Portuguese division gave way, but on its flanks British divisions held on, ensuring that the advance of about 5.5 km (3.5 miles) was funnelled on a relatively narrow front. To the north, on the following day, German Fourth Army smashed into British Second Army. The defenders gave some ground and the British were forced to abandon Armentières to the enemy. The villages of Messines and Wytschaete – the scene of so much heavy fighting in previous years – also fell into German hands. The seriousness of the situation can be judged from the fact that on 11 April Haig, not a man given to grand gestures, issued his famous "Backs to the Wall" order.

The Allies survived – just. Foch, whose authority as Allied commander was enhanced on 14 April as a response to the crisis, sent French divisions, including Micheler's French Fifth Army, up to support and relieve the British. Some British divisions were moved to quiet parts of the front. Although Haig wanted more help, he sourly noted in his diary that Foch was "very disinclined to engage French troops in the battle". Foch instead took a hard, calculating look at the situation and decided to keep plenty of French divisions in reserve. He believed that the British could hold on in Flanders, and rightly suspected that the Germans would attack further south. Plumer, after much heart searching, abandoned the positions on

the Passchendaele Ridge, won at such a high cost the previous autumn.

On the other side of No Man's Land, Ludendorff was becoming frustrated with the failure to push on. A German account of the fighting of 17 April recorded that the "foremost waves were compelled to return to their jumping-off trenches, suffering severe losses. There they lay the whole day under the heaviest fire." Georgette, like Michael before it, was becoming stalemated. On 25 April, a further crisis arose when the Germans captured Mount Kemmel, the highest feature on the Ypres Salient, which had been held by three French divisions. This setback caused some inter-Allied tension, but the Germans were unable to take advantage. Five days later, the battle came to an end. Both sides had paid a heavy price (from 21 March to 30 April, 332,000 Allied casualties, 348,000 German), but Ludendorff had failed to break through.

On 24 April, even before the Lys had ended, the Germans began another attack aiming at Amiens. Once again, a clash at Villers-Bretonneux was critical, where two Australian brigades took the lead in mounting a counter-attack and pushing the Germans back. However, for his next offensive Ludendorff turned his attention to the French, aiming to exhaust their reserves. In the early hours of 27 May, a hurricane bombardment, heavy even by Bruchmüller's standards, opened on the Chemin des Dames, held by General Duchêne's French Sixth Army (which included British IX Corps, sent south for a "rest"). The Allies were badly deployed; being forward of the

HAIG'S ORDER 11 APRIL 1918

Haig's "Backs to the Wall" message of 11 April 1918 was an uncharacteristically dramatic gesture that demonstrates how bleak the situation appeared from the perspective of GHQ. Some British soldiers commented later that they were unaware of the seriousness of the position until they read Haig's message.

TOP LEFT: By 1918, warfare had become well and truly "three-dimensional". Here, British infantry man machine guns delpoyed in an anti-aircraft role on 1 May 1918 at Haverskerque.

TOP RIGHT: One of the most evocative images of the war: British soldiers blinded by gas, April 1918.

ABOVE: Haig greets "The Tiger", the French Premier, Georges Clemenceau.

Calais
English Channel
Boulogne
Montreuil
Abbeville

XXXX
2
PLUMER

Ypres
Wytschaete
Messines
Hazebrouck
Lys

Passchendaele
XXXX
4
von ARMIN

Schelde
BRUSSELS

Armentières
Lille

B E L G I U M

XXXX
1
HORNE

Loos
Lens

XXXX
6
QUAST

Mons
Charleroi

Arras

XXXX
3
BYNG

Cambrai

XXXX
17
von BELOW

XXXX
5
GOUGH

Albert
Péronne
Somme

XXXX
2
MARWITZ

XXXX

Amiens
Villers-
Bretonneux
Montdidier

St Quentin

Hirson

LUXEMBOURG

Sedan
Arlon

XXXX
1
DEBENEY

XXXX
18
HUTIER

XXXX
7
von BOEHN

XXXX
1
MUDRA

Meuse

Etain

Beauvais

XXXX
3
HUMBERT

Oise

Soissons
Aisne
Chemin des
Dames

Rheims

Verdun

Metz

XXXX
10
MAISTRE

Marne

Epernay

F R A N C E
Seine

XXXX
6
DUCHÊNE

Château
Thierry

XXXX
5
MICHELER

XXXX
4
GOURAUD
Châlons-sur-
Marne

St-Mihiel

PARIS

N

GERMAN SPRING OFFENSIVE: 1918

German
gains from
operations:
Michael, 21 March–5 April
Georgette, 9–11 April
Blücher–Yorke, 27 May
Gneisenau, 9 June
Marne–Rheims, 15–17 July

0   50 miles
0   80 kms

THE GERMAN TANK

On 24 April 1918, at Cachy, three German A7V tanks fought an action against three British Mark IV tanks. After two British machine-gun armed "female" tanks had been forced to pull back, Lieutenant Frank Mitchell's Mark IV "male", armed with a 6-pounder gun drove back an A7V, which overturned, and caused the crew of another to abandon their tank. This action, fought during the clash at Villers-Bretonneux, which prevented the Germans from moving on Amiens, was the first confrontation of armoured fighting vehicles in history.

defensible line of the Aisne with their forward positions crammed with troops. Attacking in overwhelming force, the Germans quickly smashed through the Allied defences and crossed the Aisne, advancing 16 km (10 miles) in a day. The situation was stabilized only when the Germans reached the Marne on 3–4 June. Although alarming to the Allies, the Germans had merely acquired another tract of unrewarding territory, as Foch was shrewd enough to realize. Some Allied reserves (including US divisions) had been rushed to the sector, but not enough to make life easier for the Germans elsewhere. Another German offensive had started well but then run into the sand.

ABOVE LEFT: The huge and ungainly German A7V tank was 7 m (7.6 yds) long and had a crew of up to 18.

ABOVE: German propaganda poster. A German poster celebrating the success of the 1918 spring offensive, boasting of prisoners and equipment captured and ground gained.

BELOW: A column of French troops, led by some grizzled poilus, pass a British band resting by the side of the road.

RIGHT: A pair of German binoculars and case. These items were much sought after by Allied troops as war trophies.

BELOW: A German Stahlhelm (steel helmet). The first model was introduced in 1915, and was gradually improved during the war.

THE WAR IN THE AIR
THE START OF MODERN WARFARE

POWERED FLIGHT WAS VERY NEW IN 1914 – THE WRIGHT BROTHERS'
FIRST FLIGHT HAD TAKEN PLACE ONLY 11 YEARS BEFORE. GERMAN,
FRENCH AND BRITISH AIRCRAFT ALL WENT TO WAR IN 1914, BUT THEY
WERE PRIMITIVE AND THEIR POTENTIAL WAS BARELY RECOGNIZED.
BY 1918, THE AIRCRAFT HAD EMERGED AS A POWERFUL WEAPON
INDISPENSABLE TO MODERN WARFARE.

ABOVE: A German observer manning the machine gun.
Both sides made extensive use of two-seater aircraft.

OPPOSITE BELOW AND TOP RIGHT: French ace René Fonck (below) and the British
Captain Albert Ball VC (top right) sitting in the cockpit of his SE5 aircraft in April 1917. Ball
achieved 17 of his 44 kills in an SE5. Fonck survived the war but Ball was killed on 7 May 1917.

LEFT: A flying helmet that belonged to the French ace Joseph Guiguet, a pilot in the "Stork" squadron.

ABOVE: Royal Flying Corps pilot's "wings": a badge issued to qualified pilots.

Virtually all of the military roles of the aircraft had been developed. Air power was one of the major reasons why the First World War was different to the wars of the past, instead pointing the way to the wars of the future.

Before the war, military men had viewed aircraft with a mixture of interest, scepticism

and doubt. Foch made some dismissive comments in 1910, but at an exercise in the following year the French army used airplanes for reconnaissance and – in a portent of the future – to direct artillery fire. Any initial reservations Haig might have had about aircraft vanished after he was comprehensively beaten in pre-war manoeuvres by a force that used aerial reconnaissance. In August 1914, the value of aircraft was demonstrated graphically when Allied aircraft detected the swing of von Kluck's army inside Paris. The counter-stroke that led to the Battle of the Marne was the result (see pages 28–31). Once trench stalemate set in, aircraft completely took over reconnaissance, traditionally the cavalry's role. In order to keep the prying eyes of the enemy's aircraft away from the trench systems, other aircraft were sent up to shoot them down or drive them away. Yet more aircraft were then deployed to protect the reconnaissance aircraft and fight enemy

fighters, and so the modern battle for control of the air was born.

The aircraft of 1914 were crude in comparison to what was available only four years later, and were maids of all work. Eventually, specialist machines were introduced. Artillery spotting was left to large platforms like the British R.E. 8, while fighter planes evolved in a very different direction. Most early planes were unarmed, and air combat only took place if a pilot or observer brought a rifle with them. Even when machine guns were fitted, they were difficult to use. The invention of the interrupter gear in 1915, which permitted a machine gun to fire through the propeller arc, created the modern fighter. By the late period of the war, fighters such as the fast and manoeuvrable French Spad XIII, the British Sopwith Snipe, and the German Fokker D-VII dominated the skies. Arguably the D-VII was the finest fighter aircraft of the war. All three were a far

ALLIED ACES

An ace was a pilot with five or more kills. The highest scoring Allied ace was René Fonck, with at least 75 victories. Other French aces included Georges Guynemer, of the French "Stork" squadron with 53 kills and Charles Nungesser (45). Billy Bishop VC, a Canadian, was the leading British Empire ace credited with 72 victories. Edward "Mick" Mannock may have exceeded Bishop's total with 73 kills, but only 47 are officially recognized. The leading American ace was Eddie Rickenbacker with 26 kills.

LEFT: Capitaine Georges Guynemer in front of his Spad SVII aeroplane. He went missing on a patrol in September 1917.

MANFRED ALBRECHT VON RICHTOFEN
(1892-1918)

Von Richthofen was the highest scoring pilot of the war, with 80 kills. Nicknamed the Red Baron from his aristocratic lineage and red-painted aircraft, he achieved a legendary status in his lifetime that has continued to the present day. He came to prominence in the second half of 1916, and was appointed leader of his "Flying Circus" *Jagdstaffel* (fighter squadron) 11 in January 1917. He was shot down near Amiens on 21 April 1918. There is some mystery over his death, but most likely Richthofen was hit by ground fire.

cry from the first dedicated fighters such as the Fokker E-I "Eindekker" (monoplane) of 1915. Individual ace fighter pilots had rather different styles. For the British, Captain Albert Ball VC was a lone hunter, stalking his prey through the skies. The German ace Manfred von Richthofen fought as part of his "flying circus". On the French side, René Fonck was a skilled tactician who studied the techniques of enemy pilots.

Specialized bomber aircraft were also developed. The British DH-4, French Caudron G-4 and German A.E.G. G-IV came into this category. And yet this was not the end of the roles performed by aircraft during the war. Ground attack, contact patrols (i.e. attempting to locate and communicate with ground troops during battles), photographic reconnaissance;

interdiction bombing; and even dropping supplies by parachute were all roles fulfilled by aircraft during the war. Away from the Western Front, they were used at sea and for strategic bombing of enemy cities.

Even the humble balloon had a role. Tethered behind the lines, with an observer in a basket armed with binoculars and a telephone, the Kite Balloon was an important means of spotting for the artillery. Balloons and aircraft made indirect fire possible – gunners could now accurately shoot at things that they could not see. This apparently simple development transformed warfare by making artillery far more effective. The year 1916 was crucial; for the first time, in the Battles of Verdun (see pages 80–89) and the Somme

(see pages 136–49), the struggle for the air became an absolutely essential part of the overall battle. Dominance in the air see-sawed between the belligerents. The 1917 Battles of Arras (see pages 158–161) and the Nivelle Offensive (see pages 162–163) coincided with a period of German air superiority that became known to the British as "Bloody April". In the last phase of the war, the Allies had the upper hand, not least because of weight of numbers.

Air combat made huge advances during the First World War. In recognition, in April 1918 the British created the world's first independent air force, the Royal Air Force, from the army's Royal Flying Corps and the Royal Naval Air Service.

OPPOSITE: An FE2B, viewed from above. The FE2B was introduced as a fighter in 1915, and was used for bombing later in the war.

BELOW: Royal Air Force Sopwith Camels of B and C flights, 201 Squadron in August 1918.

BELOW LEFT (TOP): A red armband of the type worn by members of the French Air Service in the First World War.

BELOW LEFT (BOTTOM): A French bomb, designed for dropping from aircraft.

RÉPUBLIQUE FRANÇAISE

GRAND QUARTIER GÉNÉRAL
DES
ARMÉES FRANÇAISES

SERVICE AÉRONAUTIQUE

INSTRUCTIONS

En cas d'atterrissage d'Aéroplanes sur le territoire de la Zone des Armées

Marques distinctives. — 1° Les aéroplanes alliés portent une cocarde tricolore sous les ailes et à chaque extrémité, et des bandes tricolores à la queue.

COCARDES FRANÇAISES

COCARDES ANGLAISES

COCARDES BELGES

2° Les aéroplanes allemands ont comme insignes la Croix de Malte sous chaque aile, sur le fuselage et la queue.

CROIX DE MALTE PEINTE EN NOIR

Tout aviateur atterrissant dans la zone des Armées, en dehors des terrains d'atterrissage, doit décliner ses nom et qualités et présenter sa carte d'aviateur militaire aux autorités militaires ou civiles qui se présenteront. Le pilote sera responsable des déclarations d'identité des passagers.

Atterrissage d'Aéroplanes français ou alliés. — Si l'atterrissage a lieu à proximité d'une garnison, le Commandant d'Armes fera assurer le gardiennage de l'appareil. Lorsque l'aviateur atterrit loin d'une garnison, mais à proximité d'une Brigade de Gendarmerie, le Chef de la Brigade assurera, s'il le peut, la garde de l'avion au moyen de son personnel, ou procurera à l'aviateur des hommes de confiance. A défaut de Gendarmerie, le Maire de la commune doit faire assurer le gardiennage de l'avion dans les mêmes conditions.

Atterrissage d'Aéroplanes allemands. — En cas d'atterrissage ennemi, le Commandant de la Brigade de Gendarmerie ou le Maire de la commune s'assurent de la personne des aviateurs ennemis et en préviennent immédiatement le Général commandant l'Armée ou la Région.

En cas de velléité de remise en marche de l'aéroplane, user de violence pour empêcher le départ, en brisant soit la queue de l'aéroplane, soit une roue.

L'aéroplane doit être conservé intact jusqu'à l'arrivée des Autorités Militaires compétentes.

Au G. Q. G., le 22 Avril 1916.
Pour le Général Commandant en Chef,
Le Major Général,
PELLÉ.

Airforce insignia
recognition poster

A poster published on
22 April explaining
procedures for dealing
with airmen landing
in Allied territory and
showing the identifying
roundel design used by
the French, British, Belgian
and German airforces.

Lieutenant Taplin's
combat report

An Australian pilot's report
on a successful combat
with a German aircraft on
3 August 1918.

W 3J12/M2233 50,000 6/17 [X373a] W. & Co.
W7213/M2958 60,000 8/17 [439a]

APPENDIX 4

Army Form W. 3348

11

349   **Combats in the Air.**

Squadron :   4th. A.F.C.

Type and No. of Aeroplane :
Sopwith Camel E.1407.

Armament :   2 Vickers.

Pilot :   Lieut. L.E.Taplin D.F.C.

Observer :

Date :   3rd. August 1918

Time :   5-20 a.m.

Locality :   N.E. of Merville.

Duty :   Special Mission.

Height :   5,000 Ft.

Result
{ Destroyed.................................
{ Driven down out of control............
{ Driven down.....Yes...................

No. 2

Remarks on Hostile Aircraft :—Type, armament, speed, etc.

L. V. G.   Coloured light brown with dark brown and black
camouflage.   National markings.

Narrative.

Whilst flying towards Estaires I saw an L.V.G. flying West from North
of Estaires. I kept in his blind spot above his top plane until he
was warned by A.A. I then dived on E.A. from front; his observer
opened fire from range o f about 600 Yards but I reserved my fire
until I got underneath his tail. I closed in to a very short range
and fired about 200 rounds from both guns. I then noticed that
tracer bullets were ricicheting off bottom of fuselage of E.A. which
was armoured. While I was firing the pilot was endeavouring to get me
out of his blind spot and I overshot him, getting on the left of his
observer. I then fired a burst of 150 rounds from point blank range
into the side of the E.A. which silenced the observer; but, not
before he had fired a burst into my machine one of which was an
explosive bullet which hit a longeron in front of the dash board and
temporarily blinded me.
      I immediately half rolled to get away and on looking back saw
E.A. diving steeply with smoke pouring out behind.
      I did not again engage E.A. as my machine was badly shot about
      I saw E.A. go down ateeply with a partial side slip to the lef
for about 3,000 Ft. before I eventually lost sight of him; on account
of having to keep turning to avoid A.A. fire.
      "D" Battery saw this combat and confirms that E.A. went down
but were unable to observe ultimate result on account of distance.

L.Eaton Taplin   Lieut.

McClaughry   Major.
Commanding....4th Squadron. A.F.C.

209

1917

AVIATION MILITAIRE

12e Groupe de Combat

(1) ACTIVE

(2) AVIATION - ESCADRILLE N - 3 .

(1) Active, Réserve ou Territoriale
(2) Corps ou Service.
(3) Arme ou Service.
(4) Pour le Sous-Officier, la date de nomination au **grade de Sous-Officier.**

MÉMOIRE DE PROPOSITION

pour Citation à l'Ordre de l'Armée.

(3) AVIATION

NOM GUYNEMER
PRÉNOMS GEORGES
Numéro matricule
Grade Capitaine
Date d'entrée au service 21 Novembre 1914
Durée des services effectifs. 2 ans 8 mois 10 jours.
Durée des services dans la réserve (s'il y a lieu) ans mois jours.
Date de nomination au grade actuel de la Légion d'Honneur CHEVALIER : 24 Décembre 1915 OFFICIER : 11 Juin 1917.
Date de la nomination au grade actuel dans la hiérarchie (4). 21 Février 1917

		ANS.	MOIS.	JOURS.
SERVICES : Active et Réserve		2	8	10
MAJORATIONS	Etudes préliminaires			
	Légion d'Honneur	1	7	8
	Séjour dans garnison frontière			
	Aviation			
	Etc			
Blessures		2		
Citations à l'Ordre de l'Armée		21		
Campagnes		2	8	10
TOTAUX		29	11	28

Blessures de Guerre 1 le 12 Mars (VERDUN) 1 le 23 Sep.16 (SOMME)
Citations 21 À l'O/de l'Armée:21/7,5/9,12/12-15;9/2,26/3,25/5, 25/6,27/7,24/8,26/8,3 & 23/9,28/10,20 & 26/12-16;28/11/16
Actions d'éclat 12,13 & 14/2,26/3,14/6, - 1917.

MOTIF de la proposition et avis du Chef de Corps ou du Service

Pilot de combat incomparable. Le 6 et 7 juillet a abattu ses 46e 47e et 48e avions ennemis. Le 8 juillet, a livré un combat très dur, au cours duquel, il a été descendu pour la septième fois, son avion criblé de balles.

[signature]

Georges Guynemer's Citation

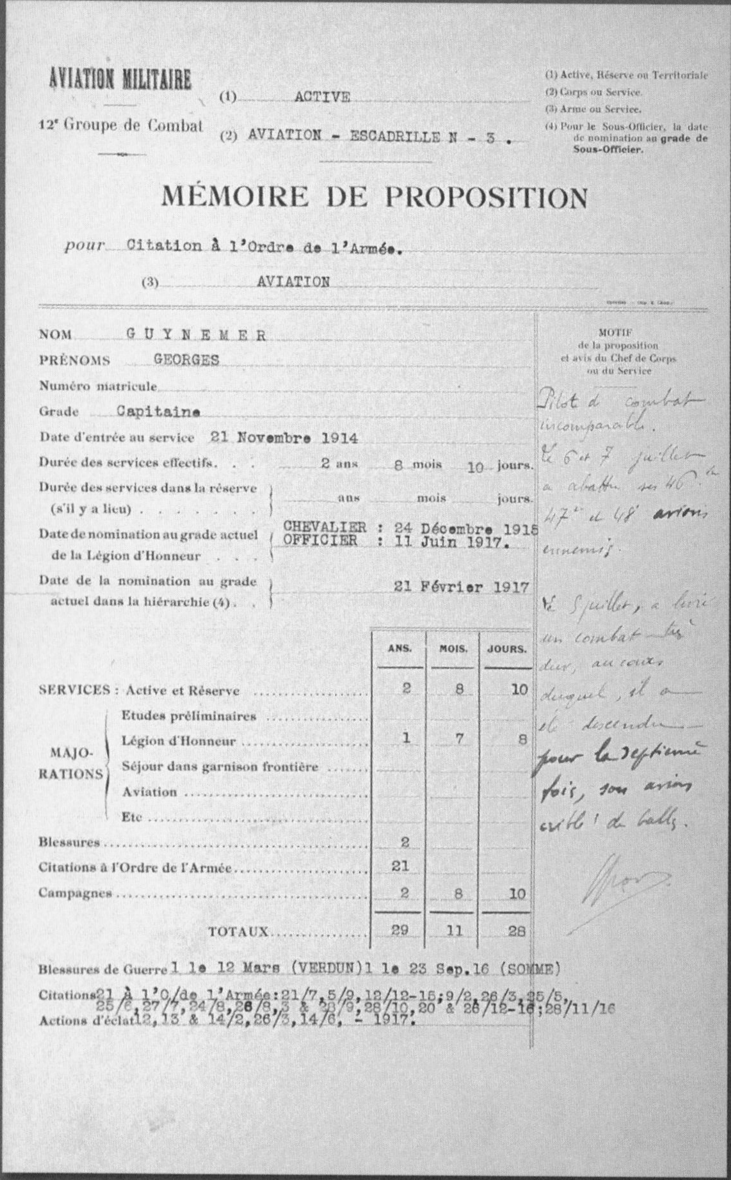

In this Citation Georges Guynemer is described as "Pilot de combat incomparable". The Citation lists his service and decorations.

Translation
MILITARY AVIATION
12th Combat Group
(1) ACTIVE
(2) AVIATION – SQUADRON No. 3
NOTE OF PROPOSAL for Mention in Dispatches
(3) AVIATION
NAME: GUYNEMER
FORENAMES: GEORGES
Registration number:
Rank: Captain
Date of entering service: 21 November 1914
Duration of effective service: 2 yrs, 8 mths, 10 days
Duration of services in the reserve (if applicable)...
Date of appointment to the present rank of the Legion of Honour:
KNIGHT: 24 December 1915
OFFICER: 11 June 1917.
Date of appointment to the present rank in the hierarchy (4):
21 February 1917

	Yrs	Mths	Days
SERVICES:			
Active and Reserve	2	8	10
ENHANCEMENTS:			
Preliminary Studies			
Legion of Honour	1	7	8
Stay in the frontier garrison			
Aviation			
Etc			
Wounds	2		
Citations to the Order of the Army	21		
Campaigns	2	8	10
TOTALS	19	11	28

War wounds:
1 on 12 March (VERDUN);
1 on 23 September 1916 (SOMME)
Citations: 21 to 1'O of the Army:
21/7, 5/9, 12/12-15; 9/2, 26/3, 25/5, 25/8, 27/7, 24/8, 26/8, 3 & 23/9, 28/10, 20 & 26/12-16; 28/11/18
Actions of shrapnel:
12, 13 & 14/2, 26/3, 14/6, – 1917.

GROUNDS
of the proposal and notice of the Head of Corps or Department

[*handwritten:*] Incomparable combat pilot On 6 and 7 July he beat the 46th, 47th and 48th enemy planes. On 8 July, he joined a very hard fight during which he was brought down for the seventh time, his plane riddled with bullets.
[signature]

A letter sent to Guynemer's parents after his death

Translation
Compiègne
17 September 1917
Dear Commandant,
Thank you for your very kind and heartfelt letter to my son. It was of great comfort to us. We shall never lose hope for as long as it is physically possible for us to preserve it, and we shall continue to rely on the devotion and affection of his chiefs.
Yours .....

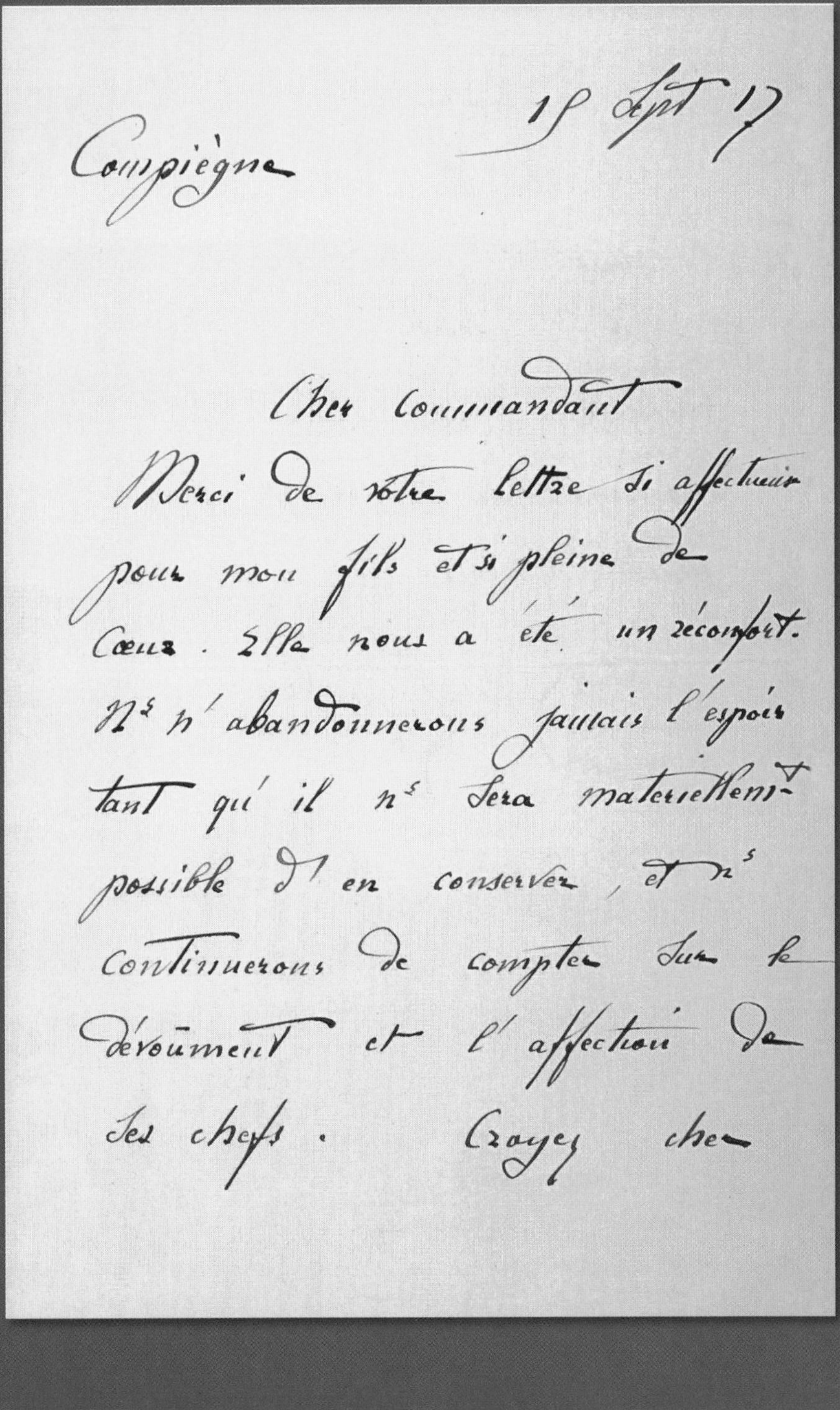

Compiègne   18 Sept 17

Cher Commandant
Merci de votre lettre si affectueux
pour mon fils et si pleine de
Cœur. Elle nous a été un réconfort.
N⁵ n'abandonnerons jamais l'espoir
tant qu'il n⁵ Sera matériellem⁴
possible d'en conserver, et n⁵
continuerons de compter sur le
dévoûment et l'affection de
Ses chefs.   Croyez cher

SECOND BATTLE OF THE MARNE

THE LAST GERMAN OFFENSIVE

AT THE END OF THE GERMANS' CHEMIN DE DAMES OFFENSIVE, AMERICAN TROOPS SAW A CONSIDERABLE AMOUNT OF FIGHTING, NOTABLY IN THE BELLEAU WOOD BATTLE (6 JUNE). THIS WAS A WARNING THAT THERE WAS LITTLE TIME LEFT FOR THE GERMANS TO DEFEAT THE ALLIES BEFORE US TROOPS ARRIVED IN FRANCE IN VAST NUMBERS.

1918

ABOVE: In this posed image, French troops take up a defensive position in a ruined church near the Marne, 1918.

Pershing was commander of the American Expeditionary Force in the First World War. Nicknamed "Black Jack" because he had commanded African-American troops, Pershing was determined to create an American Army under his command and therefore resisted pressure to "amalgamate" his troops with the British or French. American troops did well in the fighting in June–July 1918, and with the British in September 1918, but major independent US formations only saw action in the last two months of the war.

On 9 June, Ludendorff stuck again, this time against Humbert's French Third Army in the River Matz sector between Noyon and Montdider. Again, the German aim was to wear out French reserves before striking in Flanders. The attackers made spectacular gains, 10 km (6 miles) on the first day, but two days into the battle the French launched a counter-offensive under General Charles Mangin, who had been out of favour since the Nivelle Offensive (see pages 162–163). After an hour-long bombardment, Mangin's forces, which included several US Divisions, supported by ground-attack aircraft and 144 tanks, went into action. The Germans were halted, and the main battle was over by 14 June.

German High Command continued to put their faith in a planned attack by Rupprecht in Flanders, Operation Hagen, but felt that a preliminary offensive aimed at exhausting French reserves was necessary. Allied intelligence picked up signs of German activity on the Marne and in Flanders, leading to some inter-Allied disputes about where reserves should be sent. In the meantime, Mangin's Tenth Army made gains around Soissons (28–29 June), an attack that sowed the seeds for a much bigger offensive several weeks later. On the eve of the Second Battle of the Marne, the Allies had concentrated Maistre's and Fayolle's army groups, mostly comprising French divisions but also nine US, two Italian and two British. Against this, the Germans could bring First and Third Armies to attack to the east of Reims, aiming for the River Marne, 25 km (15 miles) away. To the west of the city, Seventh and Ninth Armies had to cross the Marne and link up with the eastern arm of the attack.

From the beginning, some things went wrong for the Germans. The element of surprise was lost because prisoners betrayed the time and date of the attack (03:50 am on 15 July). This allowed the Allies to open a disruptive counter-bombardment 90 minutes before German zero hour. Moreover, unlike during the defence of the Aisne on 27 May (see pages 200–203), the French defenders understood the purpose of defence in depth. French Fourth Army under General Gouraud, a Gallipoli veteran, fought a model defensive battle; the attackers were harried by fire in the outpost zone and then defeated in the main killing ground. In the western sector, initially the Germans had greater success. The Italians took a battering and were replaced by British 51st (Highland) and 62nd Divisions, which had just arrived in the area. Making good tactical use of a smokescreen, the German Seventh Army fought their way across the Marne at Dormans, and once on the far bank advanced 6 km (4 miles). This caused consternation in some parts of

ABOVE LEFT: A group of Allied soldiers, July 1918. The French soldiers have their eyes bandaged, probably as a result of the gas.

ABOVE RIGHT: A French-built Renault FT-17 tank. The Renault was used by American as well as French units, and saw much action in 1918.

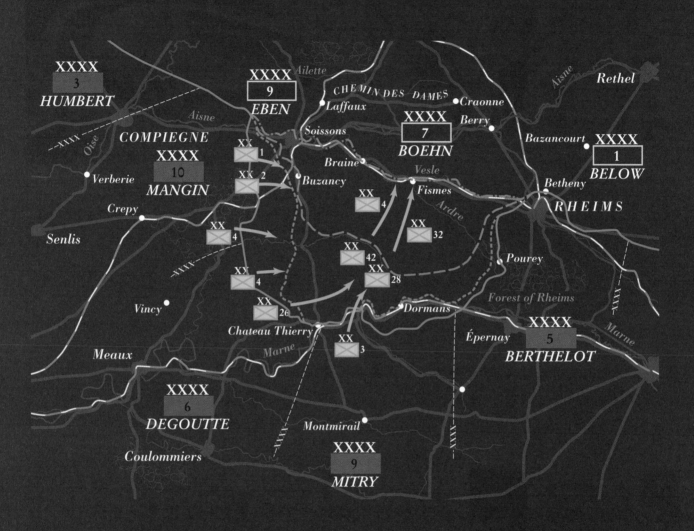

XXXX
3
HUMBERT

XXXX
9
EBEN

Ailette

CHEMIN DES DAMES

Craonne

Rethel

Laffaux

Aisne

XXXX
7
BOEHN

Berry

Bazancourt

XXXX
1
BELOW

Aisne

COMPIEGNE

Soissons

Betheny

XXXX
10
MANGIN

Verberie

XX 1

XX 2

Braine

Buzancy

Vesle

Fismes

RHEIMS

Crepy

Senlis

XX 4

XX 4

XX 32

Ardre

Pourey

XX 42

Forest of Rheims

Vincy

XX 4

XX 28

XX 26

Dormans

Épernay

XXXX
5
BERTHELOT

Chateau Thierry

Marne

XX 3

Meaux

Marne

XXXX
6
DEGOUTTE

Montmirail

Coulommiers

XXXX
9
MITRY

THE SECOND BATTLE OF MARNE:
Showing American Involvement: 18 July–6 August 1918

Front lines
——— 18 July
– – – 28 July
——▶ American advance
····· 20 July
–·–·– 6 August

the French High Command. Clemenceau was furious with Foch, and Pétain, the commander of the French Army, was worried by this development. Foch, by contrast, was calm, overruling Pétain's desire to postpone a planned counter-offensive.

Mangin attacked the western flank of the bridgehead on 16 July and gained some ground. Hemmed into a shallow salient, unable to break out, the six German divisions that had crossed the Marne were in a dangerous position and lost heavily from shelling and bombing. But this was just the preliminary to a much larger French attack on 18 July. For this, Mangin massed 18 divisions, backed by another seven. However, it was Degoutte's French Sixth Army on Tenth Army's flank that struck the first blow, 45 minutes earlier at 04:35. Disoriented from this surprise attack, the defenders were wholly unprepared when Mangin's troops joined the battle. The Germans were pushed back 6 km (4 miles) in the face of French artillery, infantry and tanks. Tenth Army took 15,000 prisoners and 400 guns. Pressure grew on the German salient as French Fifth and Ninth Armies came into action later, and increased steadily over the next few days as more troops (including two more British divisions, 15th (Scottish) and 34th were committed to battle.

On 18 July, Ludendorff was in Mons, planning Operation Hagen. Mangin's counter-offensive wrecked his plans. Accepting the inevitable, the Marne bridgehead was evacuated, and the Germans fell back on other parts of the front. By 6 August, the battle was over. Foch, his judgement vindicated, richly deserved his promotion to Marshal of France, announced that day. Operation Hagen never took place. The strategic initiative had passed decisively from the Germans to the Allies.

TOP: The 15 July 1918 marked the first day of the last German offensive of the war. Here, French stretcher-bearers bring wounded to a field hospital during the Second Battle of the Marne.

ABOVE: Highland troops, who played an important role at the Second Marne, escort German prisoners to the rear. Increasing numbers of Germans surrendered as 1918 progressed.

CHARLES MARIE EMMANUEL MANGIN
(1866–1925)

The wartime career of General Mangin was distinctly chequered. He was a brigade commander in 1914 and thanks to successes at Verdun in 1916 was appointed to command Sixth Army. Scapegoated because of the failure of the Nivelle Offensive in 1917, he was restored to favour by Foch in 1918 and played a vital role in the Second Battle of the Marne. Ruthless and personally brave, he was nicknamed "the Butcher". Mangin had the satisfaction of knowing that he had played a significant role in restoring his home province, Lorraine, to France.

THURSDAY, 4 JULY 1918–SUNDAY, 11 AUGUST 1918

HAMEL AND AMIENS

THE BLACK DAY OF THE GERMAN ARMY

THE SPRING OFFENSIVES LEFT THE GERMAN ARMY EXHAUSTED, STUCK AT THE END OF TENUOUS SUPPLY LINES, UNABLE TO MAKE ANY FURTHER HEADWAY AND VULNERABLE TO ATTACK. JUST HOW VULNERABLE WAS REVEALED BY A LIMITED ACTION THAT TOOK PLACE IN EARLY JULY AT LE HAMEL NEAR VILLERS-BRETONNEUX. MONASH'S AUSTRALIAN CORPS, REINFORCED BY AMERICAN TROOPS, CAPTURED ALL OF ITS OBJECTIVES IN JUST 90 MINUTES.

1918

JOHN MONASH
(1865–1931)

Lieutenant-General Monash had an unusual background for a Great War commander. Of German-Jewish origin, before the war he was a civil engineer and member of the part-time Australian militia. After service on Gallipoli, he took command of 3rd Australian Division in 1916 and then the Australian Corps in June 1918. A brilliant organizer, he had a methodical approach to combat. Despite sharing Haig's views on the importance of discipline, Monash became an Australian national hero, and deservedly gained a reputation as one of the finest Allied generals of the war.

An updated version of the bite-and-hold operations used in 1917, this small-scale action was of enormous significance because it provided a model of a carefully prepared, tightly controlled, set-piece battle. Tellingly, Monash later described his methods as being akin to a conductor working from a musical score. A pamphlet on the lessons of 4 July was quickly produced and disseminated to the rest of the BEF.

Le Hamel proved to be a dress rehearsal for a battle fought on a far larger scale which has a good claim to be the turning point of the war on the Western Front. It was carried out by British Fourth Army, commanded by Rawlinson, in combination with General Debeney's French First Army. For this operation "Rawly" controlled British III Corps and both the Australian and Canadian Corps, two of the most powerful and effective formations in the Allied order of battle. Preparations for the battle were meticulous. Perhaps the most impressive piece of staff work was to bring the Canadians down, in great secrecy, from the northern part of the Western Front. The Canadians Corps was fresh, having taken little part in the spring battles, and in comparison to the British and Australians was very strong in numbers. A map captured during the battle showed that the Germans were totally unaware of the presence of the Canadian Corps in the Amiens area. In sharp contrast to the Battle of the Somme launched just a few miles to the north on 1 July 1916, at the Battle of Amiens the Allies achieved complete surprise.

The attack began at 04:20 on 8 August 1918. Thanks to the advanced gunnery techniques that had been developed by this stage of the war, 2,000 Allied guns

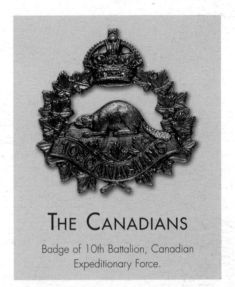

THE CANADIANS

Badge of 10th Battalion, Canadian Expeditionary Force.

were able to fire without any preliminary bombardment – another crucial element in the maintenance of surprise. The number of guns and shells that were needed had been carefully calculated, and unlike in previous years, the BEF had a superfluity of both: 700 field guns fired 350,000 shells. The counter-battery work of the heavy guns was highly effective, with most of the German guns neutralized, their crews either killed or driven off. A total of 580 tanks were used, including 72 "Whippet" light tanks and supply tanks. Infantry moved in close support of the armour, and 800 aircraft flew overhead to bomb and strafe the Germans. The plan called for reserve forces to follow on the heels

OPPOSITE: US and Australian troops dug in at Hamel, 4 July 1918. Pershing initially opposed US involvement in the battle.

BELOW: Australian 18 pounders of 6th Battery Australian Field Artillery in action near Villers-Bretonneux on the first day of the Battle of Amiens, 8 August 1918.

MONASH'S VIEWS ON BATTLE

In his book *The Australian Victories in France* in 1918 (1920) Monash set out his view on how a battle should be fought:
"A modern battle plan is like nothing so much as a score for a musical composition, where the various arms and units are the instruments, and the tasks they perform are their respective musical phrases. Each individual unit must make its entry precisely at the proper moment, and play its phrase in the general harmony." Le Hamel on 4 July 1918 showed how effective this approach could be.

1918

of the initial waves. This was to allow them to pass through the assault troops once the first objective had been captured, and so maintain the momentum of the attack.

British III Corps, attacking over the difficult terrain of the Chipilly spur in the north of the battlefield, had the toughest job. Its problems were exacerbated by the fact that, thanks to a preliminary German attack, it had to recapture part of its old front line before it could make the attack proper. Even so, it made a substantial advance. In the centre, the Canadians and Australians,

advancing over more favourable ground, pushed forward as much as 13 km (8 miles). On the southern flank, French First Army also made progress. In total, Allied casualties came to 9,000. German losses amounted to some 27,000 plus 400 guns. It was the most dramatic victory of the war up to that date. Ludendorff called it the "black day of the German Army". Amiens was also significant for its aftermath. On 11 August, with the Allies finding it increasingly difficult to get forward, the battle was halted and guns and troops moved northwards to begin a new offensive. In contrast to 1916 and 1917, the

BEF now possessed the guns and logistics to allow the point of attack to be switched quickly from sector to sector. This was to be a key factor in the defeat of the German army over the coming months.

TOP LEFT: British artillery, like these 60 pounders, achieved dominance over its German counterparts during the Battle of Amiens and made a crucial contribution to victory.

TOP RIGHT: German prisoners head for the rear past a British tank and advancing infantry.

ABOVE: A British tank crew next to their Mark V machine, 10 August 1918. They are examining a German anti-tank rifle captured by Canadian troops.

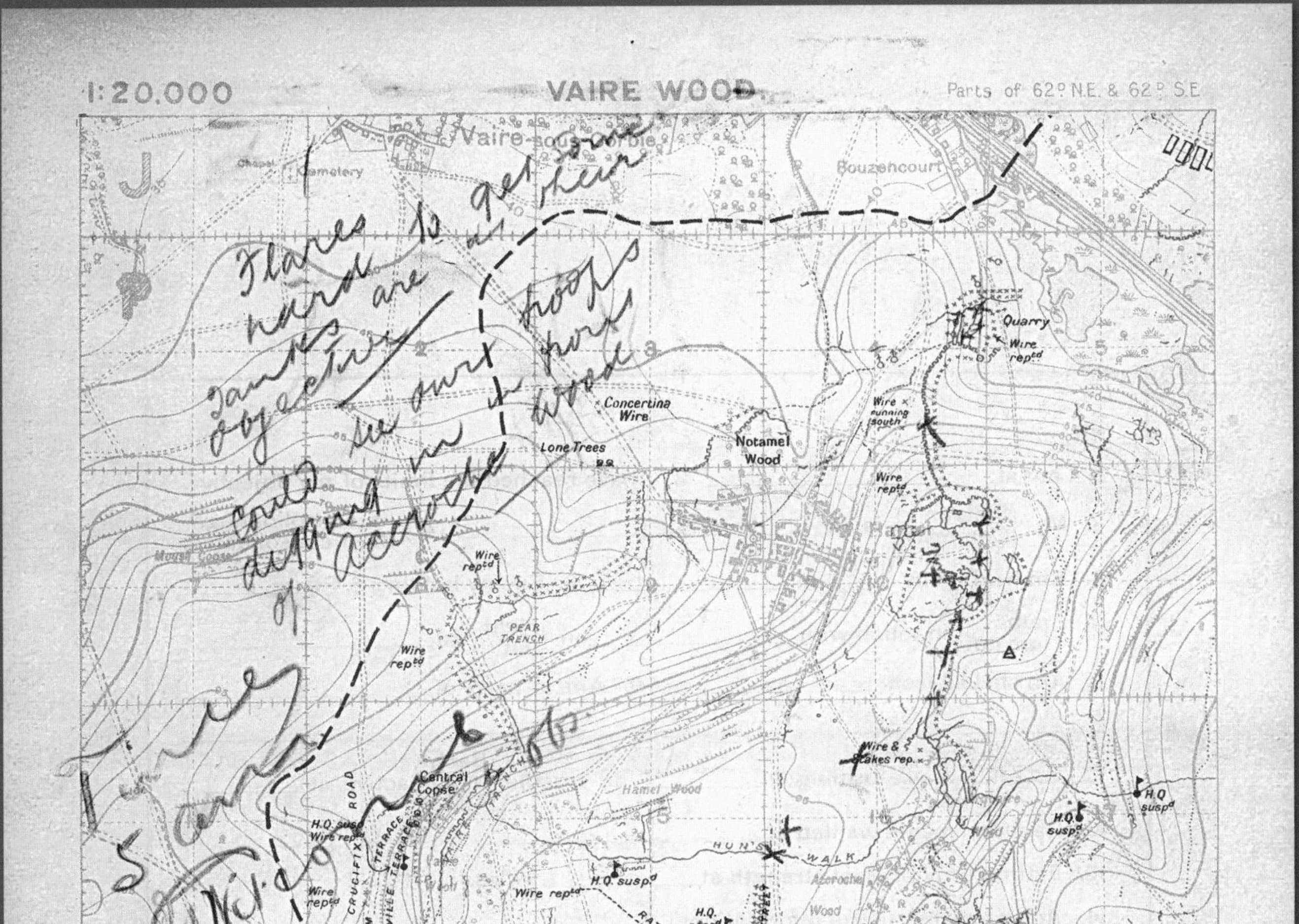

General Monash's Hamel map

General Monash's map of the Hamel battle, showing the positions reached.

219

WAR DIARY GENERAL STAFF,
OF SECOND AUSTRALIAN DIVISION.

INTELLIGENCE SUMMARY.

(Erase heading not required.)

Army Form C. 2118.

Vol. XXV.   Page 4.

Instructions regarding War Diaries and Intelligence Summaries are contained in F. S. Regs., Part II. and the Staff Manual respectively. Title pages will be prepared in manuscript.

Place	Date	Hour	Summary of Events and Information	Remarks and references to Appendices
GLISY.	1918. Aug. 6.	p.m.	During night 5th and 7th A.I.Bdes. moved forward to close assembly areas without incident.	
	7.	a.m. 5.0.	Morning Situation: Situation quiet. Scattered shelling of whole area. Some gas at intervals on O.22. N.66. normal	
			Fine sunny morning.	
		p.m.	Advice from Corps that to-day is "Y" day - units advised.	
		2.30.	G.S.O.III. synchronised watches with Artillery and Brigades.	
		5.5.	Evening report. Scattered shelling of O.29. with 77s. and 10.5 cm. between 10 a.m. and 12 noon Wagon movement in W.8. at 5.5. a.m. engaged by artillery. M.W. active on P.25.d. and P.26.c. silenced. E.A. nil.	
			Fine evening; sunny and warm.	
		7.15.	Supply Tank Park at O.29. central set on fire by shelling. 13 tanks destroyed and 3 saved.	
		8.0.	G.S.O.III. and Capt. BAZELEY left for liaison duty with flank Divs.	
		8.0.	5th A.I.Bde. Battle H.Q. closed at GLISY and opened at O.28.c.8.5.	
		11.30.	All units warned against unauthorised tapping in on telephone lines.	
			2nd Aust. Div. Intelligence Summary issued No. 195.	App. 72
			2nd Aust. Div. Order of Battle issued.	App. 73
	8.	a.m. 1.30.	Sector quiet for past two hours.	
		3.30.	Heavy shelling astride railway line - counter battery action requested.	
		4.0.	Hostile shelling reported to have ceased - no damage done.	
		4.30.	Artillery bombardment opened - heavy ground mist developing at GLISY.	
		4.35.	Right Bde. report barrage opened on time and excellent. No retaliation.	
		4.40.	Left Bde. report barrage opened on time - one tank out of action.	
		4.45.	Above message repeated Corps.	
			During next half hour Bdes. reported verbally that things apparently going well and enemy retaliation still continues feeble.	
		5.26.	Right Bde. report prisoner from JAFFA TRENCH 18th I.R. says no attack expected.	
		5.40.	Right Bde. report centre Bn. all O.K. at 5 a.m. - 6 prisoners 18th I.R.	
		5.50.	F.O.O. of 27th F.A.R. taken by Left Bn. of Right Bde.	
			Left Bde. report at 5.35 a.m. that Right Coy., Right Bn. on objective - Corps advised.	
		6.5.	1st Canadian Div. reported through HANGARD WOOD and 3rd Div. through ACCROCHE WOOD.	
		6.9.	Right Bde. report all going well - visibility bad - 75 to 80 prisoners.	

D.D.S.I., London, E.C.
(Also) Wt. Wxxxxbxxx 27xxxx 5/17 Sch. 55 Forme Cxxxx9x

WAR DIARY
OF GENERAL STAFF,
INTELLIGENCE SUMMARY. SECOND AUSTRALIAN DIVISION.

(Erase heading not required.)

Army Form C. 2118.

Vol. XXV.   Page 5.

Instructions regarding War Diaries and Intelligence Summaries are contained in F. S. Regs., Part II. and the Staff Manual respectively. Title pages will be prepared in manuscript.

Place	Date	Hour	Summary of Events and Information	Remarks and references to Appendices
GLISY.	1918. Aug. 8.	a.m. 6.20.	Identification wire from D.I.O. - 41st Div. identified - repeated to Corps.	
		6.30.	Right Bde. report prisoners say our forces in MARCELCAVE - probably Canadians.	
			Right Bde. report prisoners now 1 Off. and 74 O.Rs. - heavy ground mist - everything O.K.	
			Left Bde. report prisoners now 1 Off. and 28 O.Rs. of 152 I.R. - out of touch with left Bn. - everything satisfactory. - heavy fog.	
		6.35.	Situation reported to Corps.	
		7.5.	Identification wire from D.I.O. - 117th Div. identified, arrived during night from OSTEND - Repeated Corps.	
		7.9.	2nd Canadian Div. reported outskirts MARCELCAVE. - some trouble JAFFA TRENCH.	
		7.20.	Right Bde. report timed 7 a.m. Left Bn. on 1st objective - 140 prisoners to-date. - enemy artillery practically nil - mist clearing. 5th Aust. Div. moving forward.	
		7.30.	Left Bde. report WARFUSEE being cleared up and prisoners coming in - casualties slight. Reorganisation in P.22.d., 28.b. and d. proceeding.	
		7.45.	Right Bde. report prisoners state 2 Reserve Bns. and M.G. Coy. in Q.23. and 29. - Corps advised.	
		8.0.	Situation reported to Corps - total prisoners now 300.	
		8.10.	Left Bde. report 7.40 a.m. WARFUSEE rushed by 17th Bn. and troops now on both sides of village and through it. Our Artillery and Tanks moving forward.a	
		8.15.	Above repeated to Corps.	
		8.20.	Right Bde. Right Bn. report having reached GREEN line - Corps advised.	
		8.25.	Command of Battle front handed over to G.O.C., 5th Aust. Div. Corps and flank Divs. advised.	
			H.Q. of 6th A.I.Bde. moved to DOLL'S House - east edge VILLERS BRETONNEUX.	
			Centre Bn. Right Bde. report digging in 200 yards west GREEN line owing short shooting. 5th Aust. Div. passing through them.	
		8.45.	Wire from D.I.O. giving identifications and general intelligence - repeated Corps and flank divs.	
		9.0.	1st and 3rd Can. Divs. reported on GREEN line.	
		9.3.	Right Bde. reports all Bns. on objective and digging in - Centre Bn. being withdrawn and reorganised - consolidation in depth proceeding - repeated to Corps.	
		9.5.	Prisoners of War counted by A.P.M. to 8.30 total 651	
		9.25.	Left Bde. report all on GREEN line. Artillery now going through.	
		9.30.	Congratulatory message from Div. Commander to G.Os.C., 5th and 7th A.I.Bdes.	
		9.48.	Left Bde. report timed 9 a.m. armoured cars, tanks and cavalry have passed through.	
		9.50.	6th A.I.Bde. report 20 officers and 800 O.Rs. now passed through collecting stations - reported to Corps.	
		9.55.	Wire from D.I.O. giving further identifications repeated to Corps.	

D.D.S.I., London, E.C.
(Also) Wt. Wxxxxbxxx 27xxxx 5/17 Sch. 55 Forme Cxxxx9x

2nd Australian Infantry Division's Amiens report

The War Diary of the 2nd Australian Infantry Division covering 8 August 1918.

S E C T I O N. 11.

NARRATIVE, - August 8th 1918.

Ref.Map DEMUIN 1/20.000. Appendix. L.1.

"A". CAPTURE OF GREEN LINE(1st Objective)
By 3rd Canadian Infantry Brigade.

1. Before 4.20.a.m. (ZERO HOUR) August 8th 1918 3rd Cdn.Inf.Bde
    was assembled in Jumping-off positions as follows;-
        16th, 13th and 14th Cdn.Inf.Battalions (Attacking Battalions) -
    In Line from Right to Left respectively.
        5th Cdn.Inf.Battalion (2nd Cdn.Inf.Bde) and 15th Cdn.Inf.Bn.
    In Close Reserve to 16th and 13th Cdn.Inf.Bns respectively.
        Brigade Headquarters. U.15.central.

2. At 4.20.a.m. the barrage came down sharp on time and at 4.24.a.m.
    attacking troops moved forward and the attack quickly developed
    according to plan.

3. The lessons learned during the training carried out in May and June
    showed their value in that the forward troops pushed boldly and
    quickly, regardless of points on flank still holding out, these
    strong points being dealt with by the following waves. The result
    was that fighting was going on simultaneously MORGEMONT WOOD,
    CROATES TRENCH , PANTALOON RAVINE, (V.19.b. and d.) and AUBERCOURT.

4. As was expected, the enemy's strongest resistance was met in the
    system BOSNIA, CROATES, and CORBEAU Trenches.   This was the enemy's
    Main Line of Resistance covering his Battery Positions, and except
    on the Right he fought to a finish here.

5. The 16th Cdn.Inf.Bn (CANADIAN SCOTTISH) attacking on the Right
    pushed forward rapidly from the Jumping-off Line meeting little
    resistance going through HANGARD STRIP and WREN COPSES and BOSNIA
    Trench.
        On approaching the Road Junction North of DEMUIN (V.25.a.) strong
    resistance was encountered and many casualties suffered. Here it
    was that coming round a corner of a high bank, Lieut-Col PECK. CMG.
    DSO. and his Headquarters came under direct fire from a Machine Gun
    and his piper was killed.   The Battalion Scout Officer (Lieut
    MCLENNAN) crept forward up a sunken road and shot all five of the
    crew with his revolver.
        The enemy was gradually pushed back over the Ridges leaving many
    Machine Guns and dead behind. Very little resistance was met in the
    Village of AUBERCOURT, but one Machine Gun at V.20.c.3.1. held
    up the advance for a time. This resistance was overcome by one runner
    (SUMNER) who crept around and shot the entire crew from behind.
        The advance then pushed on rapidly until again held up by heavy
    resistance from the QUARRY at V.21.c.0.2. Tank assistance was sent
    for and obtained and this position overcome. This Quarry was a
    Regimental Headquarters and the Commander and his entire staff was
    captured.
        The GREEN LINE was then occupied on time without further
    resistance.

6. The 13th Cdn.Inf.Battalion. (ROYAL HIGHLANDERS OF CANADA)
    attacking in the CENTRE got away on time. Considerable fighting
    occurred in HANGARD WOOD WEST, but this was overcome with the
    assistance of a Tank. There was considerable wire here. HANGARD WOOD
    WEST was encircled by the leading Companies and 'Mopped up' by the
    rear Company with the assistance of two Tanks. Enemy snipers caused
    a considerable number of casualties here.

1st Canadian Division's battle report

An official report, written shortly after the event, of the activities of 1st Canadian Division at Amiens.

221

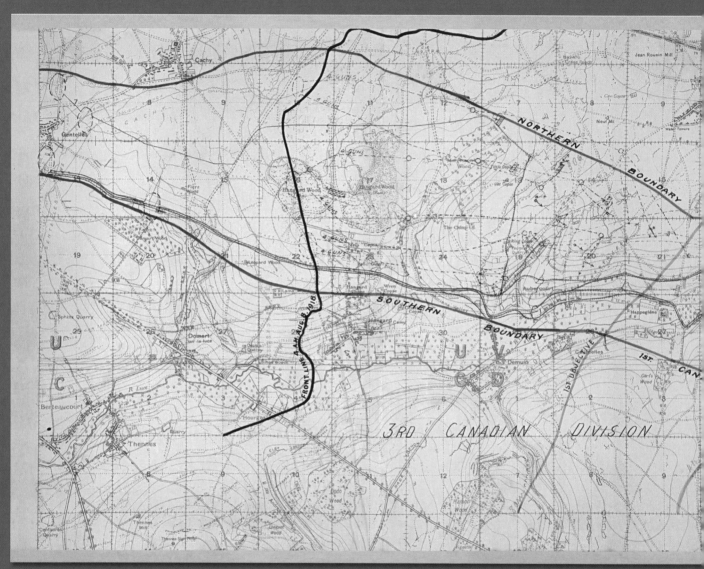

1918

1st Canadian Division's battle objectives map

A map marked with objectives to be achieved which was included in the Canadian Report.

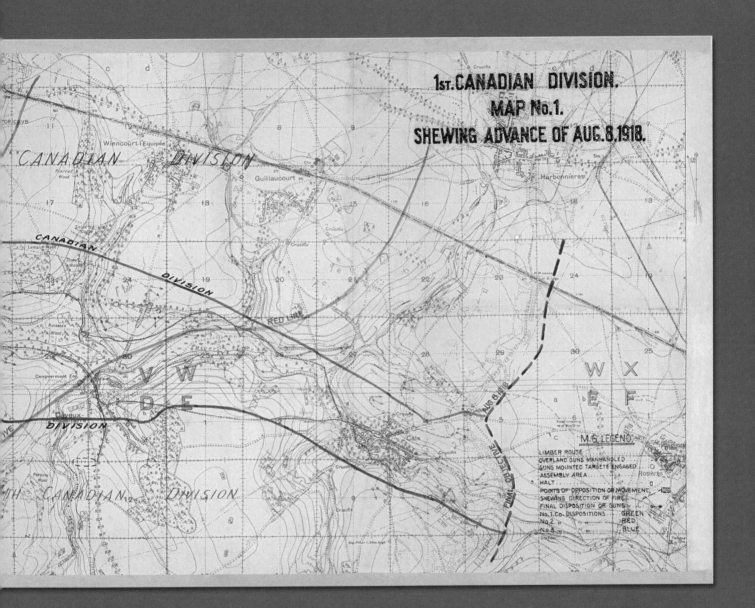

1st. CANADIAN DIVISION.
MAP No.1.
SHEWING ADVANCE OF AUG. 8, 1918.

SPECIALISTS
SIGNALLERS, POLICE, TUNNELLERS AND MEDICS

AT THE BEGINNING OF THE FIRST WORLD WAR, ARMIES WERE FAIRLY SIMPLE BODIES CONSISTING OF INFANTRY, CAVALRY, ARTILLERY, SUPPLY TROOPS, ENGINEERS AND A LIMITED NUMBER OF SPECIALISTS SUCH AS SIGNALLERS AND STAFF OFFICERS. BY NOVEMBER 1918, IN RESPONSE TO THE CHALLENGES POSED BY WARFARE ON THE WESTERN FRONT, ARMIES HAD BECOME VASTLY MORE COMPLEX AND SOPHISTICATED ORGANIZATIONS.

Units appeared on orders of battle that had been unknown before the war, concerned with new weapons such as tanks, flame-throwers and gas, while some branches of armies expanded enormously. Typical was the British Corps of Military Police, which grew from 500 men in August 1914 to 13,300 in 1918, having acquired important operational roles in addition to the enforcement of discipline. Much the same happened to the French military police. The German equivalent, the Feldgendarmerie, also expanded, with five cavalry units being assigned to policing duties to handle the increasing indiscipline in the German army in 1918.

The arrival of new weapons in the front line meant that increasing numbers of troops became specialists. In 1914, most French infantry were armed with a rifle and bayonet. By early 1917, the platoon had evolved to consist of four rifle sections, each of 12 men

LEFT: Left to right: British, French and US military policemen at Amiens, 13 May 1918.

OPPOSITE ABOVE: Men of 3rd Australian Tunnelling Company labouring beneath the ground at Hulluch, January 1918.

with two grenade launchers; two bombing sections of eight men; and a light machine-gun section armed with one gun. The platoon of 1918 was different again, with four light machine-gun sections and only two of riflemen. The British and German armies saw broadly similar changes. There was a tendency to form new weapons into separate organizations. In the German army, Minenwerfer (short range mortar) units were formed at the end of 1914. Later, independent units were attached to armies. As the light Lewis machine gun became increasingly available, the British withdrew heavier weapons from its battalions and formed them into Machine Gun Companies attached to brigades. In October 1915, the Machine Gun Corps was formed.

The demands of trench warfare brought about the formation of specialist units of miners and tunnellers. An informal group of German units had evolved to handle mining from the beginning of trench warfare, and in April 1916 Pioneer Mining Companies were formed. In February 1915, the British created similar units under the auspices of the Royal Engineers. Mining companies were also formed in French divisions. Some infantry came to specialize in patrolling and trench raiding. The Germans formed units of elite storm troops, although the British shied away from this development.

The shortcomings of the French medical service were exposed by the battles of 1914. It was equipped with insufficient and poorly designed ambulances. There were five properly equipped hospital trains, with 30 standard trains pressed into service. Brancardiers (stretcher-bearers) often had little medical training. The subsequent years saw huge improvements in the quality of French military medical care. The German medical service was 7,500 strong on the outbreak of war, and grew steadily in size. The German division of 1914 had a medical company of stretcher-bearers and a dressing station, but at the end of 1916 another was added to the establishment in addition to independent companies. Similarly, under the leadership of Sir Alfred Keogh, the strength of the British Royal Army Medical Corps grew from about 10,000 to some 170,000 during the war.

LEFT: Medical supplies, such as this French first aid box containing an assortment of bandages, were essential for the upkeep of the health and morale of front-line troops.

TRENCH WEAPONS

A variety of specialized weapons were developed for trench fighting. At the beginning of the war there was a high degree of improvization that produced fearsome clubs, sharpened entrenching tools, grenades manufactured from jam tins and spring-operated grenade throwers. Later on weapons became much more sophisticated. The British Mills Bomb (grenade) and Stokes mortar, both invented during the war, were among the most effective weapons developed for trench fighting. Some 75 million Mills Bombs were produced during the war.

ABOVE: A British fatigue party fuse Stokes mortar bombs, October 1917.

OPPOSITE ABOVE: A fine study of a French horse-drawn ambulance of the 52nd Infantry Division, taken in July 1915 at Sacy (Marne).

The increasing sophistication of artillery tactics depended to a large degree on specialists. Ernest Gold, a brilliant British meteorologist, was a pioneer in the field of providing information on atmospheric conditions, his staff of three eventually expanding to 120. All armies used highly skilled sound rangers and flash spotters, who used acoustic methods and visual observation to determine the whereabouts of enemy guns. Reconnaissance aircraft "spotted" the fall of shot for the artillery, radioing back data that allowed gunners to adjust the range.

Battlefield communications were primitive at the beginning of the war, but the semaphore flags, homing pigeons and field telephones were increasingly supplemented by wireless (radio) as the war went on. This was reflected in the growth of communication specialists – the German signal service increased from 6,300 to 190,000 men during the course of the war. The 50 wireless sets used by the French army in 1914 had grown in number to 30,000 by 1918.

Many other specialist troops, such as logisticians, staff officers and veterinarians, could also be mentioned as essential parts of the armies of the Western Front. The backbone continued to be the infantryman, but increasingly the Tommy, Poilu and Landser (the ordinary German soldier) was supported by a bewildering array of arms and services.

RIGHT: A member of the French Carrier Pigeon Service plus bird, June 1918.

BELOW LEFT: Casualties were given wound labels once they entered the medical system. This one is German.

BELOW RIGHT: A German helmet that belonged to Alphonse Bauer, first aid officer of the 75th Infantry Regiment.

ALLIES ON THE ADVANCE

THE DRIVE TO THE HINDENBURG LINE

COMING SO QUICKLY AFTER THE FAILURE OF THE GERMAN OFFENSIVE ON THE MARNE AND THE ALLIED COUNTER-OFFENSIVE, AMIENS CAME AS A TREMENDOUS BLOW TO GERMAN MORALE AT THE TOP AND BOTTOM OF THE ARMY. VICTORY WAS NOW CLEARLY IMPOSSIBLE, BUT THE GERMAN HIGH COMMAND BELIEVED THAT IF A STUBBORN RETREAT COULD INFLICT HEAVY LOSSES ON THE ALLIES, THE GERMANS MIGHT END THE WAR ON MODERATE TERMS.

1918

ALBERT RECAPTURED

The small town of Albert was, for the BEF, the gateway to the Somme. The most famous landmark was the gilded statue of the Virgin and Child on the basilica, which was hit by a shell and leaned out over the streets. Superstitions soon attached to the Golden Virgin, including that the war would only end when the statue fell. Albert was captured by the Germans on 26 March 1918 and was retaken by the British 18th Division on 22–23 August 1918. The statue actually fell in April 1918.

OPPOSITE: The advance to victory: New Zealand and British infantry, Mark V tanks and captured guns following following the capture of Grevillers, 25 August 1918.

ABOVE LEFT: Albert in ruins. This key town was recaptured by the BEF during the Hundred Days.

ABOVE RIGHT: An aerial reconnaissance photograph of the Hindenburg Line taken from 2,438 m (8,000 ft). Note trenches, mine craters and shellholes.

They were wrong; the strategic initiative had passed to the Allies, and under Foch's strategic direction, they made the most of it.

The key to their success lay in fighting a series of limited operations, breaking off the battle when the attack began to lose momentum. A fresh attack (or attacks) would then be mounted on a different part of the front. The defenders were thus placed at full stretch, unable to initiate, constantly struggling to fend off defeat. The Allied infantry did not advance too far away from the safety of their artillery support, or outrun their lines of supply. This was very different from the German approach in the spring offensives (see pages 100–103), and also a distinct improvement on some of their own fumbling efforts earlier in the war.

The next phase of the Allied offensive began in the third week of August. In the previous week or so, reinforcements – including guns – were moved north from the forces at Amiens to Byng's British Third Army around the Somme area. It is noteworthy how quickly this could now be done, in comparison to the problems of moving troops and guns from Messines to Ypres in June–July of 1917. The Canadian Corps moved up to join First Army to the north of Arras. Beginning on 20 August, Fayolle's French Army Group struck heavy blows against the southern face of the German-held Montdidier-Amiens salient. French Tenth Army, under the ever aggressive Mangin, pushed the Germans back some 13 km (8 miles) between the rivers Oise and Aisne.

British Third Army attacked on 21 August over the all-too-familiar battlefield of the 1916 Somme offensive. On the following day, Rawlinson's Fourth Army came into action on Byng's right flank, and on 26 August part of Horne's First Army attacked on Third Army's left, extending the battlefront to some 65 km (40 miles). This too was a battle in an area well known to British veterans, around Arras. On the Somme, 18th (Eastern) Division had the bizarre experience of capturing Trônes Wood for the second time, having first attacked and taken this objective in July 1916. Now, there were very different conditions on the battlefield. With superiority in the air, in artillery support and logistics, using sophisticated all-arms tactics, with experienced and confident staff officers and commanders, and up against a visibly weakening enemy, the BEF was achieving the success that had eluded it.

Haig in the Hundred Days

Opinion is divided about how much credit Douglas Haig can claim for the British Empire's victories in 1918. Some see him as an "accidental victor", who was largely irrelevant to the BEF's successes in 1918, the important decisions being taken by Foch and by Haig's subordinates at army and corps level. A fairer view is that Haig played a crucial role in improving the BEF between the Somme and the Battle of Amiens, and in the Hundred Days steered his generals to victory and guided and advised Foch.

The strain proved too great for the Germans to bear and on the night of 26–27 August they retreated to the Hindenburg Line. In doing so they gave up the ground they had captured in the German Spring Offensive. For the Germans, the news grew ever worse. French First and Third Armies on the right of the BEF attacked on 27–29 August and captured the key town of Noyon. By 1 September, the Australians held both Mont St-Quentin and the city of Péronne, putting paid to any hope the Germans had of holding the line of the River Somme. On First Army's front on 2 September, the Canadians smashed through the formidable Drocourt-Quéant Switch Line near Arras and triggered another German withdrawal. Fayolle's French Army Group capitalized on the BEF's successes by carrying out operations against the retreating Germans.

South of Ypres, the Germans were forced out of another piece of territory captured at a huge cost in lives in the spring. The withdrawals to the Hindenburg Line left the German troops defending the salient captured during the Battle of the Lys uncomfortably exposed. British Fifth Army, now commanded by Birdwood, had commenced operations on 23 August, keeping up the pressure on the Germans. By 6 September, accepting the inevitable, the defenders on the Lys, too, fell back.

The BEF followed the retreating Germans, fighting the battles of Havrincourt and Epéhy between 12 and 26 September as divisions sought to reach good positions from which to attack the main German positions on the Hindenburg Line itself. The achievements since Amiens were real, but they were costly.

The BEF had pushed forward some 40 km (25 miles) along a front of 65 km (40 miles) at a cost of 180,000 casualties. And perhaps the worst was still to come. Their next objective was the Hindenburg Line.

OPPOSITE ABOVE: Under the cover of a creeping barrage and smoke, Australian infantry advance towards German Hindenburg Line positions on 18 September 1918.

OPPOSITE BELOW: Field Marshal Sir Douglas Haig reviews Canadian troops on 31 August 1918, prior to their succesful assault on the Drocourt-Quéant switch Line.

ABOVE: During the Battle of Albert Captain B. H. Geary, 1st East Surreys, is brought in by German prisoners after being wounded. He had won the VC in 1915.

THE USA ENTERS THE WAR

THE RISE OF A GLOBAL POWER

AT THE BEGINNING OF THE FIRST WORLD WAR, THE UNITED STATES OF AMERICA WAS A SLEEPING GIANT. ALTHOUGH IT HAD OVERTAKEN BRITAIN AS AN ECONOMIC POWERHOUSE, AND ACQUIRED AN INFORMAL EMPIRE IN PLACES SUCH AS THE PHILIPPINES, THE UNITED STATES WAS NOT YET TRULY A GREAT POWER.

1914
1917

ABOVE: The American War Cabinet in Washington, 9 January 1918.   OPPOSITE: President Wilson's appeal for troops in the spring of 1917.

While the US Navy was impressive, the country's army was tiny. Above all, the United States had no allies: isolationism was king. On 19 August 1914, President Woodrow Wilson declared a policy of strict neutrality. While many of the East Coast élite, including Wilson himself, were sympathetic to the Allies, there were some 10 million first- and second-generation German-Americans to be considered.

The British Royal Navy effectively excluded Germany from trading with the United States, but American companies made much money by manufacturing war material and other goods for Britain and France – $3.2 billion in 1916. Banks in the United States were also critical in financing the Allied war effort; without American loans and credit the

British would have had trouble continuing the war into 1917.

The depredations of German U-Boats heightened US-German tensions in 1915 as American ships were sunk and American citizens died. From 1915, the "Preparedness Movement", which sought to build up American military power, conducted a propaganda campaign that helped to make the idea of entering the war less unthinkable. Although the American government carried out some cautious preliminary steps such as creating a Council of National Defense, Wilson, a genuine idealist, sought to broker a peace between the belligerents. He was re-elected in 1916 on a neutrality platform and as late as 22 January 1917 called for "peace without victory". However, the German resumption

of unrestricted submarine warfare in February that year made war inevitable.

When it declared war on Germany on 6 April 1917, the United States tried to distance itself from the Allies by calling itself an "Associated Power". American entrance into the war made little immediate difference in terms of boots on the ground, as the army (raised by "Selective Service", i.e. non-universal conscription) had to be prepared for combat. Only in September 1918 did it begin to play a major role on the Western Front, but the US Navy was a useful addition to the Allied fleets. Most importantly, the boost to flagging British and French morale was huge. Extensive industrial mobilization made also a significant impact. Seventeen thousand tons of shipping was produced each month in 1914, for instance, but this grew to 250,000 tons by 1918.

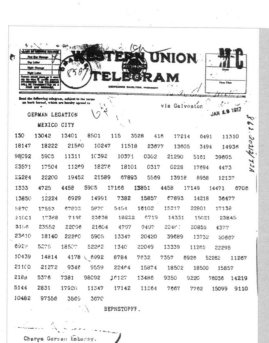

THE ZIMMERMANN TELEGRAM

On 17 January 1917 Arthur Zimmermann, the German Foreign Minister, cabled to the German ambassador in Washington that he should invite Mexico to join Germany in an aggressive alliance. The Mexicans would retake American territories lost in the Mexican War of the 1840s, such as Texas, and the Japanese might also come on board. The US State Department and the British intercepted the message, and the Wilson Administration made it public on 3 March. Coming just after the German resumption of unrestricted attacks on shipping by U-Boats, the Zimmermann Telegram helped shift the national mood in favour of war with the Kaiser.

At home, some groups, such as German-Americans and socialists, had a hard time. In all, some 1,600 opponents of the war, from various backgrounds, were jailed. The enthusiasm for war in 1917–18 turned in many cases to bitter disillusionment, with many after 1918 believing that America had somehow been cheated of the fruits of victory. In fact, the United States was one of the major beneficiaries of the war. Economically, it had received a huge boost, while rivals such as Britain had declined. And although it was temporarily to retreat back into isolationism in the 1920s, the First World War marked the arrival of the United States as a global power.

OPPOSITE: US Marines in France, testing their respirators, 1918.

ABOVE: A fleet of US Navy ships sailing past the Statue of Liberty, 1 April 1918.

RIGHT: A US Navy recruitment poster, circa 1917.

U.S. NAVY

Help Your Country!

ENLIST IN THE NAVY
Navy Recruiting Station

THE AMERICAN OFFENSIVES

SAINT-MIHIEL AND MEUSE ARGONNE

THE ARRIVAL OF THE AMERICAN EXPEDITIONARY FORCE (AEF) IN FRANCE
BROUGHT A POWERFUL ACCRETION OF STRENGTH TO THE ALLIES.
AMERICAN DIVISIONS WERE ROUGHLY DOUBLE THE SIZE OF COMPARABLE
BRITISH AND FRENCH FORMATIONS, AND THE NUMBERS OF "DOUGHBOYS"
(AS THE ORDINARY US SOLDIER WAS NICKNAMED) SEEMED LIMITLESS.

1918

ABOVE: In a town captured by the Americans near
St-Mihiel, US troops give a new name to a street named
after Hindenburg – "Wilson USA!"

OPPOSITE ABOVE: A US 14-inch railway mounted gun
fires during the Argonne offensive, 1918.

OPPOSITE BELOW: Bernard Law Montgomery (left) as a
staff officer in the First World War. Charles de Gaulle
(right) was captured in March 1916 and remained a
German prisoner until the end of the war.

Having gained control of American divisions in order to train them and to give them combat experience, the British and French were reluctant to give them up. Throughout 1918, Pershing, the AEF commander, strove to create an American operational command fully independent of his Allies. US First Army became operational on 29 August 1918. The battlefield debut of the new force was to be an offensive to reduce the Saint-Mihiel salient.

However, the rapid tempo of events elsewhere on the Western Front placed this plan in jeopardy. The success of the BEF convinced Foch that Haig's concept of large-scale concentric offensives should be adopted. Rather than attacking Saint-Mihiel, Pershing should attack northwestwards through the Argonne forest towards Sedan and Mézières. This would threaten major railways that

COMMAND APPRENTICESHIPS

Many high-ranking officers of the Second World War served their military apprenticeship on the Western Front: Charles de Gaulle was wounded and captured at Verdun in 1916; Bernard Montgomery was wounded in 1914 but went on to be a staff officer; while in the German army Erwin Rommel fought on the Western Front and in Italy. The most senior American soldier of the Second World War had a key role in planning the 1918 Meuse-Argonne battle: George C. Marshall, then a colonel, went on to become President Roosevelt's principal military advisor.

were critical to German lines of supply. Foch believed that this attack could be decisive. The clash of two different plans resulted in an uneasy compromise. The Americans would attack Saint-Mihiel, but would then redeploy to attack in the Meuse-Argonne area.

The Saint-Mihiel offensive began on 12 September 1918. The French II Colonial Corps, under the command of General Blondlat, was deployed alongside three American Corps. Although the defensive position was strong, the Allies achieved surprise, and the Germans were in the process of evacuating this bulge in the Allied line as the attack went in. The result was less a formal assault than the following up of a withdrawing force. Poor American staff

work led to disorder among the advancing troops. Nonetheless, the operation was a success, with Saint-Mihiel being captured by French troops on 13 September. With 16,000 prisoners and 450 guns falling into American hands, Saint-Mihiel gave a timely boost to US morale. Curiously, at one stage two future American generals of the Second World War met during the battle, when Lieutenant Colonel George S. Patton of the Tank Corps encountered Brigadier General Douglas MacArthur of 42nd (Rainbow) Division.

Some Americans believed that an opportunity had been missed by not capitalizing on St-Mihiel, but the "Doughboys" headed for a new battlefield in the Argonne. To move an army 95 km (60 miles) on three minor

roads, get it into position and launch an attack in less than two weeks was a huge logistic challenge. Late on 25 September, the artillery bombardment commenced. The first phase of Foch's Grand Offensive was on an appropriately grand scale. Two French Armies, the Second (Hirschner) and Fourth (Gouraud) plus I, III and V US Corps commanded by Hunter Liggett, Robert L. Bullard and George H. Cameron respectively, were supported by 700 tanks and 400 guns. At 05:30 on 26 September, the tanks and infantry attacked. On the first day the French and Americans advanced about 5 km (3 miles). It was a hard, grinding slog. The Germans had the advantage of deep belts of defences – trenches, barbed wire, strong-points, machine-gun posts – based

OPPOSITE: A Renault tank of US First Tank Brigade at Varennes-en-Argonne, 1918.

FAR RIGHT: US troops with a 37mm gun fitted with telescopic sight in firing position during a training session.

RIGHT: A shoulder badge from a uniform worn by a soldier of US 1st Infantry Division.

BELOW RIGHT: Black American stevedores attached to 23rd Engineers enjoy a singsong, 1918.

on no less than four separate positions. Up against the inexperienced Americans, the defenders caused heavy casualties even as the advance continued. Three regiments of black American troops served alongside the French. They treated the African-Americans much like their own colonial divisions, and the black troops did well, although like their white American counterparts, they lost heavily in the process.

Pershing had insisted on training for open warfare and treating the rifle-armed infantryman as the most important part of the tactical jigsaw. He disdained the hard-won lessons of the French and British armies, and the AEF paid the price in heavy casualties and slow progress. This was an army reminiscent of the British on the Somme in 1916, still learning how to fight a modern battle. Co-operation between the artillery and infantry was often poor and the Americans faced considerable logistical difficulties compounded by bad weather. Three days after the initial attack, with the battered infantry in poor shape, the offensive had clearly run out of steam. "Those Americans will lose us our chance of a big victory before winter," complained Georges Clemenceau, the French Premier. His criticism was unjust: although the Franco-American battle was not as successful as the other phases of Foch's offensive, it contributed to the overall effort by tying down German troops and grinding away their strength. Foch's comment was fairer: the Americans "are learning now, rapidly".

GERMAN VIEWS OF THE US ARMY

Many Germans were dismissive of the ability of American forces in the Meuse-Argonne battle. One report said: "The American Infantry is very unskilful in the attack. It attacks in thick columns, in numerous waves echeloned in depth, preceded by tanks. This sort of attack offers excellent objectives for the fire of our artillery infantry and machine guns." However, the number of US troops was impressive. In the summer of 1918, a German officer, Rudolf Binding, had noted "The American Army is there – a million strong. That is too much."

THE GRAND OFFENSIVE

BREAKING THE HINDENBURG LINE

ONE CRITICAL DIFFERENCE BETWEEN THE "HUNDRED DAYS" (AUGUST–
NOVEMBER 1918) AND EARLIER ALLIED OFFENSIVES WAS THE
ROLE OF CO-ORDINATOR PLAYED BY FERDINAND FOCH AS ALLIED
GENERALISSIMO. BY ENSURING THAT THE EFFORTS OF THE ALLIED
ARMIES MESHED INTO AN OVERALL PLAN, HE AVOIDED THE SITUATION
THAT HAD OCCURRED DURING THE SOMME IN 1916, WHEN THE
BRITISH AND FRENCH HAD OFTEN APPEARED TO BE FIGHTING SEPARATE
BATTLES SIDE BY SIDE RATHER THAN A TRULY COMBINED OFFENSIVE.

1918

NORTH STAFFORDSHIRE REGIMENT

Badge of the North Staffordshire Regiment, featuring the Staffordshire knot.

46TH DIVISION

The 46th (North Midland) Division was a Territorial formation comprised of battalions of regiments recruited from central England. Its achievement on 29 September 1918, under the command of Major-General G. F. Boyd, is testimony both to the high standards of even an average British division by that stage of the war and the impressive support of the BEF's artillery. Captain A. H. Charlton, a pre-war farmer, led the party that seized the Riqueval Bridge, the only bridge in that sector across the St-Quentin Canal. This was perhaps the pinnacle of the achievements of the British citizen army in the war.

Foch's relationship with Douglas Haig, who commanded the principal Allied strike force, was crucial. They did not always see eye to eye, but the partnership proved highly effective. This was demonstrated by the plan for the Grand Offensive launched at the end of September 1918. While Pétain was pessimistic, judging that the fighting would continue into 1919, Haig believed that a decisive victory was possible by the end of the year. He successfully urged Foch to extend the original scope of the attack.

Foch's motto was "Tout le monde à la bataille!"("Everybody into battle!"). He unleashed a series of blows up and down the German positions over a four-day period. First to act were to be the Franco-American forces that attacked on 26 September, in the Meuse-Argonne area (see pages 236–239). Next in the sequence came two British Armies, Horne's First and Byng's Third, kicking off their offensive towards Cambrai on 27 September. This was to be followed on the 28 September by a major attack at Ypres by French, Belgian and British divisions under King Albert of the Belgians, who had the French General Jean-Marie Degoutte as his chief-of-staff. The climactic push would be made on 29 September by Rawlinson's British Fourth and Debeney's French First

Armies. For the first time, Foch was able to wield the full force of Allied combat power on the Western Front.

As we have seen, Foch expected much of the Meuse-Argonne offensive, but the results were a little disappointing. The attack on the following day was much more significant. British First Army, with Currie's Canadian Corps in the lead, tackled the formidable defences of the Canal du Nord (the canal connecting the Oise River and the canal Dunkirk-Scheldt). Under the cover of a barrage described by the infantry as "very good", the Canadians assaulted on a narrow front and then spread out like the fingers of a hand. Third Army also penetrated the German defences, although not as deeply as the Canadians, and by the end of the day Byng and Horne had between them advanced

10 km (6 miles) on a frontage of 19 km (12 miles). The 27 September attack was, as one historian has commented, "Currie's operational masterpiece".

Such were the changed conditions of battle that around Ypres on 28 September, King Albert's Army Group attacked right across the old Passchendaele battlefield and broke out of the Salient altogether. Plumer's British Second Army advanced up to 10 km (6 miles), a distance that would have been

OPPOSITE: Against the background of a damaged bridge, a British 18 pounder gun team moves up during the Battle of the Canal du Nord, 27 September 1918.

ABOVE: King George V crosses Riqueval Bridge. The capture of the bridge was a crucial element in 46th Division's victory on 29 September 1918.

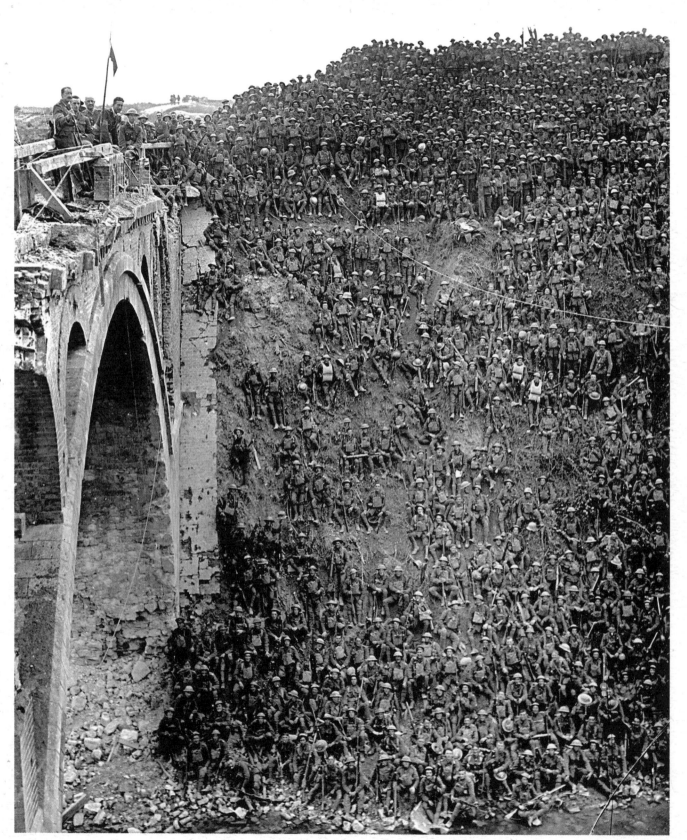

1918

unthinkable 12 months earlier, and on the next day it recaptured Messines Ridge. After an advance of about 14 km (9 miles), logistic chaos brought the French and Belgian forces to a halt; food was dropped to forward troops by air, probably the first time in history this had been done. At last the deadlock in Flanders was at an end.

The most difficult task in the Grand Offensive, carrying the Hindenburg Line in the St-Quentin sector, had been assigned to Rawlinson's Fourth Army. It was faced with the problem of crossing a wide strip of defences, including the St-Quentin Canal, which was up to 11 m (35 ft) wide and 15–20 m (50–60 ft) deep. The best going was at Bellicourt, where the canal ran through a tunnel, but it was very heavily defended. Preceded by a two-day bombardment, the Australian Corps (reinforced by two American divisions) attacked here but, faced with stiff opposition, it made slow progress. The US 27th and 30th Divisions fought

OPPOSITE: Brigadier General J. C. Campbell VC addresses his victorious 137 Brigade, 46th Division, from the newly captured Riqueval Bridge.

ABOVE TOP: German troops resignedly marching into captivity at the hands of the French at Vauxaillon, Department of the Aisne, September 1918.

ABOVE: Part of a German trench near Cologne Farm, which was part of the formidable Hindenburg Line defences near Hargicourt, 12 km (8 miles) from St-Quentin.

bravely but revealed their inexperience and tactical naivety. The major break-though came a little further south at Bellenglise on the front of Lieutenant General Sir Walter Braithwaite's British IX Corps. Here, a surprise bombardment was followed by 46th (North Midland) Division attacking straight across the canal. No fewer than 216 heavy guns were concentrated on an attack frontage of only 2,750 m (3,000 yds). The infantry crossed the canal using lifebelts from Channel steamers, or hopped across the rubble blown into the watercourse, or simply used a bridge captured in the early stages of the battle. By nightfall, these Staffordshire Territorials could boast, in the proud words of their divisional history of "Breaking the Hindenburg Line".

LEFT: Mark V tanks of 8th Tank battalion and men of 5th Australian Division with German Prisoners of War, September 1918. The tanks are carrying "Cribs", designed to help them cross the Hindenburg Line defences.

ABOVE: A German prisoner taken in the Battle of the St-Quentin Canal.

THE FINAL BATTLES

VICTORY IN SIGHT

WITH THE BREAKING OF THE HINDENBURG LINE, THE GERMAN ARMY'S
LAST REALISTIC HOPE OF HALTING THE ALLIES VANISHED. AT A MEETING
OF THE HIGH COMMAND ON 1 OCTOBER 1918, LUDENDORFF STATED
THAT GERMANY FACED "AN UNAVOIDABLE AND CONCLUSIVE DEFEAT".

1918

Events moved rapidly; in Berlin, the Chancellor resigned and was replaced on 3 October by Prince Max of Baden. He was a man of liberal views who presented a very different public face of the German government. Ludendorff had cynically suggested that opposition politicians should be given responsibility in government, blaming them – utterly unfairly – for the defeat: "They should make the peace that must now be made. They made their bed, now they must lie in it!"

Meanwhile, the relentless Allied pressure continued on the Western Front. French First Army took St-Quentin on 2 October, and progress was made early in the month by Fifth and Tenth Armies in the Soissons area, and Gourard's Fourth Army on the flank of the Americans. Foch, however, was displeased with the slow rate of advance compared to the British. The Allied Generalissimo was ungenerous to his own countrymen. Having born the main burden of the fighting on the Western Front for

so much of the war, the French Army was almost played out.

The BEF was in better shape. By this stage its divisions consisted of a mixture of wary veterans and young conscripts, and as the ordinary officers and soldiers began to realize that the end of the war was at last in sight, there was a perceptible rise in morale.

ABOVE: Cambrai was liberated by the Canadians in October 1918. In this picture the buildings of the city are still burning.

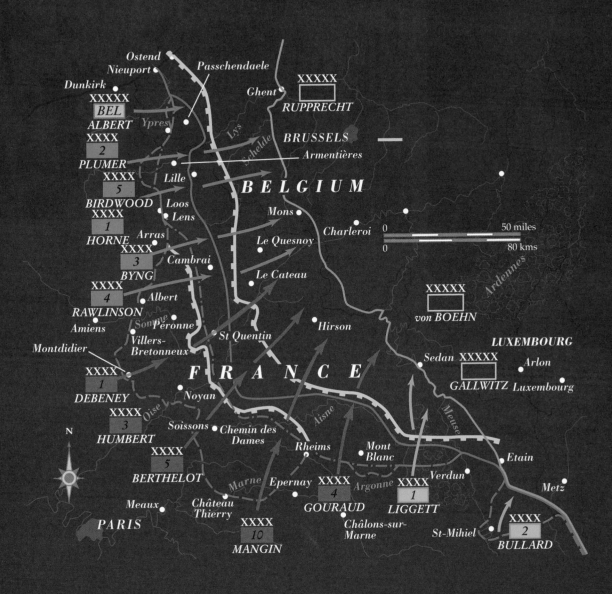

Ostend
Nieuport
Dunkirk
XXXXX
BEL
ALBERT
Ypres
XXXX
2
PLUMER
XXXX
5
BIRDWOOD
Lille
Loos
Lens
XXXX
1
HORNE
Arras
XXXX
3
BYNG
Cambrai
XXXX
4
RAWLINSON
Albert
Amiens
Somme
Peronne
Montdidier
Villers-
Bretonneux
St Quentin
XXXX
1
DEBENEY
Noyan
XXXX
3
HUMBERT
Oise
Soissons
Chemin des
Dames
XXXX
5
BERTHELOT
Marne
Château
Thierry
Meaux
PARIS
Epernay
XXXX
10
MANGIN

Passchendaele
Ghent
XXXXX
RUPPRECHT
BRUSSELS
Armentières
Lys
Schelde
BELGIUM
Mons
Charleroi
Le Quesnoy
Le Cateau
Hirson
FRANCE

Rheims
XXXX
4
GOURAUD
Châlons-sur-
Marne
Aisne
Argonne
Mont
Blanc

Sedan
XXXXX
GALLWITZ
Arlon
Luxembourg
LUXEMBOURG

XXXXX
von **BOEHN**
Ardennes

Verdun
XXXX
1
LIGGETT
St-Mihiel
Etain
Metz
Meuse
XXXX
2
BULLARD

N

0   50 miles
0   80 kms

THE FINAL BATTLES: 1918

- - - - Farthest German
advance, 17 July

━━━ German defence line

- · - · - Front line, 25 September

━━━ Front line, 15 October

━━━ Armistice line, 11 November

THE RETURN TO MONS

On the morning of 11 November 1918, 3rd Canadian Division entered Mons, after encountering stiff resistance from German machine gunners and snipers. It was a sober coincidence that the forces of the British Empire fought one of their last Western Front actions in the town where the original BEF had its baptism of fire in August 1914. In later years, the Canadian Corps Commander Sir Arthur Currie was unjustly criticized for causing unnecessary Canadian deaths by ordering the attack on Mons so close to the end of the war.

PRESIDENT WILSON AND THE "FOURTEEN POINTS"

Woodrow Wilson was elected US president in 1912 and re-elected for a second four-year term in 1916. He proposed his "Fourteen Points" in January 1918. These included an end to secret diplomacy, self-determination for nations and a post-war League of Nations to keep the peace. These idealistic principles for ending the war and organizing international relations were unrealistic (and opposed by Britain and France) but gave Wilson huge moral authority at the Paris Peace Conference. However, the 1919 Treaty of Versailles only partially reflected the Fourteen Points. Isolationist opposition prevented the USA from joining his cherished League of Nations.

Fourth Army cleared the Beaurevoir Line to the rear of the main Hindenburg positions on 4 October. The Germans were forced to abandon Cambrai on 8–9 October, regrouping on the River Selle. First, Third and Fourth Armies followed up, while in the Lens area, Fifth Army (Birdwood) was able to push forward about 16 km (10 miles) as the defenders retreated. Having untangled their logistic knot, King Albert's Army Group began to advance in Flanders on 14 October, with the ever-reliable Plumer's British Second Army in the lead. Six days later, Albert's troops reached the River Lys, where there was another operational pause, before the Army Group advanced again on 28 October.

To the south, the French and Americans continued the Meuse-Argonne offensive. They pushed forward, but at heavy cost, and Clemenceau and Foch grew angry and frustrated at Pershing's handling of the battle. In late October, the Americans reorganized and on 1 November the US First and French Fourth Armies attacked and made substantial

progress. By that stage, British Fourth Army, which included two American divisions, had already defeated the Germans in the Battle of the Selle (17–25 October), which resulted in the return of the BEF to Le Cateau (see pages 24–27) for the first time since August 1914. In October, the BEF advanced about 32 km (20 miles) and suffered 120,000 casualties.

The Germans desperately sought a way out of the war before they were overtaken by military catastrophe. Prince Max appealed to the US President, Woodrow Wilson, on 4 October to end the war on the basis of the Fourteen Points, and this was followed by the transformation – at least in theory – of Germany into a constitutional monarchy.

TOP LEFT: Prince Max of Baden, photographed before the First World War. He was German Chancellor for little over a month in October-November 1918.

CENTRE LEFT: Woodrow Wilson, the President of the United States, speaking from a podium in 1917.

TOP RIGHT: Canadian troops in the streets of Mons in 1918.

General Wilhelm Groener replaced Ludendorff in late October. While some elements of the German Army continued to fight effectively, if unavailingly, others in effect went on strike, and ominous signs of revolution appeared on the home front. Part of the German Navy mutinied on 29 October when ordered to sea. Gradually Germany's allies – Austria-Hungary, Turkey and Bulgaria – collapsed in defeat as the Allies advanced in Italy, the Middle East and the Balkans.

Foch launched another major offensive on 4 November. Haig's First, Third and Fourth Armies won a major victory on the line of the Sambre and French First Army captured Guise, while in the Argonne, the Germans finally conceded defeat and withdrew. French Fourth Army and the Americans pursued, US forces reaching outskirts of the key city of Sedan on the Meuse by 7 November. Across the entire front the Allies moved forward. In a throwback to an older form of war, the New Zealanders captured Le Quesnoy, a walled town, using scaling ladders. With his armies

beaten, and Germany sliding into revolution, the Kaiser abdicated on 9 November, the same day as Prince Max resigned in favour of a moderate Social Democrat. Two days later, at 11 a.m., an armistice between Germany and the Allies came into effect. The war was over and the Allies were victorious.

TOP LEFT: The German fleet, interned at a British naval base, scuttled itself in June 1919. Here SMS *Bayern* is sinking.

ABOVE LEFT: The Allied representatives (Foch is second from the right) stand in front of the railway carriage on 11 November 1918 in which the Armistice had been signed moments before.

ABOVE RIGHT: A poster announcing the abdication of the Kaiser. This poster displays the announcement of the abdication of the Kaiser by Chancellor, Prince Max of Baden. Prince Max resigned on the same day.

RIGHT: A New Zealand "lemon squeezer" hat.

249

AFTERMATH AND LEGACY

THE SHADOW OF THE WAR

CONFLICT AND TURMOIL CONTINUED ACROSS EUROPE FOR MONTHS AFTER THE ARMISTICE. A RUMBLING GUERRILLA WAR IN IRELAND LED IN 1921 TO INDEPENDENCE FROM BRITAIN FOR ALL BUT ULSTER. REVOLUTIONARY VIOLENCE TOOK PLACE IN VARIOUS PARTS OF GERMANY, WHILE THE AUSTRO-HUNGARIAN AND OTTOMAN EMPIRES FELL APART.

ABOVE: French tanks at the Arc de Triomphe on the first post-war Bastille Day parade, 14 July 1919.

OPPOSITE: The scene as the peace treaty is signed in the Hall of Mirrors at Versailles, 28 June 1919.

In Russia, there was an increasingly brutal civil war underway as various White (anti-Communist) groups, supported by British, French and American forces, sought to reverse the result of the Bolshevik coup of November 1917. The Russian Civil War was to end in 1922 with the victory of Lenin's Bolsheviks. An attempt to export the revolution by armed force to eastern and central Europe was thwarted, however, by the victory of the Poles against the Russians in the Battle of Warsaw in 1920.

Formally, the war with Germany was ended on 28 June 1919, with the signing of the Treaty of Versailles. This stripped Germany of various territories, forced it to pay reparations of £6,600 million, restricted the size of its armed forces and obliged it to admit responsibility for the outbreak of the war. The Treaty was denounced as a harsh peace that left Germany thirsting for revenge and led inevitably to the Second World War. In reality, the terms were not as savage as those imposed by Germany on defeated Russia at Brest-Litovsk in 1918. Given the scale of the war, German's culpability for its outbreak, and the bitterness in France and Britain in 1919, the terms were not unduly

harsh. The main problem was a failure by the victorious Allies to enforce the Treaty. Versailles soon lost moral authority in the eyes of many in Britain, and steps were taken to revise the settlement in Germany's favour even before Hitler came to power in 1933. The feeling that Germany had been badly treated influenced public opinion in Britain and fed into the policy of appeasement in the 1930s. The Great Depression, which began in 1929 and helped to destroy the German Weimar Republic and contributed to the rise of the Nazi regime, was at least as important a factor as Versailles in the origins of the Second World War. The new states created in Eastern and Central Europe such as Poland and Romania tended to move towards authoritarian rule, although in Czechoslovakia democracy survived until destroyed by Hitler in 1939.

Although Britain's Empire reached its greatest size after the war, British power had been damaged. No longer would the dominions (Canada, Australia, New Zealand and South Africa) automatically support Britain, and economic weakness was to undermine the British military. Similarly, France's position in Europe was weaker in 1919 than it had

ADOLF HITLER
(1889–1945)

The First World War was the formative event in the life of Adolf Hitler. Although an Austrian citizen, he volunteered for the German Army in 1914. Hitler rose to the rank of Lance Corporal and served on the Western Front until 1918, part of that time opposite the British in the Fromelles sector. He had a dangerous job as a runner, delivering messages, and was wounded and gassed. Part of Hitler's post-war appeal to the electorate as a politician was that he had fought in the war as an ordinary soldier.

been in 1914. It no longer had an alliance with Russia, and understandings with the newly emerged states on Germany's eastern flank such as Poland were a poor substitute. Britain and the USA, meanwhile, proved fickle friends. The wartime alliance rapidly unravelled, and when in 1923 the French did try to enforce the terms of Versailles by occupying the Ruhr, London and Washington did not support them. The USA retreated into isolation, its people disillusioned by the experience of breaching its long-held tradition of distancing itself from European power politics.

After 1918, the French abandoned the costly cult of the offensive, and instead adopted a defensive mentality epitomized by the construction of the Maginot Line, an updated version of the Verdun defences of 1916, along the French-German border. The German Blitzkrieg of 1940 apparently showed the folly of this idea, but for the most part the military methods so painfully developed during 1914–18 proved to be the foundations of modern warfare, improved upon but not substantially changed in the Second World War and subsequent conflicts. After the Armistice, people across Europe struggled to come to terms with the vast loss of life. There were 1 million from the British Empire dead; 1,400,000 French; 1,800,000 Germans and 115,000 Americans. In addition there were those badly wounded in body, mind or both; over three-quarters of a million in France alone. People in the victor states began to question the belief that war was a sensible or moral way of settling international disputes. Instead, pacifism grew in influence, alongside – in Britain and the USA at least – the erroneous idea that

the war had been "futile". Everywhere the attitude was "never again". Germany was the exception to this. Western Front veteran Hitler channelled the thirst for revenge, the belief that the German army had not been defeated in 1918, but rather had been betrayed, and in 1939 once again took the German nation – and hence Europe, and eventually the world – to war.

THE SHORT TWENTIETH CENTURY

The years 1914–1991 can be seen as one period bounded by the beginning of the First World War and the end of the Cold War. The year 1918 saw the collapse of the old monarchical regimes and the rise of the dictators that led to the Second World War. With Germany defeated, the USSR fell out with Britain and America, its erstwhile allies against Hitler, and a 50-year Cold War began. The collapse of the USSR and the return to a multi-polar world brought this "Short Twentieth Century" to an end.

LEFT: On 11 November 1989 a man smashes away at the Berlin Wall, a symbol of the Cold War that was coming to an end.

OPPOSITE ABOVE: At a cemetery in Abbeville members of the Women's Army Auxiliary Corps tend to the graves of British soldiers in 1918.

OPPOSITE BELOW: The lot of all too many soldiers was to be fitted with prosthetic limbs such as these.

RIGHT: The huge "Tyne Cot" Commonwealth War Graves Commission cemetery on Passchendaele ridge, photographed 79 years after the battle.

INDEX

(page numbers in *italic* refer to photographs
and captions; those in **bold** refer to maps)

CREDITS

The majority of photographs reproduced in the book have been taken from the collection of the Photograph Archive of the Imperial War Museums, London.

The Museum's reference numbers for each of the photographs are listed below.

Location key: t = top, b = bottom, c = centre, l = left and r = right

2 (Q 11405), 4 (CO 1178), 6 (Q 91840) l, (Q 81831) r, 8 (Q 41435) t, 10 Q 81730, 11 (Q 67397) t, (Q 53446) b, 12 (Q 81730) tl, (Q 65860) tr, (HU 1777) bl, 14-15 (PST 2765), 18 (Q 45995), 19 (Q 70232) t, (Q 53625) b, 21 (Q 53271) t, (Q 53422) c, (Q 81806) b, 24 (Q 53337), 25 (Q 70071) t, (Q 28858) b, 26 Exhibits and Firearms collection (t & bc), (Q 70451) l, (Q 80449) r, 27 (Q 70054) t, (Q 60698) b, 28 (HU 57678) t, 29 (Q 23726) tl, (Q 45327) tr, (Q 51503) bl, 31 (Q 51503) tl, (Q 65476) bl, (Q 51511) br, 36 (Q 57214), 37 (Q 51506) t, (Q 54992) bottom, 38 Exhibits and Firearms collection (t), (Q 60764) b, 39 (Q 56210) t, (Q 70075), 40-41 (99/83/1), 43 (Q 15562) b, 46 (Q 69023) b, 47 (UNI 12450) tl, 49 (Q 18724) r, 50 (Q 80704), 51 (Q 53484) t, (Q 18062) b, 52 (Q 69482), 53 (Q 49750) t, (Q 49241) b, 54 (Q 49217), 55 (Q 53517) t, 57 (Q 55085) b, 59 (Q 114867) b, 63 (Q 53304) tl, 63 (Q 23726) cr, 64 (Q 30011), 65 (HO 77) l, (Q 108846) tr, (EPH 5186) br, 66 (Q 48222) t, Q 70208 (br), 69 (HU 63277) c, 70 (Q 49224) t, (Q 29901) b, 71 (Q 17390) r, 72 (Q 53286), 73 (Q 56658) l, (Q 69626) r, 74 (Q 485), 75 (HU 55323) l, (Q 80726) r, 76 (Q 24061), 77 (Q 13732) t, (ART 2268) tr, (HU 89482) br, 78 (Q 13947) t, (Q 32800) b, 79 (69/53/1-17), 81 (Q 23740) t, 84-85 (69/53/11-17), 86 (Q 23744), 88 (23760) t, (Q 69619) b, 92 (Q 81771) l, 93 (br) PST 13589, 94 (HU 955833), 95 (Q 24869) t, (ART 2000) b, 108 (Q 103859), 109 (Q 105615) l, 110 (Q48460), 111 (58817) t, 111 (FIR2109 & FEQ 99) br, 112 (Q 64323), 113 (HU 90324) r, 114-115 (Q 86080), 117 (SP 1291) t, (Q 20648) c, (PST 11784) r, 118 (Q 20343), 119 (SP 142), 120 (Q 2393), 121 (Q 24440) t, (Q 78090) br, 121 Exhibits and Firearms collection (bl), 122 (Q 32002), 123 (Q 10509) c, 124 (Q 7993), 125 (Q 53345) t, (PST 402) (b), 126 (Q 28279), 127 (Q 31316) c, 136 (Q 1142), 137 (Q 4031) l, 137 Exhibits and Firearms (tr), 138-139 (Q 3990), 140 (Q 5817), 141 (Q 65442) t, 146 (Q 1309), 147 (Q 5572) t, 149 (Q 35825) c, 154 (Q 6548), 155 (Q 1177) t, 157 (Q 57515) t, 158 (Q 6434), 159 (Q 82969) cr, 159 (tl) Exhibits and Firearms collection, 159 (CO 1155) tr, 160 (Q 5127), 162 (Q 56400), 163 (Q 58154) tl, 163 (Q 5659) tr, 166 (Q 5460), 167 (Q23934) t, (Q 23665) b, 168 (E AUS 4487), 169 (Q 4649) t, 174 (Q 5723), 176 (Q 5773) t, 177 (Q 45320) tr, 178-179 (69/53/18), 180 (Q 2909), 181 (CO 2265) t, (CO 2120) c, 183 (Q 2973) t, 184 (Q 49225) l, 185 (Q 55394) t, (Q 56577) b, 186 (CO 2196 A), 187 (Q 10617) t, (Q 55224) bl, Exhibits and Firearms collection (br), 188 (CO 1763), 189 (CO 1757) b, Exhibits and Firearms collection (tl), 190 (CO 1761), 193 (Q 71653) tl,, (Q 11146) r & tr, 195 (Q 6311) t, (Q 6432) b, 196 (Q 10797), 197 (Q 47997) t, (Q 48178) b, 198 (Q 57466), 199 (Q 10290) t, (Q 23904) b, 200 (Q 6530), 201 (CO 6588) tl, (Q 11586) tr, (Q 363) b, 203 (Q 37344) tl, (Q 6676) br, 204 (Q 23896), 205 (Q56140) tr & cr, 206 (Q69317), 207 (Q 64213) tl,

(Q 107381) br, (CO 2859) br, 207 Exhibits and Firearms collection (cl), 213 (Q 6864) tl, (Q 11120) tr, (Q 70210) b, 215 (Q 8191) c, (Q 34781) b, 217 (E AUS 2350) tl, 217 Exhibits and Firearms collection (tr), 218 (CO 3007) tl, (CO 2975) tr, (CO 2972) c, 221 (69/53/18), 218 (CO 3007) tl, (CO 2975) tr, (CO 2972) c, 222-223 (69/53/18), 224 (Q 11142), 225 (E AUS 1681) t, 226 (Q 6025), 227 (Q 8877) br, 228 (Q 11262), 229 (Q 11204) l, 230 (E AUS 3248) t, 231 (Q 11216), 232 (Q 65790), 236 (HU 56409), 237 (Q 81616) t, 238 (Q 72557), 239 Exhibits and Firearms collection tl, (Q 48371) tr, 240 (Q 9347), 241 Exhibits and Firearms collection tl, (Q 9743) tr, 242 (Q 9534) b, 244-245 (Q 9365), 245 (Q 9354), 246 (CO 3373), 248 (HU 68376) tl, (CO 3660) tr, 249 (SP 1626) tl, 251 (Q 14996) tl, (NYP 68037) tr, 252 (Q 8467) t

Photographs supplied by sources outside the Imperial War Museums.

AKG-Images: 35, 48, 83 (br), 104, 105 (t, bc & br), 243 (t), 249 (cl), 250; /Erich Lessing 63 (bl), 106 (t), 171 (r), 192; /Interfoto 46 (cl), 97 (b), 163 (b); /Mondadori Portfolio: 113 (l) ; /Sputnik: 100; /Jean-Pierre Verney: 82-83, 123 (t); /Peter Weiss: 47 (cr); /Ullstein Bild 33 (b). 42, 46 (c)

Alamy: Interfoto: 106; /Moozic: 109; /The Print Collector: 99

Australian War Memorial: 13 (AWM 4, 1/25/1, Part 5 RC09039), 43 tr, 161 (E00454), 189 (E02855) tr, 209 (AWM4 8/7/18, Part 1 RC09042), 216 (E02690), 217 (E02926) b, 219 (3DRL/2316.015), Series 3, Folder 21, 220 (AIF unit war diary, General Staff, HQ 2nd Australian Division, August 1918 (AWM4 1/44/37),

Bridgeman Images: Private Collection/Peter Newark American Pictures: 233

Conseil General de la Meuse: 181 (tr)

Firstworldwar.com: 69 (tr)

German History Museum: 203 (tr) 1988_93-4, 249 (tr) 1989/2044.101

Getty Images: Apic: 43 (br), 115 (b); /George C. Beresford: 129; /Bettmann: 9 (t), 29 (br), 237 (br); /John Warwick Brooke: 177 (t); /Buyenlarge: 235 (b); /Corbis: 129, 212, 239 (b); /FPG/Hulton Archive: 95 (br); /General Photographic Agency: 80, 132, 175; /Henry Guttman: 57; /Hulton Archive: 7 (tl), 34 (t), 43 (c), 49 (l), 56 (r), 96, 98, 107, 147 (b), 149 (tl), 155 (b), 156, 215 (t), 229 (r), 237 (bc), 243 (b); /Hulton-Deutsch Collection/ Corbis: 7 (b); /Imagno: 32 (r); /Keystone: 171 (tl); /Library of Congress/Corbis/VCG: 155 (cl); /Mansell/The LIFE Picture Collection: 93 (bl), 97 (t); /Martinie/Roger Viollet: 131 (t); /Michael Nicholson/Corbis: 7 (tr); /Mondadori Portfolio: 102, 115, 173 (b); /OFF/AFP: 170; /Photo12/ UIG: 62, 102, 103 /Popperfoto 32 (l), 101 (b), 105 (bl), 173 (t); /George Rinhart/Corbis: 47 (t), 205 (bl); /Three Lions: 127 (t); /Time Life Pictures/Mansell/The LIFE Picture Collection: 248 (cl); /Topical Press Agency: 93 (tc), 169 (bl); /Roger Viollet: 43 (tl),

Historical de la Grande Guerre Chateau de Péronne: 53 (cr), 55 (b), 195 (cl), 203 (bl), 225 (r), 252 (b)

In Flanders Fields Museums: 9 (b), 31 (cr), 39 (tr), 56 (l), 137 (b), 176-177 (b), 249 (br)

Library of Congress, Prints and Photographs Collection: 234 (b)

Mary Evans Picture Library: 92 (r), 183 (br)

Mémorial de Verdun: 67, 82 (tl), 87 (tl), 90-91, 149 (tr), 184 (br), 186 (tl)

Musée du fort de la Pompelle: 5, 8 (b), 12 (br), 71 (bl), 81 (br), 88 (c), 183 (bl), 203 (cl), 205 (c), 205 (tl), 207 (bl), 208, 225 (bl), 227 (t & b)

The National Archives of the UK (P.R.O.), Kew: 22-23 (WO 32/5590), 60-61 (WO 142/241), 133 (c), 134-135 (WO 95/1653), 142-145 (WO 158/21/70, 150-151 (WO 95/110)

National Army Museum, N.Z.: 152-153 (1989.860)

National Geographic Society: 235 (t)

National Library of New Zealand: The Alexander Turnbull Library, Wellington: 28-29

Photo12.com: 141 (br), 157 (b), 191 (c); /Oasis: 81 (bl), 83 (tr)

Private Collection: 34, 87 (b), 116, 133 (cl)

RAF Air Historical Branch: 66 (bl)

REX: Assoc R&R/Paramount/Kobal/Shutterstock: 130; / Realisations D'Art Cinematographique/Kobal/Shutterstock: 129 (tl); /Paramount/Kobal/Shutterstock: 131 (b)

Reuters: 253 (t)

RMN: Paris, Musée de l'Armee, Dist. RMN - © Photographe inconnu: 68, 69 (t)

Service historique de la Défense, Château de Vincennes: 210-211

Somme Trench Museum: 16-17, 137 (cr), 149 (br), 163 (br), 169 (br)

Topfoto: 1, 63 (tr), 93 (tr), 128, 133 (t); /The Granger Collection: 129 (tr), 234 (t); /The Print Collector/HIP: 58, 59 (t), 87 (t), 191 (t), 230 (b); /Roger-Viollet: 82 (bl), 95 (tc); /Ullstein Bild: 33 (t), 47 (b), 172

Maps © Martin Brown/Carlton Books Limited

Every effort has been made to acknowledge correctly and contact the source and/or copyright holder of each picture and Carlton Books Limited apologizes for any unintentional errors, or omissions which will be corrected in future editions of this book.